Claire E. J. G. de Vergennes Rémusat

# A Selection from the Letters of Madame de Rémusat to Her

# Husband and Son

from 1804 to 1813

Claire E. J. G. de Vergennes Rémusat

**A Selection from the Letters of Madame de Rémusat to Her Husband and Son**
*from 1804 to 1813*

ISBN/EAN: 9783337844646

Printed in Europe, USA, Canada, Australia, Japan

Cover: Foto ©Andreas Hilbeck / pixelio.de

More available books at **www.hansebooks.com**

# A SELECTION

FROM THE

# LETTERS OF MADAME DE RÉMUSAT

## TO HER HUSBAND AND SON,

From 1804 to 1813.

FROM THE FRENCH BY

MRS. CASHEL HOEY AND MR. JOHN LILLIE.

LONDON:

SAMPSON LOW, MARSTON, SEARLE & RIVINGTON,

CROWN BUILDINGS, 188, FLEET STREET.

1881.

# PREFACE.

Fifteen years ago, my father wrote, on the cover of the first packet of his mother's letters which he had collected, the following words :—

"I had always promised myself that I would write a 'Life' of my mother; but I now think it will be enough that I should leave all her writings in a condition to be published. I have just re-read her letters. Only once, and that thirty years ago, had I perused the entire series. Occasionally I read a few of them, but I always adjourned the task to which I am now setting myself. By fulfilling this task, by arranging this rich correspondence, and throwing new light on it with the aid of other documents, I am preparing a collection for publication, and raising to my mother's memory the monument most worthy of her. I am not sure that her Letters will not do her even more honour, in certain respects, than her

Memoirs, which have been so highly appreciated by all who have read them.''

My father's death, or rather, I should say, his life, his cares, his labours, and the noble efforts which distinguished his later years, prevented him from carrying out his purpose, and I am under the necessity of terminating singly the work which we commenced jointly. The classification of the Letters was, however, finished during my father's lifetime, and this necessary detail was a difficult one, for, in most instances, the date of the month or year is missing.

In the introduction to the Memoirs of my grandmother I have related all that was known to me of her life and her feelings. Without recapitulating what has been already given to the public on those subjects, I think it well, in order to avoid encumbering the text with over-numerous notes, that I should set down here a few details, and certain dates, that are necessary to enable the reader to understand the references made to persons and events in the Letters which follow.

Claire Elisabeth Jeanne Gravier de Vergennes was born on the 6th of January, 1780. Her father, who had been Intendant, was Master of Requests when the Revolution broke out. He was the son of the Marquis de Vergennes, Swedish ambassador, and brother of the Minister. His mother, Adélaïde de Bastard, was the daughter of a Councillor of State, formerly President of the Parliament of Toulouse, and Chancellor to the Comte d'Artois. M. de Vergennes, his father, beheld the Revolution without enthusiasm, but without displeasure. He was *chef de bataillon* in the National Guard, and a member of the Council of the Commune in 1789. He died on the scaffold with his father, a few days before the 9th Thermidor. At the beginning of the Revolution, he had bought the estate of St. Gratien, in the Valley of Montmorency. Thither Madame de Vergennes retired, and there she conducted the education of her daughters : Claire, who became Madame de Rémusat, and Alix, who, somewhat later, married M. de Nansouty. .

Augustine Laurent de Rémusat, born in 1762, was, prior to 1789, Advocate-General at the Cour des Comptes, and to the " aides " of Provence. After the abolition of the sovereign courts, he was delegated to Paris by his company, to treat for them in matters affecting their interests. He remained there when the times became seriously troubled. He was more secure in that great city, where he was unknown, than at Aix. There he had known M. de Vergennes, he had been received at his house, and the ties which bound him to the family were but strengthened by the death of M. de Vergennes, when his widow, with two young daughters, and charged with difficult business matters, stood in great need of his advice and society. He was constantly at St. Gratien, and he soon became attached to the eldest girl, Claire or Clary, who returned his affection, and whom he married when she was sixteen years old, in Pluviôse, year IV., or February, 1796.

The two children born of this marriage were Charles François Marie de Rémusat, born the 24th Ventôse, year V. (March 14, 1797), and Albert Dominique de Rémusat, born the 11th Frimaire, year X. (December 2, 1801). We know what the eldest was. The second, four years younger, was what is called "rickety;" in his infancy he was puny, and his development was very slow; and yet in his childhood he showed no positive deficiency, beyond a general tardiness of development. He was a little deaf, but he could hear; he articulated badly, but he could speak; he was slower than other children, but he used to do almost all that any child two or three years younger would have done. He continued to progress in this degree for a long time; but his infirmities increased little by little, and he remained always a child. The devotion of his mother never flagged, and she made it her special task to give him help towards all the development he was capable of. It is well known that a mother is equally fond of the son who from his birth is her joy and pride, and of the one who can inspire only a melancholy pity. By untiring attention she cherished and kept alive the flickering flame in the fragile vessel; she taught him to read, to write, to count, and even to draw a little; but she could never lead his intelligence beyond the stage of childhood, though he seemed to understand clearly that he had fellow-creatures better endowed than he by nature, especially his brother, whom he loved, or rather whom he revered, and who continued his tender care of him until 1830, when this poor young man, this poor child, died.

Jeanne Françoise Adélaïde Gravier de Vergennes, the second daughter of Madame de Vergennes, born the 30th of March, 1781, married, when very young, M. de Nansouty, general of cavalry. He served with distinction under the Empire, and died in 1815, at the age of forty-seven, leaving one son, Stephen de Nansouty, who was born the 27th Messidor, year XI. (July 16, 1803), and died in 1865. Madame de Nansouty died in 1850, outliving her sister by nearly thirty years, so that it was possible for me to know her. She was a clever woman, energetic and brusque, and reminded my father strongly of his grandmother, Madame de Vergennes.

M. de Rémusat became Prefect and Madame de

Rémusat Lady of the Palace respectively in 1802 ;
the former was afterwards Chamberlain and Superintendent of Plays.   He remained at Court until
1814, alternately in favour and disfavour, much the
same as M. de Talleyrand.   My grandmother
accompanied the Empress Joséphine in her retirement, and rarely saw the Emperor after the divorce.
Under the Restoration, her husband was made
Prefect, and she was with him while he served at
Toulouse and Lille.   She died in December, 1821.

Her life may be divided into three periods.   Of
the first, previous to her marriage and up to the
time of her appearance at the Court of Bonaparte,
there remain but slight traces—a few stray notes
and some youthful compositions not worth publishing ; they afford indications of quickness and culti-
vation rather than talent.   Her Memoirs give an
account of the early years of her life, as well as
those of the second period, after her entrance at
Court.   I have no letters of this period in my
possession ; they were not preserved in the family.
Madame de Vergennes was in the habit of burning those she received, and Madame de Rémusat
was at that time seldom away from her husband.
She went with him to Belgium, and the same year
followed him to Boulogne, as she has related in
her Memoirs.   The earliest letters now collected
date from the summer of 1804.   The Empire was

then decided upon, the Duc d'Enghien had been shot, and they were only waiting for the Pope and the coronation. Between the months of August and October the Emperor and Empress paid a visit to the Rhine; and it was at that time the letters found at the beginning of the following collection were written.

I must not abuse the privileges of an editor, nor overpass the liberties of a writer of prefaces, by describing this journey, and one made the following year in Italy, where the Emperor went to possess himself of another crown, taking with him all the pomp of a Court, all the attributes of royal state and conquest. It was, in fact, a real Court, with its wearing routine, its cares, and all the false reports, inevitable imprudences, and demands for caution of Court life. If the reader remembers the description in the Memoirs, he will readily picture to himself the situation of the First Chamberlain, an odd enough sort of courtier; for he was a man particularly fond of peace and quietness, of books, and of the gentle ties of home life, but obliged to devote endless labour to the preparation of novel and splendid fêtes, keeping up with all the demands of an imperious Court, and the rivalries of vanity and ambition. His wife, one of the Ladies of the Palace, a woman of sterling principle, of elevated and romantic sentiment, looking upon the re-

straints of Court life as sad inflictions when they
came into conflict with her affections, putting
everything to the test, and expressing her opinions
with earnest zeal and sincerity, was condemned to
strive for peace and happiness amidst all the dis-
tractions of a career of frivolous dignity.

It would need a Sainte-Beuve to describe these
contrasts and develop their consequences. To in-
telligently appreciate this correspondence one must
enter thoroughly into it, and not place one's self
in the elevated sphere of pure philosophy, which
permits the sacrifice of all to the reason and the
heart, nor in the region of mere actual interests,
where everything tends to the egotism of self-
love or cupidity.

At this second period of her life, she was for a
long time separated from her husband, who had to
accompany the Emperor. A little later, she was
herself obliged to travel with the Empress, and for
her own health. This book is made up from the
letters she wrote to her beloved husband at this
time. Such a correspondence is necessarily
monotonous; in spite of a great diversity of
travelling and of ideas, the same expressions
frequently recur. Possibly the tender effusions
may appear a little too frequent and detailed, and
the domestic affection may not possess the flavour
of a romance, but it is necessary to preserve the

true character of the letters, and the repetition, and even reiteration of sentiment, have a charm of their own. In no way could the warmth of heart, the intelligence, and the resources of the writer be better displayed than by her expression, so earnest, so constant, so deliberate, so ingenuous, of a passion which seemed to have nothing romantic about it.

The third period of my grandmother's life extends from 1815 to 1821, from the close of the Empire to her death. A new Government had come in; new ideas, or rather old ones resuscitated from 1789, fired the nation, and particularly the leading spirits. Liberal opinions, scarcely dreamt of under the Empire, suddenly came into being under the force of circumstances, and the author of the Memoirs was fitted by nature to understand them. Moreover, a new influence sprung up close beside her, an element that was zealous, impassioned, all-powerful with her—her son, whose youth fulfilled all the promise of his childhood. So a new correspondence was begun, which proved even richer than the first one. Her husband received, after the Restoration, a position better suited to his tastes. She was no longer separated from him; but with her son, now a student at Paris, she opened a correspondence upon politics and society, which gives the most original and truthful picture of the time—a time about which France has not yet lost interest, and to which the liberal party, still in shadow, has always referred its origin.

We shall concern ourselves here only with the first part of this correspondence, and with the letters of the wife to her husband during the glorious but ill-omened days of absolute power. It is possible, and indeed probable, that the reader will not find here what he is looking for—a new volume of the Memoirs, with bolder expression of political opinions, or piquant revelations. Some, perhaps, will be disappointed to find only the loving utterances of a good and true woman about her husband and children. Her opinion of the Emperor and the Empire, which we have seen expressed in the Memoirs, were formed after the passing of time. Like all other French people, she was carried away by the splendid achievements of the First Consul and by his genius. She was grateful for the great calm which followed the excitement of the French Revolution. She had no prejudices or ill-will against the Empire; her principles were neither Royalist nor Republican; but it is only fair to add that even if her innermost feelings had protested against this dearly bought glory, she would never have put the thought into words. Her letters were written with the greatest reserve as to what went on at the Court and in politics. Under the Empire, letters were tacitly considered to be sent open, and subject to the Emperor's personal inspection. We shall observe more than one proof of this further on, and it is well known that this abuse, "this cowardly abuse," as Beranger calls it, was handed down by the uncle to his nephew, for there was found on the 4th of September, 1870, in the cabinet of the Emperor Napoleon III., the copy of a letter written by my mother to my father a few days before.* Care was therefore taken to avoid offending so powerful and irritable a personage. Hence the reticence and the omissions of this correspondence, the occasional reflections made on purpose, and in reality addressed to him under whose stern and severe observation those lines, written in the intimate confidence of two persons between whom there were no concealments, might fall. Passages of this kind are, however, few, and it would not be just to commend the foresight of the writer at the expense of her sincerity.

The political interest of this correspondence is not its strongest point, and the sentiments of the Lady-in-Waiting are not exactly those of the author of the Memoirs written in 1818, and yet,

---

* "Papiers Trouvés aux Tuileries," etc., première livraison in 8vo. Paris, Imprimerie Nationale. 1870.

will the effect of those Memoirs be weakened to any extent by this new publication? I do not think so; and, however strong my wish might be to augment the intellectual fame of those so near to myself, I would not sacrifice to that desire the cause which we have all tried to serve. But these letters will have just the contrary effect. The life of the Court or the capital, as described in them, cannot inspire any regret for the *régime* that rendered that life so troubled, precarious, and unhappy. Never has sounder proof been afforded that the epoch was profoundly agitated, that absolute government is the most unstable of all, that its greatness was only in appearance, while every one believed while it lasted that France was a mere gambler's stake, at the mercy of the hazard of the die. Never did good patriots suffer more painful apprehensions for the destinies of their country, for the very existence of France; never were wives and mothers so racked with fear for their husbands or their sons, as while the fate of all the men in France depended on the most terrible consumer of human lives that the world has ever known. What are the troubles of parliamentary government, debates in the Chambers, electoral contests, and changes of ministry in comparison with perils and emotions such as those of that period!

It is needless to say that the text of the letters and the opinions of the writer have been scrupulously respected. Certain omissions have been thought advisable, but the passages left out refer only to money troubles, which would not interest the reader, to details of health, the shortcomings of the post, and the badness of the roads, or they contain repetitions of the feeling that pervades the whole, which are suppressed, lest they should prove wearisome. Enough has been left to show that communications were difficult, that the much-envied position of the great functionaries of the Empire included many trials, and that the health of this active and passionate woman was always uncertain, so that her life in the world and in her own heart was a chequered one, and those who loved her were kept in constant anxiety about her. Lastly, I have thought it well to suppress the greater part of the passages that relate to her younger son, Albert, her care of him, and her efforts to develop and instruct him. This topic also would not possess interest for the public, although it is right that they should know that her afflicted child was the object of her unremitting attention. I shall be forgiven for having retained all that concerned her eldest son, Charles, with its testimony to the lavish and exquisite tenderness of her affection for him. May I venture to add that it has been very sweet to me thus to unite, by a common admiration, a common passion, the first and the last affection of my father; the mother who rejoiced in his first smile, the son who received his last look.

PAUL DE RÉMUSAT.

# INTRODUCTORY NOTE BY THE TRANSLATORS.

In his preface to the Letters of Madame de Rémusat, her grandson, M. Paul de Rémusat, addressing French readers, has explained his reasons for publishing in their entirety a number of letters containing only repetitions of the writer's sentiments of conjugal affection, and complaints of the pain inflicted upon her by the frequent separation from her husband that inevitably resulted from the position of M. de Rémusat in the household of the Emperor Napoleon I.

In preparing a translation of the Letters of Madame de Rémusat, for English readers, it has been thought advisable to select from among the whole those that possess interest of a more general kind.

The letters chosen with this view depict the social aspects of the time (from 1804 to 1813), give an idea of the condition of the capital during the frequently recurring periods of the absence of the Court, and narrate the incidents of the writer's attendance, at different periods subsequent to the divorce, upon the Empress Joséphine.

It will be remembered that the Memoirs of Madame de Rémusat came to an abrupt conclusion with a deeply interesting account of the noble conduct of the Empress Joséphine on the occasion of the divorce, and a sketch of the proceedings of the Emperor Napoleon I. with regard to Spain, in which the fatality that attended his action is already foreshadowed. The Letters do not deal with the political and military events which ensued; they are essentially *intimes;* their interest is of a different order. That interest is, however, of a striking and novel kind, and cannot fail to be appreciated by those readers who have followed with avidity the marvellous history of that glory of the French arms abroad, which was destined to be so evanescent, but who have hitherto had little opportunity of obtaining an insight into the history of the interior of France. These letters will show them Paris at home, in low spirits and financial difficulties, pervaded by the dull discontent of a people in a state of constant suspense, and the Court, no longer brightened by the presence of the sweet and gentle Joséphine, oppressed with gloom, and daunted by the morose temper of a harsh master, whose luck had begun to turn.

In selecting from among the Letters of Madame de Rémusat those which they believe likely to have the greatest interest for English readers, the translators have been careful to retain a number of passages which strikingly illustrate the characteristic qualities of the writer; qualities on which M. Charles de Rémusat has dwelt, in his preface to his mother's Memoirs, with profound filial affection, and which M. Paul de Rémusat commemorates, in his preface to his grandmother's Letters, with just pride.

# CONTENTS.

————◦◦◦————

# LETTERS OF

# MADAME DE RÉMUSAT.

## I.

Paris, 10 Fructidor, Year XII.
(Tuesday, August 28, 1804.)

Thanks for your little note from Pont St. Maxence.* It was an agreeable surprise, for I had not hoped to hear from you so soon. We are rejoicing over your splendid weather; I wish from my heart that this journey might be all enjoyment for you, and that I could take as my share the annoyances and the *ennui* you must needs experience. Take care of your health, avoid over-fatigue, and try to amuse yourself; I want

---

\* M. de Rémusat was on his way to join the Empress at Aix-la-Chapelle, in order to accompany the Emperor on his progress through the Rhine Provinces. The Empire had been established, but the Imperial household was not yet formed. The coronation was not to take place until December. The Emperor did not return to St. Cloud until October 12, 1804 (20 Vendémiaire, Year XIII.). Pont St. Maxence is the chief place of a canton in the department of the Oise, and was formerly a post-town.

B

to think that you are happy. Write whenever you are able, and tell me how you are received. I saw Corvisart * yesterday, on his return from Aix-la-Chapelle; he wondered he had not come across you on his journey; it is true that he travelled post haste night and day. He told me that the roads are bad the other side of Liége; you will be travelling over them to-morrow, and I shall be jolted all day long. Pray be very prudent; remember to how many persons you are necessary, and that to me life would be nothing without you.

On Sunday I went to a fête at M. de Valence',† where I met Madame de Montesson; Lavalette‡ was there too, and I questioned him closely about the state of the roads. I cannot say he relieved my mind, and those wretched Rhine roads are always before me. By-the-by, although I felt bored and out of spirits at this fête, I could not help smiling a moment at the thought of your expression of countenance, if in the midst of the verses addressed by the actors of the Comédie Française to Madame de Valence, and to Madame de Montesson and all her family, you could have heard Mademoiselle Émilie Contat § singing the

---

* Corvisart was a friend of Madame de Rémusat, and her physician.

† General de Valence had married the daughter of Madame de Genlis. He was distantly related to Madame de Montesson, the widow of the Duke of Orleans, who was grandfather to Louis Philippe.

‡ M. de Lavalette, Director-General of the Post.

§ The name of *Contat* has been borne by three actresses of

praises of the *Prefect*, and informing you in very
second-rate metre that one must not be surprised
at meeting with a Mecœnas in the reign of an
Augustus. All the company present were very
gracious towards us and applauded warmly. Tears
came to my eyes, and I embraced Mademoiselle
Contat. The verses might be poor stuff, but they
were about you and harmonized with my secret
thoughts. I dined yesterday at Madame de
Soûza's,* to meet the *Corps Diplomatique.* The
poor ambassadress was anxious and distressed.
She implored me to tell you what occurred; you
will notice it or not, as you think fit. She
invited Madame and M. de Talleyrand to dinner.
The former declined at once. He made no reply

unequal celebrity. The first, Louise Contat, who was born in
1760, and died in 1813, took the *rôles* of the *grandes Coquettes*,
and in 1784 created the part of Susan in the "Mariage de
Figaro." Her sister, Émilie Contat, mentioned above, was
born in 1784, and died in 1846. For thirty years she played
the *soubrettes* at the Théâtre Français with the greatest success.
Her niece, Amalrie Contat, acted the same parts, but made
no mark. The *Prefect* alluded to is, of course, M. de Rémusat,
Prefect of the Palace.

* Madame de Souza, previously Madame de Flahault, is
known as the author of some successful novels. She was pretty,
clever, and rather scheming. Her father was an official, and
she had been married, first, to M. de Labillarderie de Flahault,
and afterwards to M. de Souza, a distinguished and honourable
Portuguese, who represented his country as ambassador to
France. Her intimacy with Madame de Rémusat was increased
by the fact that both ladies resided very near each other in the
Rue du Marché d'Aguesseau. She survived her husband and
passed her old age in penury, partly occasioned by her passion
for lotteries.

until Monday morning, when he sent word that having some guests dining at his own house, he could not accept her invitation. Madame de Souza knows as a fact that he specially invited his company. This throwing down of the gauntlet, as it were, is the first incivility he has ventured on in public, and she is consequently excessively annoyed. When I parted from her she was bent on writing to the Emperor. She probably hopes that you will mention the affair; do as you like about this. I have just heard that your minister is to join you at Aix. Everything indicates that this Court journey will be a long one. General Murat thinks that the Empress will not be allowed to accompany the Emperor, and that the latter will only return here a short time before the coronation. But surely your services will be required at the same time, and could you not point this out?

I enclose a letter for the Empress, and one for you from Charles,* who shed tears on reading your message to him. He is tenderly attached to you, and I love him the more for it. He prefers you to every one; and he is right, for you are very lovable, and my happiness is great when by your side. Our little Albert† is better.

---

* My father, Charles François Marie de Rémusat, was born on March 14th, 1797. He was at this time seven years old.

† Albert de Rémusat, Madame de Rémusat's second son, was born in 1802. Neither mind nor body ever attained a full development. He died in 1830, at the age of eight and twenty, but with the appearance of a sickly child of ten or twelve. As I have stated in the Preface to this work, I have suppressed

You may be sure that he knows where you are, and says "*Papa is gone away.*" Alas! yes, he is gone, and I must not look as yet for his return; it seems so far off that I cannot think of it without tears. How hard it is to be separated, when we are so happy together! But since it must be so, let us try to arrange matters in such a way that we need not part again. I feel a sweet conviction that, after this period of storms and agitation, our remaining years will pass calmly away, and that our life will be peaceful and happy. I picture to myself a pretty place in the country, where we could educate our children; a kind and beloved friend, whose side I should scarcely ever leave; and *la cara libertà.* How delicious! Let us labour for so sweet a future, and I possess already the surest guarantee of the happiness I anticipate, if you will only take good care of yourself. Adieu. My mother and Alix * embrace you.

Wednesday, 11 Fructidor.

Don't forget poor Madame de Grasse † and little

---

most of those passages in the Letters in which his mother refers to him and speaks of her anxiety on account of his weak state of health. She was as much engrossed by his unfortunate condition as by the brilliant promise of her elder son. But it seems to me that public attention should rather be called to the latter.

\* Alix de Vergennes, the sister of Madame de Rémusat, had married General de Nansouty.

† Madame de Grasse, whose maiden name was also De Grasse, was the wife of an *émigré.* She had only recently come to Paris with an introduction to my grandmother, who received her kindly, and afterwards became her friend. She was petitioning

D'Houdetôt.* Give me an answer also about Latouche - Tréville's letter, for M. de Ville-blanche's† mother wants to take the opportunity of writing directly to the Emperor which their misfortune affords.

---

## II.

### TO M. DE RÉMUSAT, AT AIX-LA-CHAPELLE.

Paris, 14 Fructidor, Year XII.
(Saturday, September 1, 1804.)

*Mon ami*, to-day is Saturday. I awoke sad, remembering that it is a week since you left me, and that I must not count the days if I wish to bear the remainder of your absence patiently. My grief is increased by just a little anxiety,

for the restoration of some property confiscated during the Revolution. Although a strong Royalist, she wished for an appointment as Page for her eldest son. He did not, however, obtain it, and entered the army through the school of St. Cyr. He was lieutenant-colonel of dragoons in 1830, and sent in his resignation. He and my father were comrades throughout all their youth, and more especially in childhood, and their friend-ship only ceased at my father's death in 1860.

* This *little* d'Houdetot is Henri d'Houdetot, a grandson of Madame d'Houdetot. He wished to be a Page, and died in the army.

† The mother of our cousin, the ruined *émigré*, M. de Ville-blanche, had married Latouche-Tréville. The admiral of that name had just died at Toulon, where he was in command of the fleet, which was afterwards put under the orders of Villeneuve and beaten at Trafalgar.

which will, I hope, have been removed by the time you receive this letter, as I shall then have had one from you. I am expecting to hear from you to-morrow about that wretched road from Liége to Aix-la-Chapelle, that Corvisart says is so dreadfully bad. He told me you would have to get out of the carriage and walk, and I fear that perhaps you did not do so. Perhaps you have forgotten the journey that engrosses my thoughts and are ready for another. For my sake and your own, pray be careful. You will see M. de Souza to-day, the 14th; he is to present his letters of credit; gloomily enough, I fancy. Between ourselves, he dislikes M. de Talleyrand, and is quite inclined to take leave of us. His wife is very anxious, and begs you will not mention what I wrote to you at her request, because she has changed her mind on the subject. She begs only that you will let me know what sort of reception M. de Souza has met with, and whether any gracious expressions have been bestowed on him, or all have been reserved for M. de Lima.*

You will also tell me, for my own information, whether you were satisfied with your reception, whether the Empress spoke of me, whether she still likes me, and was glad to see you; and I will tell you that Charles is well, and Albert much as usual. This is all my news, for I have not been out for a

---

* Madame de Souza feared that M. de Talleyrand's enmity might cause her husband to lose his post as Portuguese ambassador to Paris; and in fact this occurred.

week; I have been rather unwell and have nursed myself. To-day, however, I mean to throw off my laziness, and pay a visit to Cambacérès; then I shall return to a home which is dull to me now, and go to bed early. My mother says I am very tiresome, and she is right; at the beginning of a separation one feels acutely how easy it is to become accustomed to happiness. When we are happy, we enjoy our blessings as a matter of course; our days slip by and we do not appreciate them; we are spendthrifts, and set no value on our possessions. But when happiness departs, then we discover its height and depth by the weariness and sorrow to which it leaves us. This is my experience; and I reproach myself when I have lost you for not having oftener remembered what happiness it was to pass my life at your side.

What else can I tell you? I know nothing, and there is no news except that there is some grumbling at the alteration of the coinage. As I have just finished reading Daniel,* I shuddered at the repetition of a measure which occasioned so many troubles to Philippe le Bel, but we have progressed in our education since those days. There will be some clamour and nothing more.

I have seen Madame de Grasse, who, on her knees, asks for your good offices, and Madame

---

* Father Daniel, a Jesuit, born in 1649, was the author of a History of France in seventeen volumes. He published an abridged edition in nine small volumes. The work is little read at the present day.

Parseval-Deschènes,* who begs you to mention her son to the successor of Latouche-Tréville as soon as he is appointed, if you have an opportunity, direct or indirect, of doing so. Give me an answer about M. de Villeblanche. Every one in Paris considers M. de Cercey the only suitable person for the place. Meanwhile he has gone to Nantes to join his ship.

You will let me know if you are soon about to start off again, and whether I am to send my letters through the post, or to Maret's. I saw M. de —— yesterday. His daughter-in-law has arrived in a pitiable state; she has constant convulsions, and causes great anxiety to her family. Alas! what is life to her now, and why do they wish her to retain it?

Adieu. I am ashamed of the *pétoffes*† I have written, but I am too melancholy to be pleasant; I can think of nothing but that horrid road, and I am longing for a letter to set me at ease. I am writing to Deschamps,‡ because I want him to write to me about you. Adieu; I love you, now and always. M. Bertrand§ desires to be remembered to you.

---

* Madame Parseval-Deschènes, widow of a farmer-general of taxes, was through her husband first cousin of Madame de Bastard. Her son, Ferdinand Parseval, was in the navy and died an admiral.

† *Pétoffes*, an expression commonly used in the family, signifying gossip, scandal, etc. It is a Provençal word, and is met with in Madame de Sévigné's letters.

‡ Deschamps, secretary to the Empress.

§ M. Bertrand (Dominique), formerly a merchant, secretary

Pray ask M. de Talleyrand if he ever regrets his former travelling companions, and remind him that he promised accounts of his journeys to Madame Devaines * and Madame de Talhouet,† and that I claim my share.

---

## III.

TO M. DE RÉMUSAT AT AIX-LA-CHAPELLE.

Paris, Monday, 16 Fructidor, Year XII.
(September 3, 1804).

A thousand thanks for the kind exactitude which has relieved me from deep anxiety! I received your letter yesterday, Sunday, at six o'clock; I had been expecting it all day, and I needed it, for my imagination was busy with the bad roads from Aix-la-Chapelle, and I could not repress tears of joy when I saw your handwriting. Pray continue to let me have a line now and then

of the Council of Commerce, was an intimate friend of my grandfather. He was a clever, well-informed, and thoughtful man, and very intimate with M. de Talleyrand, at whose house he afterwards took up his abode. He died about 1818.

* Madame Devaines (Mademoiselle Racine) was the widow of the Academician, philosopher, and Councillor of State, and mother of M. Devaines who died a peer of France. The latter and M. Guizot married two sisters, Pauline and Henriette Dillon. The mother was considered a clever woman, kept a good table, and was surrounded by a circle of distinguished men.

† Madame de Talhouet was a Creole and very intimate with Madame Bonaparte, who had appointed her Lady-in-Waiting.

to set my mind at ease. I really require it, for my health is not good enough to bear up against anxiety, and your absence has tried me very much. I heard through the Archchancellor that the Emperor is only to arrive at Aix* to-day, and that you will set out again on Thursday, at latest. Do try, if possible, to obtain the nominations for young De Grasse and D'Houdetot, and to wind up Madame de Grasse's business—the poor woman is in a pitiable condition.

I am delighted that the Empress received you so well. I should like you to have nothing but pleasure on your journey, and would willingly keep all the disagreeables for myself. . . .

I have no news for you. There are some miserable rumours of war, and of conspiracies on the eve of explosion. As for your *tripot*,† it continues to be rather stupid, and I have not been there since your departure, but I have seen Mahérault.‡ He told me that Mademoiselle Georges had asked for leave of absence in order to go to her dying father, but it seems that he must have recovered rapidly, for she is

---

\* The Emperor joined the Empress at Aix-la-Chapelle on 15 Fructidor, Year XII., that is, on September 2, 1804.

† Voltaire's name for the Comédie Française.

‡ Mahérault, brother-in-law to Legouvé, the author of " Le Mérite des Femmes," had a place in the department of Public Education, and was Government Commissioner at the Théâtre Français. He was prematurely struck with paralysis, but lived to a fairly advanced age. His son was a Councillor of State, and the present Academician, M. Ernest Legouvé, has written a charming sketch of him.

acting at Amiens. I was not aware that the ladies of the company would be permitted to absent themselves thus. I went to Le Vacher yesterday about your Court suit, and from all I saw I think the new costume will be very expensive. Try, at any rate, to obtain the Presidency of your Electoral College,* that we may contrive to make our way a little. I saw the Minister of Finance about your nephew. He has no directorship to give away because he has made up his mind henceforth to choose the directors from among the inspectors. But by taking a place as inspector, a directorship may be had afterwards. I am going to tell your sister † this, and she shall dictate my reply.

I have told you of all Madame de Souza's troubles ; she has suddenly warmed again towards me. She is anxious and dissatisfied, and has good reason for believing that M. de Lima will remain

* My family owned an estate in the Haute-Saône. My grandfather wished to be, and in fact became, President of the Electoral College of Vesoul. The Presidents were appointed, both under the Empire and under the Government of the Restoration, by the Emperor and the King. Their duties were to superintend and direct electoral operations, and they were sometimes proposed by the Government as candidates for the votes of the electors.

† Madame de Foresta, the sister of M. de Rémusat, died in Provence in 1825. Her eldest son, for whom she sought a financial directorship, was, at his death, a Councillor of the Court at Aix. A brother of his, the Marquis de Foresta, who died in 1858, played a considerable part in the Legitimist party. I give numerous family details in these early pages, in order to show the tone of the correspondence, and restrict myself, further on, to subjects of more general interest.

here, while M. de Souza has a great desire to leave Paris. She wished, at first, that you should interfere, but has happily changed her mind, and is now waiting for the Emperor's return. Say nothing, therefore, about her vexation, and write to me in such a way about the audience given to the Portuguese, that I may repeat what you say. The affection she shows for me has made Gallois my friend again; * he is once more quite attentive.

Adieu; I must leave you for Charles's lessons. He is very well and loves you as much as ever. Albert knows your handwriting. When I show him a letter from you, he says, " Papa ! " and kisses it. I hope soon to give him a fresh letter to kiss.

I don't know whether General Duroc is to be told of an accident that happened to his wife.† Do not speak to him on the subject unless he has already heard of it. Yesterday, Sunday, she was driving in a buggy with her brother, and was thrown out, hurting her head a little. I have just sent to inquire. She has been bled and feels well this morning. There is not the slightest cause for anxiety. For Heaven's sake, don't get yourself

---

* M. Gallois was a former Girondist, who had remained a Liberal. His enlightened mind and an intimate acquaintance with England had attached him to Lord Lansdowne and his friends. He was very fond of Madame de Souza, and remained intimate with her to the end. He was *Maître des Comptes*, and died in 1828.

† Madame Duroc, Duchess of Friuli, was by birth Mademoiselle. Hervas. After the death of Duroc, she became Madame Fabvier.

thrown out on those wretched roads. Come back well and strong, for my health, my happiness, and my life depend on yours. My mother sends you her love, and says we are a tiresome pair.

Do not forget Halma.* I enclose a letter from Rustan † that I opened without looking at the address.

---

## IV.

Paris, Sunday, 22 Fructidor, Year XII.
(September 9, 1804.)

Your orders have been attended to at once. They arrived to-day, and the actors will set out to-morrow, Monday. I will myself go with Mahé-rault to M. de Lavalette's, and you shall have all the tragedies you ask for at Mayence by the 28th, except the "Cid," because we do not possess a "noble father," but we have substituted "Horace" for the "Cid." I hope the Emperor will be pleased with your promptitude in carrying out his wishes, and that you will therefore remain at the head of the department of his amusements, in spite of all M. de la Tourette's speeches here. He is trying to make out that all the Chamberlains are on the

---

* The Abbé Halma, librarian to the Empress, was tutor to my father, who was not sent to school until the following year.
† The Emperor's Mamelouk.

same level as the *First*, and that he shares with you the direction of the theatres.

You are very good to have written to me. I was rather disappointed at having no letter from you, because it seemed to me there was time for you to have written between your own arrival and that of the Emperor; but I have heard from you now and am relieved. Tell Auguste * to send me a line now and then. I do not ask for details, but only, "We are well." Absence is always pain to the one who remains behind; it is great pain to me, who am far from you, while my heart tells me that I would never willingly be parted from you.

You must, I am sure, have been very glad to see the Emperor. We are wishing for him here, but cannot hope to see him very soon. It is said that he means to visit Boulogne again, and the good-natured Parisians suggest numberless evil motives for his absence. May it be brief! May we soon welcome back our good Empress and friend! Speak of me to her, I beg of you; tell her how much I wish to be assured that she does not forget me.

Madame de Vaudemont has, at last, bought a house. She seems quite resolved on leaving her present abode before winter. I had a note from her to-day, promising me, within a week, a definite answer as to the date of her departure. I went over her house; it is very convenient, with good offices; we should all, and you especially, be very

* M. de Rémusat's secretary.

comfortable there. Mamma and I have contrived
a capital way of managing, and with due regard to
the strictest economy. I attend all the sales that
are going on, and have seen some very good bar-
gains. If I could hope, however, that you would
soon be back, I would rather wait for you to decide
upon everything. It is curious that I, who look
such a *determined* person, can never make up my
mind, and am always afraid, unless you are with
me, of doing something foolish.

In order to have as little to reproach myself with
as possible, can you guess what I am doing during
your absence? I am becoming pious. I go to
Mass, I pray to God, and as one must love something, I turn to Him, while waiting for your return
some fine morning. I have found that this is
the only way of bearing the trials of life. I
worked myself up to a sort of enthusiasm, and—you
will smile perhaps—I am calmer since I have had
recourse to Divine Providence; besides, I pray for
you, and that is another way of thinking of you.
In short, I am in such a state of fervour that I
believe I shall even go so far as confession, and if
you stay away much longer, I will not answer
for myself on that point. Do not imagine, however, that I have any heavy sin on my conscience. My greatest fault is, in truth, that I
do not remind myself often enough that you are
the best of husbands, and that I neglect opportunities of giving you pleasure. Is not the humility
of this avowal due to my new sentiments? I
intend to remain in this frame of mind.

Can you guess what I am doing as I write to you? I have surrounded myself with your letters, and I kiss them all, one after the other; those I received long ago, as well as that of this morning. I have one in my hand written to me when I was as yet only *Clary*. It contains nothing at all remarkable, only a commission you give me from Paris, yet my heart beats when I look at it. Ah! what happy recollections I retain of those early days, notwithstanding the grief they sometimes brought me! How greatly were my sorrows assuaged by the feelings with which you inspired me! You made them endurable. What sweet emotions are recalled by those days! My thoughts were of you only; to see you for a moment alone, to read your love for me in your eyes, were my sole pleasures. I remember what I felt when I saw you at the end of one of our lonely paths at St. Gratien. But those days are already far away. How many cares and anxieties have succeeded to that peaceful time! How many quiet delights were showered by Heaven on our youth!

I have come to the end of my paper, and I have still much I could say to you, but adieu. Send me word how you are. Tell General Duroc his wife is quite well. I have seen her; there is not the least cause for anxiety. It was a terrible accident, from no fault of hers, and we must thank Heaven for her escape. But she is now perfectly well, and would write herself only that her right hand is a little sprained.

## V.

Paris, Wednesday, 25 Fructidor, Year XII.
(September 12, 1804.)

*Mon ami*, this is a happy day for me ; I have
had news of you twice over, once from you and
once from Deschamps. I feel quite weary with the
bare account of all your work ! I fear that amid
all the hubbub you will not have time to take care
of yourself. I know how you can exert yourself
when necessary, and I feel anxious about you. But
remember, your health is the first need of my life.
While you are rushing about, I am here in the
most perfect repose ; I bestirred myself, however, in
order to send off your actors. Make your mind
easy on that point; all will be well. So soon as your
letter for Mahérault arrived, I went with him to
M. de Lavalette ; who gave orders for relays of
post horses for the actors. He told them not to
travel too closely, one carriage upon the other, for
fear of not finding horses ready. He fears, nevertheless, that they may have some trouble, notwithstanding this precaution, in getting from Strasburg
to Mayence, and may be delayed for a day. I
asked M. de Lavalette for an intelligent courier to
precede them on the road. Afterwards (it was on
Monday morning) I went to Beckwelt's * to fetch

* Beckwelt, *chef de bureau* at the Finance Office, had been
under M. de Vergennes when the latter was Director of Taxes

the twelve thousand francs, a sum, which, by-the-by, I had some trouble to get, for it had been invested. I secured it at last, and then proceeded to the green-room of the Comédie, where I found your subjects assembled, and quarrelling over their various conveyances. I acted as Vice-Chamberlain, and I gave instructions about all to Saint-Prix, because he seemed the most business-like, and we arranged that he should start on Tuesday in the first-carriage, followed by a second, which was to be five hours in advance of the others. This was accordingly carried out. Mademoiselle Raucourt,* only, had not returned from the country yesterday morning. I am waiting to see Mahérault before closing my letter, to hear news from him of the fifth carriage, which she and her people are to occupy. But even if she does not arrive until four and twenty hours after the others, you would still be able to have " Phèdre," " Bajazet," " Ariane," or " Mithridate " played ; "Cima " and " Horace " would come afterwards. The greater part of their luggage is going by the diligence, which will arrive on the 29th.

I am now going to see Mahérault, and to read your letter, which has this instant reached me, to

at the General Receipts Office in the Rue Ste. Avoye. He continued to the end of his life to be the man of business of the family.

\* Mademoiselle Raucourt, who was born in 1756, had long been first tragic actress at the Théâtre Français. She had now been relegated to the second or third rank, in consequence of the success of Mesdemoiselles Georges and Duchesnois. She died in 1815.

him. I shall advise him to go, if possible. The actors reckon on receiving money from you on their arrival. Those who are left behind complain very much of the Emperor's neglect cf the Comédie Française. I held out hopes that it would be made up to them, and I objected to their closing the theatre entirely, as they wished to do. They will play twice or thrice a week, but they are so few in number, and the season is so fine, that they will really need help. You see that Mahérault and I have done our best. I have just come back to my room after seeing Mahérault, who tells me that Mademoiselle Raucourt can start to-day, Wednesday, and, since you wish it, Mahérault will go with her. His health allows of this.

I have many messages for you from your son. You will wonder that he does not send them himself, but he has gone on a party of pleasure to the Jardin des Plantes, and was obliged to give up the pleasure of writing to you. I have made a discovery about him : he is a very nice boy. You see the result of my hours of meditation! He is working very fairly, because life being a little hard for me just now, I spend my time in making it hard for him too ! He reads and writes with me for three hours every morning, and works again a little in the evening, for I found it did not do for him to have so many unoccupied hours. He agreed very willingly to the evening lessons, which consist of ten lines of verse learned by heart, and a few written phrases of his own com-position, to teach him to spell. He had a funny idea a few days ago. He made a droll little sketch representing the Emperor at his toilet, and the Sovereigns of Europe each handing him one of his garments. My mother and I were greatly amused.

People say here that the Emperor will return to Boulogne after this Rhine journey. In that case you would come home, I hope, or would you be going into Franche Comté? Try not to lose sight of the Presidency of the Department. To obtain that, I would patiently bear a little delay. But what will the Empress do? Shall we soon have her among us again? I begin to think her absence very long. It is pleasant to live with her, and I wish she were returning to St. Cloud.

I have just read, in Deschamps' letter, his account of the Emperor's reception at Aix-la-Chapelle. You are going to make a triumphant progress, and I must own to a secret regret that I cannot be of the party, since you are one of it. My only fear is lest the Court, so well received everywhere, and so justly disgusted with our horrid Parisians, may take a dislike to this gloomy capital and remove from it altogether. To give you some idea of our amiability, only imagine, everybody is grumbling at the absence of the actors of the Français, though the house was invariably empty! You see that I take advantage of your permission to write at length, although I have nothing to tell you, and am perhaps wearisome. But what can a humdrum woman like me

hear in the way of news? I seldom go out, I
see no one but a few old greybeards, and I cannot
be happy with my husband away. My greatest
amusement is the shower-bath which I take every
morning, and enjoy very much. My health is
good; I even think I am growing stout. Every
one says so. . . .

## VI.

### TO M. DE RÉMUSAT AT MAYENCE.

29 Fructidor, Year XII.
(Sunday, September 16, 1804.)

I am surprised that you do not mention M. de
Souza in any of your letters. I saw his wife this
morning; she had heard from him the bad news
of his recall, and of his new mission to one
of the Northern Courts. You can imagine the
effect on her and the excess of her grief. She
fears, moreover, that matters may become still
worse for her, and that some false report may
be made to the Emperor, of things she will
be accused of having said on the subject; she
begs you will prevent this additional misfortune,
by assuring the Emperor of her regret, but, at
the same time, of the resolution she has taken
not to manifest even the slightest vexation, and
to comfort herself by the recollection of his
Majesty's kindness, which she will never forget.
M. de Souza, who for some time past has had

many reasons for expecting his removal, left Paris,
nevertheless, in a more tranquil state of mind,
because, two days before his departure, he had
had a frank explanation with M. de Lima, who
gave him his word of honour that he had no
pretensions to the Embassy in France. It would
seem, however, that he changed his mind at
Aix-la-Chapelle. But if anything can console
Madame de Souza, it is the tender affection of
her good husband. Nothing can be more touching
than the letter in which he gives her all the
particulars. I should like you to see it; it is
impossible to have purer, tenderer, or more estimable sentiments than his. However sad it may
be to part with her country, her friends, her old
habits, and perhaps even her son,* there can be
no unhappiness in accompanying a husband like
hers or mine.

It is especially on account of her son that
Madame de Souza fears to be injured with the
Emperor. She begs you to tell this to the Empress, and to say that, though greatly distressed,
she is quite resigned. If possible, write me a few
words to prove that you have exerted yourself in
this affair and that our good protectress is interested in the poor lady. In truth, she needs
such a consolatory proof of your friendship.† I

---

* Charles de Flahault, Madame de Souza's son by her first
marriage, became a general at the end of the First Empire, at
a very early age. He was a senator and Grand Chancellor of
the Legion of Honour under the Second Empire. He died
September 1, 1870.

† This letter is one of those (the reader must remember)

think you must now be at Cologne. Every one
tells me that you are making the most delightful
journey in the world, and that I ought to be very
glad you are travelling through such a lovely
country. All the better, if you are enjoying yourself. I am not so selfish as to wish you to be
dull; I will take all the dulness for my share, and
shall be amply rewarded by the joy of meeting you
again.

I am longing too to be once more with the
Empress—I would almost say with the Emperor
also, only that it might seem disrespectful. You
say nothing about his return; true, you may know
very little about it. It is rumoured here that the
coronation is to be deferred. I cannot believe
this, and if I might venture, I would say that delay
would have an ill effect. On the other hand, we
are told that the Pope is coming, and that the
Grand Master of Ceremonies is to be sent forward
to meet him. Do you know whether this is
true? You are really unbearably discreet; there
is nothing to be got out of you.

I saw Portalis about your nephew. He promised
to put down his name on the list for a Prefecture,
and to speak strongly in his favour. I will not let

written when my grandparents were in constant fear that their
correspondence was, or might be, seen by the Emperor. This
will be still more apparent in succeeding letters. Yet it would
not be just to say that all their expressions and remarks were
dictated by calculation. There was a certain mixture of sincerity
and caution in the sentiments they expressed, which it would
be difficult to sift, but which is intelligible to the reader of the
Letters and the Memoirs.

him forget his promise; while you are away I like to exert myself actively in your service, or in that of any one belonging to you.

I dined a few days ago with M. Humboldt, and passed the whole evening in delightedly listening to him. He is simple and modest, like Merit itself; he has observed with judgment, has a fine memory, and his narratives are admirably *written.* I can use no other word, for he speaks both carefully and fluently, and one seems to be listening to an interesting book read aloud. . . .

## VII.

### TO M. DE RÉMUSAT AT MAYENCE.

Paris, Tuesday, 1st Complementary, Year XII.
(September 18, 1804.)

I have not heard from you since Thursday, and though not greatly surprised at your silence, still it makes me just a little anxious, and I shall remain so until you can find a leisure moment in which to tell me that you are well. Anxiety about your health pursues me everywhere, and any one to hear me talking about the heat and the cold would imagine you were a gouty old invalid. In spite of your infirmities, however, I hope you are getting on well. . . .

You will see in the newspapers a capital letter from the Minister of Police to the clergy; we are all delighted with it here. He wrote to me that his wife receives on Wednesdays; I intend calling on her to-morrow. If you wish for news, for you are capable of knowing nothing about it, although on the very spot whence it emanates, let me tell you that Madame Bonaparte *mère*, who has also her brevet as Princess, has been sent for; that M. Clary is her Chamberlain and Madame Clary her Lady of Honour; that Madame Borghèse * has quarrelled with her husband, and is returning to Paris; that private proposals have, it is said, been made to Lucien; that M. de Jaucourt is First Chamberlain to Prince Joseph; that the marriage contract between Mademoiselle Tascher and M. de Fuentes is signed, also those between Eugène and Mademoiselle de Rohan, and M. Tascher and Mademoiselle de Valence. This is what we amuse ourselves by hearing and repeating in Paris, during your absence. Much of it seems probable, but I do not believe it all.† About once a week I emerge from my shell to pay a few visits, and gather in all the gossip. The rest of my time I remain at home, and my days are all so alike that you may always guess what I am doing at whatever hour you may think of me. In the morning my bath; on returning home Charles's lessons. Afterwards I write a few lines to you, and read Pascal, whom I have seized upon to keep up my piety. In the

---

* Madame Borghèse, or Princess Pauline, was sister to the Emperor.

† Most of these previsions were not realized. Everybody knows that Prince Eugène de Beauharnais married Princess Augusta of Bavaria, and not Mademoiselle de Rohan.

course of the evening a little discussion with the
Abbé Morellet,* Bertrand, and Gallois, who is very
friendly again ; and by ten o'clock every one in the
house is in bed. This, you see, is a very salubrious
sort of life, and my health consequently is good.
With a few little exceptions—you will guess them
—I could be very happy, spending my life in this
way ; but I feel that I should sometimes want to
see my good and kind protectress, and the Emperor
also. Adieu. Mamma pretends that she no longer
thinks about you, but she speaks of you continually.

Wednesday Evening.

I had closed my letter, but I open it again,
because I have received one that has raised my
spirits. Your want of occupation wearies you, but
you have no vexations as I feared. I shall send
you my little sermon all the same, however,
because I have not time to write my letter over
again. Besides, in the vortex in which we are
plunged, we shall find good use for it. I can
understand the dulness of your present life. You
are not accustomed to keep your mind in such a
state of inactivity, and really and truly I pity you,
for I know what it is. I hope you are often consoled by smiles from the master ; you rejoice in
them, I know, and I congratulate you, if you

---

* The Abbé Morellet, who wrote his Memoirs, is he whom
Voltaire nicknamed Abbé *Mord-les* (the Biter). He died, over
ninety years of age, on January 12, 1819. He was a member
of the French Academy.

obtain them sometimes. You are very good to
give me an account of your day, and your narrative
is most spirited. But will no Chamberlains be
appointed to do the no-work which now fills up all
your time? You ought to have brought such
labours to an end. . . .

I see Madame de Souza every day. She is out
of spirits and unhappy, and all this business is
not a consequence of her indiscretion only; she
certainly helped, but she is not the only cause.
Her husband's behaviour is most noble and dignified. He shows her and Charles * the greatest
affection. Wherever she may be, with such a
husband, it will only depend upon herself to be
happy. You do not say a word about Madame
Devaines,† and she is quite put out by it. She
is not a woman to offend, and you are wrong to
be negligent of this. If I receive another letter
with no mention of her, I must invent some sort
of satisfactory message.

I heard here that M. de Ségur ‡ was to be sent
forward to meet the Pope, and as the happiness
of seeing you, especially after so long an absence,
comes before everything with me, I was delighted.
They say now that the coronation is deferred,
but I think I told you this before. There is
nothing new in Paris, but profound dulness and
idleness reign. Your poor theatre gives an occasional performance to an empty house, and, by

* Charles de Flahault.
† Madame Devaines wished to be Lady-in-Waiting.
‡ M. de Ségur was Grand Master of the Ceremonies.

the way, you must give them a good *raking* on your return ; they are so lazy ! All the newspapers are down on your actors with well-deserved blame. Before they left Paris, they were always acting the same pieces, and they want a sound scolding.

Picard's theatre is carried on with great spirit. He has brought out a new piece, which is a success ; but I have not seen it, as I scarcely ever go to the play. Yesterday, however, although depressed by your letter, I went to the Opera. I saw "Panurge," which was very good, and the great Duport, who, in spite of poor M. de Luçay's prohibitions, introduced ever so many new steps. I saw M. de Luçay * a few days ago ; he is melancholy and discontented, and confided some of his sorrows to me. Oh, *mon ami*, what human being is happy ?

But enough of *pétoffes*. You will have no occasion to complain of the brevity of this letter ; I am spinning it out as much as I can, as when it is finished I must return to solitude. You are now at Mayence, whence you will write to me ; but it will be four or five days before I can hear from you. Adieu, my beloved. Charles is climbing on my shoulder, to ask if I have sent a message from him ; he is an affectionate child. I think

---

* M. de Luçay was Prefect of the Palace and responsible for the Opera and the Opéra Comique. Duport was an opera dancer and composer of ballets. He was an excellent dancer in the serious style. " Panurge " is an opera of Grétrys, the libretto by Morel. It was represented for the first time in 1785. Picard had been appointed director of the Italian Opera, on its removal to the Salle Louvois in 1803.

you will see that he has made some progress.
Adieu. Oh! I was forgetting. Send me a line
authorizing me to take Madame Lavoisier's *
apartment, which she agrees to let to us.

---

## VIII.

### TO M. DE RÉMUSAT AT MAYENCE.

Paris, Wednesday, 2nd Complementary, Year XII.
(September 19, 1804.)

I wrote to you under the melancholy influence
of your last letter, and I regret now that I did
so, because I do not wish to cause you the
slightest pain of any kind. But you will forgive me, if you recollect that your tone of gloom
was accompanied by no particulars, and that you
left all details to my imagination. I still feel

* Madame Lavoisier, the widow of the illustrious Lavoisier,
who was executed under the Reign of Terror, had been Mademoiselle Paulze. She died in 1834, after a second marriage
with Count Rumford. She was, all through her life, very intimate with our family. My father felt a real regard for her.
She was rather blunt, but sincere, faithful, and energetic. She
was living at that time on the ground floor of a large house on
the Boulevard de la Madeleine, at the corner of the Rue Duphot.
This was the apartment my grandparents were anxious to take,
and where, in fact, my father passed the greater part of his
childhood. The whole building has since been pulled down, and
replaced by the houses of the Cité Vindé. Madame Rumford,
on vacating it, took Madame de Vaudémont's house in the Rue
d'Anjou. Afterwards the Rues Rumford and Lavoisier, and
part of the Boulevard Malesherbes, were built on this ground.

rather anxious, in a vague way, and constrained
to write to you again to-day, although a letter for
you has already been despatched this morning.
Assuredly you cannot accuse me of neglect. I
write to you almost every day; in fact, I believe
I write every day; it is my delight and my only
consolation, and while thus holding intercourse
with you, I cherish the delusion that we are once
more together. I enjoy this happiness all the
more, because you tell me that my letters give
you the same feeling, and I believe it, for I love
to believe all you say. What renders my life so
happy, and beautifies both present happiness and
that which I look forward to in the future, is my
entire confidence in you—a confidence which, I
will confess, I sometimes abuse. I am so sure of
your feelings ; it is so delightful to be able to say,
when reading my husband's affectionate words,
" All this is true." But to return to your letter.
It grieved me ; but I do think your extreme
sensitiveness is the cause of your being so easily
upset. What has happened ? Some slight mark
of dissatisfaction on the part of the Emperor,
which hurt you at the moment, but which can
have no serious results, because your zeal for him
is as active as your admiration is sincere. He is
not ignorant of this ; he has more than once done
justice to you, and you are too right-minded to
misjudge the occasional violence of temper that
belongs to his character, and which is surely sufficiently accounted for by the multitude of affairs
that occupy and agitate him. Moreover, it appears

to me that at this very moment he is giving you
a proof of confidence in appointing you President
of an Electoral College. There is no alteration,
therefore, in the interest he kindly takes in us, and
you must not forget that the life of Courts is not
so calm and peaceful that one can dispense with
strong armour to guard one's feelings from the
little vexations that meet one at every turn. Is
it from your companions that you have received
some annoyance? Has your self-respect been
wounded? Has some prerogative been con-
tested and taken away? After all, what does it
matter? Trust to time, to the justice of the
Emperor, to your own merit, for the reward due
to every honourable man who does his duty. *Mon
ami*, one thought is constantly before me, which
prevents my feeling very deeply the little con-
tradictions we may meet with at Court. It is
this. What have we done for the Revolution?
What pledges, to use the current expression, have
we given it? What claim have we to distinc-
tions from the new authorities it has brought
forth? We have suffered and sighed, which is
interesting to nobody; and after that terrible
upheaving, your position is one to be envied
and coveted by all who have been toiling to get
on these last fifteen years. Such reflections
make me earnestly wish that you could obtain
some place in the Government, as well as your
place at Court, and belong to some official department. They also moderate my feelings of ambition, which would be excessive, if I could forget

that, after such political crises, modest merit and
delicate probity have no claims to favours of the
first rank.

You will think my tone very serious to-day, but
it harmonizes with my thoughts, which in consequence of your letter are rather grave.   Yet, when
I look around me, I see many reasons for content-
ment: our mutual affection, our children, our
happy home!   Who could complain, with so many
blessings? . . .

The Emperor, I suppose, is at Mayence by this
time?   I hope the actors have arrived.   I see by
your letter that when you wrote you had received
none of mine on the subject; I trust you have
them all now.   I should not like them to be lost.
Adieu, once more, my beloved.   Your children and
my mother are well.   My health is tolerably good;
Corvisart is more satisfied with it, and if my mind
were quite at ease, I should be well.   Tell the
Empress how much I long to see her.   I do not
send the same message to the Emperor, and yet,
believe me, I wish he were back at St. Cloud.

## IX.

TO M. DE RÉMUSAT AT MAYENCE.

Paris, Friday, 4th Complementary, Year XII.
(September 21, 1804.)

. . . I called on Madame de Talleyrand yesterday morning.   She was very civil, and said she
should tell her husband to tell you she had seen

me. She asserted so strenuously and so often that her husband was delighted, happy, and on the best terms with the Emperor, that I was half tempted to doubt it.

Poor Madame de Souza is far from this state of triumphant delight, although she has sufficient self-command to speak very little of her departure. The Imperial family show her the greatest friendship. Madame Louis * shed tears on seeing her, and Prince Louis promised to write to the Emperor that there was some intrigue at the bottom of all this, which ought to be looked into. M. and Madame Murat also are interesting themselves. I do not think anything is to be gained, however, and the best thing our poor ambassadress can do, is to love her husband and go with him to Russia, where she may enjoy the honours paid to him and the sensation she herself will create. Bertrand is heart-broken, and Gallois in a state of repressed fury; Abbé Morellet no longer knows how to spend his Thursdays. In the midst of all this M. de Souza remains admirably calm and dignified. He has behaved nobly throughout; he is a very high-minded man.

You will not tell me whether the coronation is to be deferred, and I do not know whether I ought to go on with my preparations. Meanwhile I would much rather spend the money on installing ourselves comfortably than on unnecessary clothes. I have no answer as yet about the price of the furniture which I agreed on with Fallanquin.

* Madame Louis Bonaparte, afterwards Queen Hortense.

I have just seen Picard, who praises you and the Empress alternately. He tells me your health is very good. Pray take care of it. I am well. Adieu.

## X.

TO M. DE RÉMUSAT AT MAYENCE.

Paris, Sunday, 1 Vendémiaire, Year XIII.
(September 23, 1804.)

. . . I suppose you are now in the midst of your theatrical performances, and that they are going off well. It is just the contrary here ; our actors play only twice a week to empty houses. The public grumbles at them, and they at the public. I enclose you a newspaper which speaks of them fairly enough. They certainly require reform ; because, after all, in former times, when they were only half their present number, the removal of the Court never prevented them from playing at the Français. Picard's theatre, with smaller resources, is better managed ; it has been open without intermission, and he has brought out two new pieces that have both succeeded. I was inclined to send for Dazincourt,* but I reflected

---

* Dazincourt, who was born in 1747 and died in 1809, created the part of Figaro, and had great influence at the Comédie Française. His acting was considered to be correct, refined, and somewhat cold. Préville said of him, " He is a good comic actor,—joking apart."

that it would not do for me to set myself up as regent, that you would not approve, and that it must not be. People hope that on your return you will regulate the administration of the theatre differently.

I went this morning to the Salon, where I saw some fine paintings. The best is undoubtedly the picture by Gros of the Emperor's visit to the sufferers from the plague, in Egypt. Drawing, composition, and colour, all are excellent. David at once awarded it the crown of honour, and it was well deserved. There is a most painful picture, by Hennequin, only moderately well executed. It represents the dreadful events at Quibéron.* One shudders at the sight of Frenchmen slaughtering each other, and I own that it was an effort to me to explain this melancholy subject to our son. It is said to have been painted by order, but not only is it ill executed, but I fail to see that it can have any good effect. I remarked also a beautiful flower piece by Vandaël, belonging to the Empress, and Isabey's picture, which is charming, every face being a perfect likeness. Lastly, a very beautiful little painting by Richard, who painted the Valentine of Milan. It represents Francis I., and is pronounced by connoisseurs to be equal to a Gerard Dow. You should advise the Empress to buy it.

* Every one knows that painful incident of the civil war, of which the Emperor wished to perpetuate the memory. In 1725 the *émigrés* and the English landed at Quibéron. They were defeated by General Hoche.

Will you be so kind as to mention M. Chéron to Maret?* This is the reason. The Presidency of his Electoral College is vacant. I wrote to Montalivet, and, at my request, he very kindly put Chéron's name at the head of the list presented to Portalis. The latter promised to put it on the list that will be shown to the Emperor, and then will come the opportunity for M. Maret to help us; do not forget this.

---

## XI.

### TO M. DE RÉMUSAT AT VESOUL.

Paris, Friday, 6 Vendémiaire, Year XIII.
(September 28, 1804.)

Thanks for your two letters, which arrived together and gave me great pleasure. I needed these two companions of my solitude, for I have been alone since last Monday. My mother is at Auvers, and has taken Charles, leaving me alone with my thoughts. I should be very dull were it not for the sweet reveries caused by your letters, and for the knowledge that Charles is enjoying himself. Thus maternal love, the least selfish of all love, delights in the sacrifice of self. But I do not so patiently endure a certain person's absence, and time seems to lag wearily until the happy moment of your return. It is said that the

* Maret, afterwards Duc de Bassano. He was at this time Secretary of State.

Empress will come back here next week; I shall take my turn of waiting the following week, so as to be free from the 20th to the 25th. Then, with nothing to disturb me from the anticipation of the close of this weary separation, with what impatience shall I not await the blessed day that will reunite us!

I have just received letters from my mother; she says that Charles is in good spirits, and is all day long in the vineyards. I am glad he has taken advantage of these last fine days. While he is playing, I am thinking of him and you; I make plans for the future, and place you both in a prosperous position, as you deserve. I picture that dear child rewarding us for all we have done for him, and enjoying the good things of life that you have amassed for his sake, while you enjoy calm repose with me after all your trials and labours. Oh, my dearest, may these hopes be realized and not disappointed! Where are those days in which I should have had no doubt? What sad progress I have made!

It seems we are not to see the Emperor just yet; he intends returning to Boulogne. Here we are all excited about the invasion, and politics are the order of the day. You may imagine that we don't let the affairs of Turkey pass without plenty of comment and much dissertation. But I have little to say on the subject. The older I grow the less I care for what is not myself, that is, *you* and all I love. Whatever the future may have in store for us, if we are left together, we shall always be happy; otherwise, all will be over. Do not scold me for a shade of melancholy; you know who will make me gay again. While on the subject of the finality of all things, did you see in the papers the almost sudden death of poor Fargues,* and that of Madame Macdonald? Thus do youth and riches vanish in a single moment. I remember what you told me once of Fargues' discontent, and of his unsatisfied ambition; if he had known then how soon he was to reach the term of all human passions, how greatly he would have despised his own state of mind!

Is not this a grand subject for moralizing, and in my present humour I have but to let myself run on and I shall be making the liveliest and most original remarks. But I spare you, and in order to enliven you a little more, I must tell you of the sums our new house† is costing us. I send you an estimate I got from Fallampin,‡ before beginning, that you may see the amount. I exclaimed when I saw it, and asked for exact particulars of each article, and I see plainly that the present generation is foolish to throw away such sums of money on all these superfluities.

---

* M. Fargues was in the Administration. His son was Auditor under the Empire and Prefect in 1830.

† She is still speaking of the house on the Boulevard de la Madeleine, or rather of the ground-floor of that house. The rent was seven thousand francs (£280). The house was bought successively by M. Ouvrard, and M. Pourtalès, who lived in it. It was used afterwards as an hotel, and then passed into the hands of Morel de Vindé.

‡ An upholsterer.

However, I shall conclude none of my purchases until your return; there is no hurry, nor will there be any difficulty in finding what we require. You must own that I am right in saying we are all foolish. Our good old forefathers, wiser than we, passed their days in armchairs where their fathers had sat before them, and they amused themselves quite as much as we do. Nowadays, if one would have a few friends in one's house, one must begin by decorating it like a shop, and it is too true that many people have no means of amusing their guests except by feasting their eyes on the elegance of their furniture.

I hope your actors have given satisfaction; I don't see why they should not act as well at Mayence as here. When you have amused your-selves sufficiently, send them back, for those who remain are really pitiable; the theatre is nearly always closed, and when open, is empty. Picard, on the contrary, is delighted, and proud of his success. The Opéra Comique have done well also; they brought out the night before last a most charming little opera.

Adieu; I think this is enough gossip. You will read it before going to bed the day you arrive at Vesoul; it will put you asleep. You are quite right to have made up your mind to be amused with my long rambling letters—for, if you had not, what would become of you?

# XII.

St. Cloud, Saturday, 9 Germinal, Year XIII.
(March 30, 1805.)

In one of Madame de Sévigné's letters she says, *" What a day is that on which separation commences!"* Alas! I have experienced the pain of such a day, and I do not think there can be many moments more painful than those which follow on the departure of a person we love. The solitude that succeeds to the bustle of departure, the

---

* The coronation had taken place in Paris in December, 1804. A few months later, on 11 Germinal, Year XIII. (April 1, 1805), the Emperor left for Milan, to be crowned King of Italy. His First Chamberlain had to start a few days earlier, to make the necessary preparations, taking with him the Imperial insignia and the crown diamonds. It was during this journey to Italy that the following letters were written. My father retained a keen recollection of the emotions of this leave-taking, and wrote the following memorandum on the subject, towards the close of his life:—" A journey to Italy, the passage of Mont Cenis, and indeed any kind of travelling, was at that time, by reason of the badness and insecurity of the roads, a much greater affair than at the present day. My mother, who took everything seriously and was an enthusiastic and romantic woman, and who, moreover, had never considered the positive side of life, greatly exaggerated it besides; and as her imagination gave the key-note to us all, I looked upon a leave-taking, or an absence, or a journey, as a catastrophe, or almost as a family mourning. At that time there prevailed a tone of sentiment or affection on all subjects, which at the present day would appear affected, but which was, nevertheless, perfectly sincere, and perhaps indicated finer moral qualities than the cynical irony of our generation."

silence, the tears that stand in the eyes of all, but that one dares not acknowledge lest they turn into sobs, and for all the rest of the day the usual order of the house neglected! In short, every little circumstance that one dwells on although it only adds to one's grief! For myself, my dearest, I am not strong enough to bear such emotions frequently. I have taught myself to believe that we should always be together; I cannot exist alone and far from you. Do believe me, there can be no happiness for me away from you. Poor little Charles wept so bitterly, his unrestrained grief cut me to the soul. All the evening he kept telling me that he could not believe he should not see you in the morning. At last he was so distressed that I was obliged to try and amuse him, and only succeeded by taking him to the theatre. . . .

I came here to St. Cloud, yesterday morning, and found everybody preparing for departure; this made me think of yours. They start to-morrow, and I return to Paris this evening. I do not want to stay here, or to see anybody; it would only make me weep, and make people think I am sorry because *they* are going away. The Empress is in a state of perturbation which prevents me from seeing much of her. However, she seemed pleased to have me here these last two days. No one could form an idea of the confusion that prevails. Every place is encumbered; no one knows to whom to apply for orders, and yet everybody is giving them.

Amid this tumult Caulaincourt is loudly ordering that the men servants and the maids are to be seized by main force and packed off. The journey to Fontainebleau is to be made to-morrow, and on to Troyes on Tuesday. General Duroc thinks that the Emperor will be at Turin on the 22nd. You will then be much farther away, but you will be resting yourself, and I shall be more at ease; for your journey disquiets me—the roads are so unsafe, and then the cold is so intense! To-day we are in mid-winter. When I opened my shutters, in order to write to you, I found everything covered with snow, and I sorrowfully reflected that you were travelling. I cannot, alas! ask you to be careful of yourself, for this letter will only reach you after you have, I hope, escaped all the dangers that I dread. I am entering on ten days of terrible anxiety; the grief of separation is not the only trouble absence brings with it.

I did not see the Emperor yesterday; he was at work all the morning, and retired at eight o'clock. Before closing my letter I will tell you if I do see him, and to-morrow I will just wish you good morning before I seal.

Saturday Evening.

I have passed a dreadful day, listening to people talking of the difficulties of your journey, of the want of horses, and consequently the diminution of your escort, and of the wretched Savoy roads and their ignorant postilions. I cried all day, and I spend my time in prayers for your safety, but I cannot beg you to be careful, for this letter will not reach you for a long time. How soon shall I hear from you after that fatal Mont Cenis? How I must suffer until I do! It is in these times of anxiety especially that I feel how dear you are, how necessary is your existence to mine. Oh, my dearest, be careful; without you I feel I cannot live.

I spent the day at St. Cloud, without, however, seeing the Emperor, who has been continually at work, and did not make his appearance. The Empress has been all kindness, but I was in a very unfit state to enjoy it.

---

## XIII.

### TO M. DE RÉMUSAT AT MILAN.

Paris, 13 Germinal, Year XIII.
(Wednesday, April 3, 1805.)

. . . M. Salembini * wrote to me from Avallon; I am most grateful for his kindness, and rely on him to make up for your laziness by his punctuality. If you have been properly supplied with post-horses, you must have slept at Lyons on Sunday night; but where are you now? It was thought at St. Cloud that you would reach Turin on Friday; but, for my part, I do not hope it; post-horses must be

---

* M. Salembini was a retired officer, whom my grandfather had taken with him as travelling companion and secretary. This gave rise to some difficulties, as will be seen, and as has been mentioned in the Memoirs. He had a sister and two little girls, of whom more hereafter.

scarce and the roads bad. I cannot think you will reach Turin before Sunday, and only then if no accident has occurred to detain you. You see by all I write that I have but one idea, and I would therefore deny myself the happiness of writing to you and remain silent until I am more at ease only that you will want to hear some news of us. But I must try to speak of other things, and will avoid, if I can, making you a sharer in my trouble. But you must be indulgent until I know you are at Turin; until then I have but one subject of thought.

The next thing will be to regard my fears as presentiments! But hitherto I know to what to attribute them, and when I am calmer, I will tell you why your absence is more painful to me this time than ever before, and why I am absolutely unhappy without you.

The Emperor left Fontainebleau this morning; the Archchancellor, whom I met at Madame Devaines', told me he believed the Emperor's absence would last three months, although his Majesty had told him he should be back at the end of two, that he had no intention of visiting the departments of the south, and that the Empress expected to return on June 15th. If no special accident happens to you, through your mode of travelling, I shall be very glad that you have gone on first. You can have no idea of the confusion and disorder this journey is entailing; yours was nothing at all in comparison. Everybody is grumbling and already tired out, and they must thank God if they all come back safe. He knows what I ask of Him. You first, and then the master of us all. But I need not make myself anxious on his account; there are plenty of persons devoted to him, and eager to bring him back safe to us. It is for your health and your enjoyment that all my prayers are offered : first, that you may meet with no accident, and then that you may enjoy yourself. Yes, my dearest, enjoy yourself; I love you enough to wish that you may be amused. Let me bear all the pain of separation, so that your share be the pleasure of the journey. I shall be quite satisfied with this division.

I enclose a letter from Mademoiselle Mars ; * Corvisart asks your attention to it. He is to start in about three weeks, and will tell you how he leaves me. If my mind were at ease, I should be pretty well.

Adieu. I will write no more, because I can but repeat myself. I will chatter away when my anxiety is relieved ; until then, I will only write in order to say that I love you and am well in health. I may say the same for Charles ; Albert is getting on wonderfully ; my mother scolds me, sends you her love, and says she ought to have been an old maid.

---

* It is scarcely necessary to say that Mademoiselle Mars was the well-known tragic actress, then at the zenith of her beauty and talents.

# XIV.

Paris, Saturday, 16 Germinal, Year XIII.
(April 6, 1805.)

I had need of your letter. I was widowed and lonely, and my days hung heavily. I feel better now; your letter will keep me company. You know that I shall put it quite near me at night, that I may fall asleep thinking of you, and awake with the same thought in the morning. Oh, how sad a thing is absence! and to what end? Men throw away their happiness as they do their money; they squander both on an uncertain future, to which they sacrifice the present, which only is their own. They lose three or four months in a year living far away from those they love; they take change for their gold without looking at it; and life and fortune alike pass away from them unnoticed.

This is my third letter to you since you left me; but I do not feel great pleasure in writing, because my thoughts are always fixed on the dangers of your journey. In ten or twelve days' time, when I know you are safe at Milan, and can rest from all your bad nights, your joltings, and your shakings, if not the worse accidents of which I tremble to think, then I can chat with you unrestrainedly; I shall have no other pleasure but that of writing to you, of telling you about our children, about myself, the happiness I owe you, my most tender love, and, above all, of the confidence I feel in your affection for me, which is the foundation of all my joy.

The Emperor is on the road since Tuesday, and was to sleep last night at Sémur ; * he travels slowly, although people say he is pressed for time. The want of occupation to which I am reduced by his absence and yours, is something new. I should be lazy enough to like it, if you were here with me. I have thrown myself into the society of the Faubourg,† without, however, neglecting that other faubourg‡ to which I owe a duty. To-morrow and the next day, I shall take leave of the Princesses ; then I shall spend a week making a round of visits, after which I shall pay no more until you are with me. On May 1st, I go to Sannois, whence I shall, once a week, bring Charles to M. Halma. Madame d'Houdetôt§ insists on having the whole family with her. I intend returning to Paris in June, and you, I hope, will decide what we are to do in July.

* Sémur, chief place of a district in the department of Côte d'Or, on the road to Italy.

† The Faubourg St. Germain.

‡ The Faubourg St. Honoré, where most of the Government officials resided.

§ Madame de Houdetôt, the same mentioned by J. J. Rousseau in his " Confessions," although already aged and in very moderate circumstances, had a country-house according to the old style at Sannois, where she entertained a numerous and distinguished company. It was one of the places where the scholarly society of the eighteenth century still survived and lived again. She is spoken of at great length in the Memoirs.

I have now given you an accurate account of my actions. If you wish for news of my thoughts, I may say that they will be entirely of you, for Charles is my principal occupation, and naturally leads me to think of his father. Once more let me repeat that, when my anxiety is relieved, I will write to you about him, the progress he makes, and his little brother's health. Until then I feel stifled, and my heart tortured by anxiety; I get through the days, not in order to reach the happy one of your return—it is too far off, I dare not. think of it—but to reach that one when you will write, "My dear one, I have arrived and am well." Picture to yourself, if you can, how these words will be received, and then say, if you dare, that you are not loved as you deserve.

My mother embraces you. She makes charming complaints of her misfortune in having daughters; she says that she is no sooner easy about the ruts on your road, than her sympathy is claimed for the inundations on M. de Nansouty's.* She writes to her friends, begging them not to leave her a prey to our dismal lamentations, but is so kind-hearted in reality, that she always ends by sharing our anxiety. Morning and evening we look through the "Post Guide," and alarm ourselves at any sign of the "fourth horse;" † we make inquiries in every direction as to the dangers of the route;

---

* General Nansouty was then on his way home from Hanover.

† In those days an extra horse used to be charged for by the postmasters, and called the *third* or the *fourth* horse, when the road was heavy or fatiguing. This horse was paid for, but was never harnessed or seen.

there is, I know, between Chambéry and Mont
Cenis, a bad road, with snow and steep descents,
and no wall on the outer edge.  Did you leave the
carriage at all those bad places ?  Did you think
of your wife, whose life depends upon your health,
and who could not bear up against any addition to
her troubles ?  I expect you will find all this very
tiresome reading, these dangers being already
in the past.  But what can I do ?  It would be
easy to prove to each of us that we are really
happy and really understand each other, only
when we are not parted.

## XV.

### TO M. DE RÉMUSAT AT MILAN.

Paris, Wednesday, 20 Germinal, Year XIII.
(April 10, 1805.)

After thoroughly enjoying your letter from
Lyons, I have fallen back into a state of nervous
anxiety, which will only cease, as I have already
told you, when I get a letter from you from Turin.
You must be there, I think, now. . . .

The weather here is splendid; you must be
enjoying the beautiful Italian spring, and I hope
such a lovely climate will reward you for all your
trouble in getting to it.  Enjoy it all, my dearest,
the beautiful scenery and the pure sky; I love
you sufficiently to wish you may have pleasure,
although far from me.  I know so well in what
you place your happiness, that I do not desire

any proof of your regrets that would interfere with your enjoyment of the journey. There is one kind of amusement only that I cannot, in conscience, allow you, and I trust you will know how to resist any whispers of *mio bene* that may be offered to you, emphasized by sweet voices and bright eyes.

I hope your first care was to write to me from Turin. Indeed, it is necessary to me; for to be ignorant of the fate of him I love best in the world is a very heavy burden. But I am again complaining! I do wish to spare you my lamentations; I strive against them as much as possible, but I cannot command my feelings. How truly I feel that you are my life and my all, and that if sometimes the hours fly past without my appreciating your beloved presence as I ought, it is because our poor human nature uses happiness as it uses health; we learn its full value only when some accident deprives us of it.

I must tell you, by way of diverting my thoughts, that M. Guys * has gone at last, that the Emperor left the affair in the hands of the Archchancellor, and that it was settled on the spot. They are a fortunate family, and your sister shares in their happiness. By the way, she is sorry that you did not take Josephin † with you, and so am I. He would have been one more man, and the dangers you have been exposed to, owing to the treasure

---

* M. Guys belonged to a Marseilles family, many members of which have distinguished themselves as consuls in the Levant.

† Josephin de Foresta, his nephew.

in your charge,* have not been the least of my anxieties, especially as the newspapers very stupidly announced your departure. Everybody thought this very imprudent.

If you would like news of your *tripot*, I can tell you that M. Chéron's piece was a great success; † that it is in excellent verse, that two acts are extremely clever, that everybody speaks well of it, that Geoffroy praises it highly, and that we hope you will call the proper attention to it at the right opportunity. I have no further information respecting the comedy; my door has been closed against all actors and actresses since your departure, and I begged Mahérault to say that I was not in Paris.

I send you some memoranda on the unfortunate affair of M. de Villeblanche. When you see Maret, tell him I was much obliged by his letter, but that in informing me that Madame de Latouche had obtained a pension of three thousand francs, he does not fulfil his engagements with me, because that lady is stepmother to the admiral, being the second wife of his father, and I am petitioning for Madame de Tréville, his aunt. I see that Maret, and consequently the Emperor, has confounded the two, and thus I have unintentionally obtained a favour for a lady whom I do not know.

---

* The crown diamonds and the regalia.

† M. Chéron, a great friend of my parents, wrote a piece in imitation of " The School for Scandal," called " Le Tartuffe des Mœurs." The play was so good, that the Emperor appointed the author to the Prefecture of La Vienne. He and Picard were joint authors of the comedy of " Duhautcours."

# XVI.

## TO M. DE RÉMUSAT AT MILAN.

Paris, Saturday, 22 Germinal, Year XIII.
(April 12, 1805.)

. . . I saw Isabey* this morning. Your mantles will be sent off next Saturday. He has lost no time, and seemed to me rather annoyed at having to go; he no longer cares about it. The Princess Elisa † will start on Thursday. I went to see her the day before yesterday; she was alone and had given orders that I should be admitted. I remained with her an hour and a half; she was most kind. When you see her you can say that I told you; she is really very amiable.

I must tell you, in confidence, something that happened to Carrion-Nisas and Regnault de Saint-Jean d'Angely,‡ which is just now amusing all Paris. The day before the Emperor's departure, they each received an autograph letter from the Chamberlains on duty, requesting their attendance that same evening at Fontainebleau. The Emperor had sent for them. You may imagine their state of excitement, each rushing to M. de Lava-

---

* Isabey, the artist, was designing the embroidery for the Court dresses.

† Elisa Bacciochi, the Emperor's sister.

‡ Regnault de Saint-Jean d'Angely was President of the Council of State. Carrion-Nisas, first an officer, then a Tribune, and then again in the army, was born in 1767. He died at Montpellier in 1841.

lette, asking for horses, and making as much fuss
as you please.   They set off at about nine in the
evening.   Carrion was the first to reach Fontainebleau ; no Chamberlain to be seen, but Duroc
comes forward, and, after inspecting the proferred
letter, goes to the Emperor to announce him.
"I did not send for him," says his Majesty ; "it
is some mistake ; I have not time to see him.
Put him up somewhere, and he can go back in
the morning."   Carrion laughs over his nocturnal
drive, and retires very good-humouredly.   At midnight a second carriage dashes up, Regnault
springs out, asks for M. Duroc, to whom he
hands his letter, and is announced to the Emperor.
"Depend upon it, it's a *poisson d'Avril*,"* says
the latter.   M. Duroc emerges from the cabinet.
"It is a *poisson d'Avril*," he says.   Regnault
dashes headlong into his carriage, and drives full
speed back to Paris, to find out who has played
this trick.   The postilions, who had not had an
easy time of it coming to Fontainebleau, so great
had been his eagerness to get on, repeat, as they
crack their whips, "It's a *poisson d'Avril !* "   The
Minister of Police says the same thing, and it
is very soon echoed by all Paris.   I say so too ;
but you must not mention it at Milan, for the
Emperor was, very justly, displeased with this
stupid joke.

I enclose a poetical petition from a young man
who has called on me a few times since you left

* April fool.

—M. Morel de Clinchamp. He tells me you received him kindly, and promised him your patronage, and he wants his petition to be presented to the Emperor by the Empress, together with the little poem that I send you. He has written me some verses too ; he seems to possess facility and some talent, if I may judge by an epistle he showed me, addressed to Mademoiselle Duchesnois. Do as you think fit about the petition ; but I promised to commend it to you.

---

## XVII.

### TO M. DE RÉMUSAT AT MILAN.

Paris, Tuesday, 26 Germinal, Year XIII.
(April 16, 1805.)

At last I have news from Turin ; yesterday I received a packet from M. Salembini, which has made me very happy. You have crossed those dreadful mountains, and that terrible Mont Cenis that caused me so much anxiety, and for the last six days you have been quietly at Milan. I hope you will now be thinking of writing to me, for since you left home, nineteen days ago, I have had only one little letter ; you rely too much on the zeal of your secretary. . . .

I must tell you that in my next parcel I intend to enclose a letter to the Empress, in which I shall repeat part of what I said in the one I wrote to her some time ago, and which I did not

send.  You will read it, and then seal it up, because
I don't want you to seem to know anything about
it.  If you approve, you will give the sealed parcel
to Deschamps, at any time you think fit.

---

## XVIII.

### TO M. DE RÉMUSAT AT MILAN.

Paris, 29 Germinal, Year XIII.
Friday, April 19, 1805.)

When this letter reaches you, you will be with
the Emperor.  The newspapers say that he is to
arrive at Milan on 1 Prairial.*  It would appear,
therefore, that his progress is more rapid than was
intended at first.  People are wondering here what
can be the cause of such haste, and as they are
never at a loss, the Parisians are saying that preparations for war will bring you all back sooner
than was expected.  To see the delight which
some persons take in confirming these rumours of
war, one would never think that no Frenchmen
were to be engaged in it.  Thus it is that party
spirit destroys every generous sentiment.  Talking
of sentiment, we had a little dispute yesterday
morning with mamma and a few other persons ;
one must quarrel sometimes, you know.  We were
speaking of the love of country, and my mother
contended, half in jest, that there was no such

* The Emperor reached Milan some days earlier than this, on
18 Floréal (May 8), instead of 1 Prairial (May 21, 1805).

thing as love of country; that it was simply a fine theoretical sentiment, and that, for her part, she should always prefer the country in which she was happiest, to any other. Madame de Vintimille and I argued, like good Frenchwomen, on behalf of love of one's country, and declared that we had our share, although it was but a small one, in the glory of the nation. My mother was amusing herself by displaying the greatest indifference to our fine sentiments, when all at once Charles, who had been playing in a corner, got up, and approaching his grandmother, said to her in a tone that I cannot describe to you, "Oh, Gaga, don't you love your country?" and then he burst into tears. I cannot explain why he was so much moved, but the saying gave me pleasure, and I pass it on to you.

I took him to the theatre yesterday evening, and was quite pleased with his behaviour during the performance of " La Caverne," in which there is much noise of firearms, and a very exciting combat in the last scene. The boy did not show the least fear of the firing; his little face turned rather red, because of the restraint he put upon himself, but he came well out of the ordeal.

While on the subject of plays, I wrote to you, did I not, about M. Chéron's. It is most successful; at the fourth performance the author was still called for; try to make the most of this. Only two days ago, Regnault de Saint-Jean d'Angely said that the play was by a man not only talented but good; that M. Chéron was a most estimable character, and had acted an upright part all through the Revolution.

I have seen Mahérault; your actors are constantly asking him for leave of absence. They would like to come to me, but I have declined to receive them, thinking you would prefer my taking this course. I only saw Madame Suin,* whose benefit night was very brilliant, and who came to thank me. I found her a really clever woman; she told me a great deal about the Comédie Française, and of the advantages belonging to such a post as yours. "In fact," said she, pointedly, " since I have lived in Paris, I have seen many ministers and many courtiers fall into disgrace, but the gentlemen of the Chamber have always been in favour, and the post of purveyor of amusement, held by M. de Rémusat, is almost always a road to fortune." I got out of Madame Suin's benefit very well; I did not go; and I found some people to fill my box and pay my share of the benefit.

In twelve days from this, I am to take up my abode at Sannois.† I intend to see Lavalette tomorrow to try and obtain an exemption for my letters; I shall tell him that you *often* receive letters on the affairs of the Emperor, and that you require me to answer yours at once. If I can

---

* Madame Suin had come out at the Comédie Française in 1775, as a leading actress; at the end of her career she undertook the *noble mothers* and the *tragedy confidants.* The performance in question was her farewell to the stage. She was an intelligent and estimable woman.

† Madame d'Houdetôt's well-known country place.

obtain nothing from him, I shall ask Madame de Ségur to take charge of my letters. I intend to pass the month of May, with the children, at Sannois ; the country will do us all good. . . .

---

## XIX.

### TO M. DE RÉMUSAT AT MILAN.

Paris, Tuesday, 3 Floreal, Year XIII.
(April 24, 1805.)

Before replying to all the interesting details you give me, with an account of the dull trifles that fill up my life, I must tell you how grateful I am for the affection of which you so tenderly assure me, and how happy I am to be so greatly beloved. Every word that you write prints itself on my heart with all the force with which it emanates from yours. However strong your expressions, I believe them to be true. I say to myself that happiness exists for us only when we are together, that we need each other's presence, and that, though now separated, we are so continually together in spirit, that we shall meet again in a few months' time without a moment's interruption of that feeling which make the happiness of my existence. My dearest, put the same faith in my tender affection that I put in yours. Your absence and my loneliness make me feel how limitless it is. The long days, the sad nights that I pass without you, the solitude of my room, the study where you are not, the big empty rooms, the entire liberty which I know not how to employ —all these things continually draw my thoughts towards you, while numberless circumstances must turn yours away from me. I speak and think and feel like Lafontaine's pigeon, " *L'absence est le plus grand des maux*," and especially for the one who is left behind.

You are good to give me so many details ; I quite appreciate them. I am surprised at what you say of the weather ; I fancied you were in mid-spring, and the accounts of the snow and the cold at Turin upset all our calculations. We had some splendid weather here, and during Holy Week a taste of perfect summer, but for the last week it has been cold again. Thus it is with life ; a little sunshine and then the cold returns, to last much longer than the warmth. Everything changes and passes away, except your affection and consequently my happiness.

If you care for *pétoffes*, as Madame de Sévigné would say, I must tell you that Madame de Souza has at length taken her departure, but in great distress because M. de Souza refused to take Charles de Flahault with him. As a foreigner, and also as an ambassador, he thought that would not have been a prudent step. Our friends are all in confusion, and don't know where to settle down. Gallois has not yet appeared ; M. Leroi is going away ; Bertrand is half crying, half laughing over the departure of Count Rumford, who has returned to Munich to preside over some academy or other, and so has left the field free to others. The Abbé Morellet is, I fancy, rather struck with Princess Elisa.* She was uncommonly gracious to him, and even told him to write to her. Do not forget to remember me to the princess.

Our friends the Chérons have gone ; don't forget them. M. Chéron's play is more popular than ever; try to get a place for him. Now that the Forests are being established, and the Imperial Hunts and *Capitaineries*,† there must be some opening. Do not be vexed with me for adding my importunities to those with which you are already overwhelmed.

I do not know whether you see any French newspapers. If you do, you will have read a circumstantial account of the Emperor's extreme graciousness at Brienne.‡ Madame de Brienne was beside herself with delight. It is true that it would be impossible to be more gracious than was the Emperor on that occasion. I saw some letters to M. de Damas, full of charming little speeches made by him ; he laid himself out to be agreeable, and the effect has been excellent in our critical society. Our severest lady critics owned the amiability of our sovereign, and they are willing now to admit that he can make himself

---

* Princess Elisa Bacciochi, Grand-Duchess of Lucca, was of a literary turn, and associated with very distinguished people.

† " *Autrefois charge de capitaine des chasses.*"—Littré.

‡ Madame de Brienne, niece to the Archbishop of Sens, was related to the Damas family. The Emperor, wishing to revisit his old military school, had spent some hours at the Château de Brienne.

pleasant when he likes, but they add that he does not always like. What a treatise I could write on human vanity! What examples I could find in the very society that values itself so highly! There is not one woman of our acquaintance who would not have been as much enchanted as Madame de Brienne, yet they are all laughing at her enthusiasm.

Salembini writes to me about the shells and mosaics of Milan. With regard to the latter, General Caffarelli * suggested, after you had gone, that I should allow him to order a set for me at Rome, saying that those he had brought to his wife are very handsome, and had only cost twenty-five louis. I agreed, and asked him to mention it to you. Please ask him for the little memorandum I gave him, and if you find that the set will come to too high a price, you might leave out the tiara and the bracelets. When we were at St. Cloud, I told the Empress that General Caffarelli had undertaken to bring home mosaics for Alix and myself; thereupon she very kindly said she would take that on herself, so you may *consult her* on the selection.

Adieu, since one must always end with that sad word. I was reading to-day one of Massillon's sermons, a favourite of mine, on the best way to bear the afflictions of this life, and on the

---

* General Augustus Caffarelli, aide-de-camp to the Emperor, died a peer of France, later than 1830. He was the youngest of five brothers. The eldest died a few years ago, Councillor-General of the Haute-Garonne.

thanks we should return to God when He vouch-
safes to try our faith by the sorrows He sends us.
After that I cannot but endeavour to submit to
the grief of separation, but I am far from having
arrived at perfection. . . .

## XX.

TO M. DE RÉMUSAT AT MILAN.

Paris, Sunday, 8 Floréal, Year XIII.
(April 28, 1805.)

. . . I have just been reading Marmontel's
Memoirs of the Regency. You may perhaps have
the work at Milan; it seems to me well written,
but ill conceived. I am quite shocked at the
judgment he passes on Louis XIV. He speaks of
him with severity, that contrasts with his indulgence towards the Regent. If you read the
work, remark the passage he quotes from Saint-
Simon, concerning the "Bed of Justice" that was
held, to remove the education of Louis XV. out
of the hands of the Duc du Maine, and to restore
precedence to the peers over the legitimized
children of the king. The malignant joy felt by
the Duke, not only at this victory, but at the grief
and depression of the vanquished party, the in-
toxication of vanity which he owns to having
experienced—all those disgraceful passions, en-
gendered by the pride of man, disgusted me so
much, that I felt quite sick of ambition and its

aims. Far from us be all enjoyment procured at the expense of others! We can be happy, I hope, at a less cost, and without causing a single tear to flow on our account.

M. de Salembini writes that you are suffering slightly from gout; this, added to your silence, makes me uneasy. At such a distance everything becomes magnified, and I feel that, against my reason, I am needlessly anxious. Madame Devaines, who came to see me yesterday, says conjugal affection makes me very tiresome; but adds that you must be very amiable to be so much beloved. She introduced her daughter-in-law into society yesterday, and seemed rather proud of being so beautiful herself and the chaperon of so plain a young woman.* Her son often comes to see me; he is sensible and kind-hearted. One must overlook a few little oddities that do no harm to anybody, and then one sees he is a reasonable man. I like him. He seems also to be pleased to be with me; and, moreover, he loves you with his whole heart. This last is a recommendation I cannot resist; any one who appreciates you has a claim on my affection.

Adieu. I am going to pay some visits, because I leave Paris in a week, and must bid farewell to all my friends. I intend to remain all May at Sannois, and I shall find there, if I choose to seek them, many sweet recollections, and perhaps some legitimate regrets.

* M. Devaines' first wife, Mademoiselle Malherbe, was considered plain.

I enclose a letter for the Empress, which I should like you to hand to her at once, and some days before that which Corvisart will take to you. As for the latter, it is undated, and you can give it when you like.

---

## XXI.

### TO M. DE RÉMUSAT AT MILAN.

Paris, Wednesday, 11 Floréal, Year XIII.
(May 1, 1805.)

. . . There is much talk now of the Toulon fleet, of the wonderful success of all the Emperor's designs, and the extraordinary incapacity of the English, in always letting us slip between their fingers. There are different views on the subject. It is hoped, generally speaking, that our two sorties will have an effect on the English Government, and give some chance of peace. On the other hand, the gloomy and discontented politicians assert that the English are only allowing us to assemble our naval forces in order to attack us at sea; but, on the whole, there is a hopeful feeling. For my own part, you may imagine, from my love of our country and my hatred of England, that I am delighted at this promising beginning; and I must admit that I assumed an air of superiority towards certain Anglo-maniacs whom you know.

I have very little social news for you. There

is hardly anything going on this season, and everybody is on the eve of departure. I can only tell you of a few marriages, and of some interesting events that are expected to come off. Alexandre Laborde is engaged to Madame Gilbert.* She is a very pretty woman, the widow of that M. Gilbert whom we saw with Madame de Vannoise.† Then, Madame Juste‡ is in an interesting condition, and (which has caused more sensation in the neighbourhood) Madame de Lamoignon is in the same state.§ M. Molé is much depressed, people say, because Providence has left him out, as regards this particular blessing. M. de Ségur,‖ the Grand Master's brother, is absolutely dying, and it is

* Madame de Laborde, who died in 1855, was Mademoiselle Sabathier de Cabre. She was tall, handsome, amiable, and an agreeable woman. Her son, Léon de Laborde, has been a deputy, a Member of the Institute, and Keeper of Archives.

† Madame de Vannoise, née Parseval-Deschênes, was a cousin of ours. She was considered an attractive woman. She had been married to a disagreeable provincial husband, from whom she was divorced, and she was rather liked than otherwise in the family. Her daughter, Constance, was married, at a subsequent period, to M. de Villeblanche. The two sons of Madame de Vannoise entered the army. One of them perished in the Russian campaign.

‡ Madame Juste de Noailles was the daughter of Archambauld de Périgord, the brother of M. de Talleyrand.

§ Madame Christian de Lamoignon was sister to M. Molé, who at that time was childless. She retired into private life at an early age, on account of bad health. She had but one daughter, who married M. Adolphe de Ségur, second son of Octave de Ségur.

‖ The brother of the Grand Master of Ceremonies was the Vicomte de Ségur, a man of talent, who wrote some pretty vaudevilles.

probable that the Grand Master will not find him
alive on his return. Is not life compassed in these
few lines—its commencement and its end ? This
would be a fine opportunity for a little moral
essay; but I will spare you, because, to quote our
friend La Bruyère, everything has already been
said.

Tell Madame Savary * that I often speak of her
two little girls to Bigot, and that they are quite
well. He is anxious about Madame Davoust's
daughter,† who is very delicate, and over whom he
watches carefully.

Adieu. I must leave you, or rather I must leave
this letter, which will soon be speeding towards
you. What more shall I say ? No, I will say
nothing, not another word, for fear of garrulous-
ness ; it is too soon, as yet, for that.

## XXIX.

TO M. DE RÉMUSAT AT MILAN.

Sannois, Friday, 27 Floréal, Year XIII.
(May 17, 1805.)

I have just finished giving Charles his lessons,
and can now have a chat with you, by way of
recreation. Next to seeing you and hearing you
speak, there is no greater pleasure for me than
that of writing to you, so I give you leave not to

* Madame Savary, Duchess de Rovigo, *née* Fandous.
† Madame Davoust was the first wife of Marshal Davoust,
Prince d'Eckmüth.

be more grateful than the occasion demands, provided you appreciate the reason why it is so delightful an occupation to me.

The children and I are extremely well. A country life suits us so perfectly that I regret we cannot pass the whole summer here—less on my own account, although my health has improved, than for the sake of our two darlings, who are in splendid condition. I must tell you, too, that I went to St. Leu * yesterday morning. The improvements in the grounds are making it a most delightful place. Prince Louis has purchased a large part of the forest. He has eight hundred acres of wood, through which he is opening the prettiest roads, and a broad stream runs through the middle. I repeated to the princess all you told me about her brother. She was much affected, and the more so that she had been distressed by receiving quite different accounts. She is devoid of all ambition, but feels and suffers from the dangers and stumbling-blocks to which her brother is exposed, in the high position to which he has attained. She conversed with me, with great good sense, on the drawbacks and advantages of her own position. Although at an age when illusions are natural, she seems to me to be absolutely free from them, and to weigh, too wisely perhaps, the enjoyments we meet with on life's somewhat thorny road. I was speaking to her of an ill-natured and certainly unfounded rumour, which has been ridiculously exaggerated in Paris,

* Princess Louis Bonaparte's country-house.

and which I heard from persons who profess to be well informed. I must repeat it to you, although I think it most absurd. It is this :—

There are proofs, it is said, that the Polignacs * and others imprisoned in the fortress at Ham were planning an escape, that they carried on a correspondence with the princes, that they had the command of money and endeavoured to bribe the soldiers, and that Prince Murat has had them removed to the Temple. It is likewise asserted that the Empress has continued to evince great interest in them ; and that there are letters from her which would be compromising.

I am ignorant whether MM. de Polignac could be capable of such dishonourable conduct. In times such as these, when Revolution has left demoralization behind it, one cannot, unfortunately, rely on the principles of any ; but besides the absurdity of the complicity attributed to the Empress, you and I know how very little she is in the habit of writing at all. I have been present occasionally when she has received Madame de Polignac with the kindness inherent in her, and which is always doubled by the sight of any kind of misfortune. I hardly think this tenderness of heart is to be imputed to her as a crime, nor can I conceive, if the rest be true, how any one can have invented so absurd a calumny. I have not the means of clearing it up at present ; I will

---

* The Duc de Polignac and his brother, whose lives had been granted them by the Emperor, were at first imprisoned at Ham, but were soon removed to the gentler durance of a *maison de santé.*

thoroughly; when I see them so unconscious of
misfortune, so careless as to the future, so gay
and happy, I feel my heart beat with pleasure and
pain at once. What will be their fate? What
future lies hidden in this stormy present? Shall
we have exhausted both their share and our own
of anxiety and trouble?

You see I am in a rather melancholy mood. I
own it. You only could disperse the little cloud
which, as Madame de Sévigné says, makes my
reflections of a *grayish-brown.* But whatever my
mood, you are never a loser; my heart never
changes. Perhaps melancholy even adds another
degree to tenderness, either because the latter is
an effect of the former, or that it consoles and
brightens the gloomy reflections caused by a somewhat lengthy contemplation of the afflictions of
this life.

## XXX.

### TO M. DE RÉMUSAT AT MILAN.

Sannois, Monday, 30 Floréal, Year XIII.
(May 20, 1805.)

*Mon ami,* I have this instant received a letter of
the 23rd, announcing the sudden return of Salembini. I am grieved and alarmed at the few words
you write me, because I seem to read between the
lines that he has been in fault, and gravely so, to
incur so prompt a punishment. I will not, however,

judge him too severely, without further information, and it would pain me to have to doubt the principles or the attachment of a man to whom you have done so many services. I think he is much given to vanity, and I will own to you that I have observed, in the few letters that I received from him, some indications of want of balance that surprised me, and also of a disposition to take offence at trifles. I had quite expected that this might prove a source of annoyance to you, but I was far from anticipating what you now tell me. At any rate, I will see him when he reaches Paris; I cannot be hard upon him now that he is in trouble. I will ask him some questions, and, if he has sinned against ourselves only, I feel I cannot condemn him altogether. From your habitual gentleness towards myself, I have earned indulgence for others that I hope to retain all my life long. Although I look upon ingratitude as the most odious of vices, yet it fills me rather with pity than with anger, and on this occasion, when Salembini perhaps is not wholly exempt from it, I will not allow myself to reproach him, if he seems sorry; and this especially on account of his sister, whom I like much. I have had frequent opportunities of seeing her, because her brother used to send me all his letters for her; and very long they were, if I may judge by their thickness. They were very frequent too. Perhaps these letters have been opened? Perhaps their contents were indiscreet? I cannot tell. Mademoiselle Salembini never

opened them in my presence; she contented herself with saying that her brother spoke highly of you and appreciated your friendship, and I believed her, because that was but natural and right, because every one who knows you ought to love and esteem you.

I regret this event very much, and I regret it for my own sake also. He was very attentive in giving me news of you, and you are too much occupied for me to hope to hear very often directly from you. Under present circumstances you are far less to be pitied than I; first, because, whatever you may say, you do not want to write to me so much as I want to receive your letters, and secondly, because your time is occupied in the service of the Emperor, whom you love, and who, I fancy, is a very potent solace to the pain of absence. Nevertheless, my dear one, notwithstanding the agreeable necessity of proving your zeal by your assiduity, think of your poor wife who is very lonely away from you, and whose one solitary pleasure is that of receiving your letters.

From what you tell me, I see that the Emperor has arrived at Milan as you predicted, that his presence has produced its customary effect, and that the Italians, in their turn, have been compelled to admire the hero who is going to protect them. While on this subject I must tell you that you wrote me two very eloquent pages; your theme inspired you. I would almost wager that you are not aware of this; they were dashed off so quickly, because your heart as well as your head guided the pen. *Mon ami*, what I have just said would, if uttered aloud, seem like flattery, and yet, between us, it is but truth. Here, in the solitude of the fields, I often reflect on all the sorrows we have experienced. This neighbourhood reminds me of our misfortunes, and painful though they were, you know by what feelings their recollection has been sweetened for me; but when, after sadly counting them over, my thoughts revert to the peaceful times we are now enjoying, to the well-regulated liberty that I find all-sufficient, to the glory with which my country is covered, even to the pomp and magnificence that I like, because they are proofs that all is an accomplished fact— in short, when I remember that this prosperity is the work of a single man, I am aroused to admiration and gratitude. *Cher ami*, this is quite between ourselves, for some persons would impute to these sentiments a very different motive from the real one, and, besides, it seems to me that praise from the heart is less anxious for publicity than that which proceeds from the intellect. . . .

Tuesday, 1 Prairial.
(May 21, 1805.)

"Les Templiers" continues to be a great success. Every one says that nothing better has been written for twenty years. Opinions differ a little as to the choice of subject and the truth of the characters. Parisian critics get warm, it is said, over Jacques de Molay and Philippe le Bel, and their greater or less guilt; but the fact remains that the tragedy draws immense houses, and is incessantly applauded.

To return to poor Salembini. Can he have written some piece of foolery? But, then, how comes it that his letters were opened, since they were brought by the Emperor's couriers? I am inclined to think it is some wicked calumny; in fact, I am sure he must have been imprudent rather than guilty. He always seemed to me such an honourable man.*

## XXXIII.

### TO M. DE RÉMUSAT AT MILAN.

Sannois, Saturday, 5 Prairial, Year XIII.
(May 25, 1805.)

I saw Salembini yesterday. He was quiet enough, relying on your friendship and his own innocence. He regrets most having occasioned vexation to you, and I was touched by the tone in which he said that he could never forgive himself for having caused you trouble and annoyance in

* As M. de Salembini and the trouble he caused are described in the Memoirs, I give this in full, although it is of no interest at present, except as affording an additional proof of the distrustfulness and meddlesomeness of the Imperial system of police. Salembini had written imprudently, not on politics, but on the scandals of the Court. His letters were opened, and he received orders to leave. In reading the present correspondence, it is necessary to remember that the writers had always to bear in mind the possibility of a similar treatment of their own letters.

return for all the kindness you have shown him.
I endeavoured to console him; and, in truth, he
appeared so confident, so calm, so entirely ignorant
of any misconduct deserving of the severity with
which he was banished, that I cannot believe him
to have been anything worse than a little imprudent.

I am now very anxious to hear from you, and
whether this unfortunate affair has had any unpleasant consequences. You do not mention the
Emperor, and this makes me uneasy. Ah! how
many vexations and troubles are caused by absence!
I can only endure it when I know you are well
and happy; but, alas! my lamentations are un-
availing. I must wait, I must watch the hours
pass by, before I can again be with you, and able
to speak to you at every moment of my life.

I am dining at St. Leu to-day, in order to take
leave of the princess, for I return to Paris on
Thursday. We shall be talking of our kind
protectress, to whom I beg you will frequently
speak of me, if she is still at Milan. I hope you
have given her all my letters. I preferred sending
them through you, because I feared they might
otherwise get lost. Tell her how greatly I am
attached to her; how I wish her a long-lasting
happiness, and that since Thursday I have sympathized in all the emotions that she must have
experienced.

Salembini has described the beautiful presents
you are bringing me, and for which I am half
inclined to scold you. *Mon ami,* you have been

extravagant in spending money on a wife whose reasonableness you are good enough to praise. I was far from wishing for so much, and there was no need thus to glorify your return home. On my side, all I can offer you in exchange are my two little jewels, Charles and Albert, and, like the Roman lady, I shall say, as I show you their fresh and smiling faces, "Here are my treasures, and with them the happiness that you have bestowed on me."

I have just been reading an excellent article on the "Templiers." It is in the *Mercure*, and is an answer to the censure showered on M. Raynouard by Geoffroy.* That wretched journalist took into his head to discover his dreaded philosophers among the defenders of the order of Knights Templars, and to attribute the wildest projects to the author of the tragedy, who endeavours, he said, to move people to compassion for their fate. You will have to take part in all the dissertations on your return; for you know it is not allowable to remain neuter on any subject, and at present disputes rage almost as fiercely on Philippe le Bel and the Templars as on Glück and Piccini. It must be admitted that we are a singular nation in the importance we attach to little things, while we often let great ones slip by with scarcely a glance. One need only cut off one's dog's tail to turn off

---

* Geoffroy, who was born at Rennes, in 1743, had succeeded Fréron, as editor of the *Année Lettéraire*, and also to his hatred of Voltaire. He was at this period editor of the *Journal des Débats*. He died in 1814.

the attention of the Parisians. But to return to the Templars : *Le Mercure* quotes two phrases of Pascal's and Bossuet's in their defence, and surely the authority of those great writers is sufficient to justify a poet in making them interesting. " The Templars," says Bossuet, " confessed under tortures, and denied when brought out to die ; there was perhaps more of avarice and revenge than of justice in their execution." These words occur in an abridged History of France, composed for the Dauphin by the Bishop of Meaux, and notwithstanding the restrictions that he said he had to impose on himself in a work produced under such circumstances.

Geoffroy can scarcely call these two witnesses *philosophers,* according, at least, to his own interpretation of the term.

## XXXIV.

### TO M. DE RÉMUSAT AT MILAN.

Sannois, Tuesday, 8 Prairial, Year XIII.
(May 28, 1805.)

. . . You are severe, I think, in your judgment of Raynouard ; the piece is much more successful than you fancy. Every box was taken, last night, for the sixth performance, and people were fighting for admittance at the doors. The play is far from being as spiritless as you think. All whom I have seen tell me they shed tears over it, and that they were moved by the same emotions that Corneille habitually arouses. It is written in simple and touching verse; the sentiments are generous without being bombastic, and such as are inspired by religion; the character of the king is cleverly drawn; in short, the interest is sustained for five acts without love-making, extraordinary events, or machinery. Surely the author's success is justified. You will judge for yourself when you return, and, for my part, I intend to see the piece when I get back to Paris.

While on the subject of the theatre, I find myself suddenly struck by that phrase of Mazarin's that you quote to me. What does it mean? How does it affect you? This and other words in your letter go to my heart. The depression in which you write does not proceed only from the grief of separation from those you love; I fear that you are hiding some secret sorrow from me. *Mon ami*, I have a right to share all things with you, and you must not deny me my half of your troubles.* Perhaps, however, they exist only in my imagination, which in your absence is gloomy, and would be still more so without the assurance in which I find all my comfort.

*Mon ami*, I really think I am becoming religious; our new separation is developing the feelings caused by that of last year. Do not let this alarm you, for, if my character be at all changed by it, it

---

* These feelings are explained further on, in a letter entrusted to Corvisart. The quotation from Mazarin is as follows: —" When any one was recommended to him for employment, the cardinal always asked, ' Is he lucky?' "

must be for the better and to the advantage of us both. I already feel that my study of religion and the meditations I make, after reading pure and devout books, are rendering me more gentle and good. The habitual recollection of God makes me wish as much as possible to avoid offending Him. My thoughts revert naturally to Him and to you, and at such times, in presence, as it were, of the Divinity, I renew my vows to love you and make you happy. Adieu. Do not smile over these few last lines ; let me enjoy the comforts of religion.

## XXXV.

### TO M. DE RÉMUSAT AT MILAN.

Paris, Sunday, 20 Prairial, Year XIII.
(June 9, 1805.)

. . . Prince Eugène's appointment * did not surprise me. It was spoken of here for some days past, and Madame d'Houdetôt sent me the news yesterday. She had seen the Princess Louis, who told her of it with tears, and confessed that after her first feeling of gratitude to the Emperor, the next had been grief at the separation from her brother. If he is still at Milan, pray offer him my good wishes and my homage. From my heart I trust that his happiness will be equal to his glory.

* Prince Eugène de Beauharnais had been made Viceroy of Italy on 18 Prairial.

I shall write to the Empress, whose mother's heart must be alternately glad and sorrowful. Poor mothers and wives often pay with tears for the prosperity of their sons and husbands. My sister is now doing this. M. de Nansouty has just been appointed to the command of the Reserve Cavalry, and is to accompany Prince Louis. Although it is a most honourable mission, and he is delighted, Alix only sées the separation and possible danger, and she is in tears. The expedition to England is more than ever talked of. It is said to be certain, and that on his return the Emperor will go to Boulogne. There are reports, on the contrary, of a Congress to be held at Brussels; in fact, each day brings forth some fresh rumour which is sure to be succeeded by another on the following.

I have been to the " Templiers." I was de-lighted, and cried a great deal. There are grave defects in the work, but greater beauties, which are so striking that the former are only perceived on reflection. It attracts great crowds; the Français is as full as in the height of the winter season, and the eleventh performance produced four or five thousand francs. " Madame de Sévigné " * was performed at your theatre the night before last, with only moderate success. It is an ill-conceived work, in which, by making

---

* "Madame de Sévigné" is a play in three acts, by Bouilly, the author of " Contes à ma fille " and " L'Abbé de l'Epée." The principal character was one of the last undertaken by Mademoiselle Contat. Michot and Mademoiselle Mars had comparative success.

Madame de Sévigné declaim in three quarters of an hour all that she wrote in twenty years, the author has contrived to represent her as the most affected and stilted person in the world. I saw also Duport's ballet of " Acis et Galatée," which is very pretty. I have now concluded my course of theatres, for the weather is beginning to be too hot to shut one's self up in a box. I am going to stay at home and get through my time as best I can. Do not forget that all the emotions and regrets you describe so well are experienced by me also, and that, although I endeavour to resign myself to your absence, I can never become accustomed to it.

## XXXVII.

### TO M. DE RÉMUSAT AT MILAN.

Paris, Thursday, 24 Prairial, Year XIII.
(June 13, 1805.)

I passed a pleasant day yesterday, conversing, about you principally, with real friends. The Abbé Morellet, Gallois, and Bertrand dined with us, and afterwards M. Devaines made his appearance; he takes compassion on our solitude and improves on acquaintance. We talked till midnight. Paris is so empty that they do not know what to do. Gallois feels quite lost, and is going to take himself and his reveries to Switzerland.

Madame de Souza (the mention of her is purely accidental, believe me) has arrived at Berlin, where she is *fêted* and caressed by the Queen and all the best society.    Her literary reputation had preceded her, and procured her a most gracious reception. It is no longer quite certain that her husband goes to Russia ; he is said to be inclined to give up diplomacy and retire into private life.    As you may imagine, the conversation yesterday turned for a time on our friend the ambassadress ; the " Dictionnaire de l'Académie " was the immediate cause. Abbé Morellet declares that the writings of women are what embarrass him most as to the meaning and employment of words.    Our favourite Madame de Sévigné reduces him to despair, and as he has no high opinion of the sentimental trifles which are the greatest charm of feminine compositions, he would willingly burn them all and forbid us ever to attempt the art again.    Gallois, as a chivalrous knight, took our part.    He argued that literature would be deprived of an important branch, if women were forbidden to write, and asserted that their so-called negligences of style are but a more graceful way of expressing their thoughts. During the discussion I kept saying to myself that I would willingly submit to such a prohibition, if I were allowed to tell my dearest one that I love him with my whole soul; and that if I were to make a dictionary, I would multiply in every possible way the modes of expressing that affection, which I never succeed in describing as strongly as I feel it in my heart.  . . .

## XXXVIII.

### TO M. DE RÉMUSAT AT MILAN.

Saturday, 26 Prairial, Year XIII.
(June 15, 1805.)

*Mon ami*, I received two letters from you to-day : one that Corvisart sent me in the morning, and another that I have this instant read. You can understand my surprise at the first. I keep my reflections on the subject to myself; you were my first thought and my first anxiety, Heaven knows. I will follow your advice and see the person you mention.* As to the lady of whom you speak, I have paid her but three visits since your departure : one on the occasion of her daughter's confinement, which then occupied her thoughts exclusively ; another, one evening in the midst of preparations for a little party that she was giving in honour of her daughter's recovery, and for which I did not remain because it would have bored me ; and a third time, when I went to take leave of her, as she was going into the

---

* In a note to the Memoirs, I have published the letter that my grandfather sent by Corvisart. It is a striking instance of the worry and wearisomeness of the Emperor's service. An accusation of too great an intimacy between my grandmother and Madame de Damas had been brought, and they had allowed themselves to criticize the Italian journey and the Emperor's brothers. As the letter in reply had to go through the post, it throws little light on the circumstances. The person whom my grandfather advised his wife to consult on the subject was the Minister of Police.

country. This is all. You can imagine my feelings, therefore, and I hasten to leave so unpleasant a subject.

We were struck, as you were, with the Emperor's speech at Genoa ; * it was very remarkable, and in all respects worthy of him. The union of the States seems to give general satisfaction, and all the Provençaux whom I know say it can do no harm at Marseilles. What an Empire it is that extends from those countries to Antwerp ! And what a man must he be who holds it all in his hand ! How few do we find in history like him !

These reflections are suggested to me by the study of history, which I have taken up in order to occupy my leisure time. Such a study is of special interest and use after a Revolution like ours, which throws a new light on many brilliant deeds, by which we had at first been dazzled, and at the same time makes us appreciate others that we had hitherto hardly noticed. How many circumstances and characters are explained by it ! How many actions justified ! It is a kind of labyrinth, in fact, of which the plan has at last been found out. I believe it would be most useful to recur in this way when one's reason is matured to the histories read during youth. We should thus escape the danger of retaining the impressions received at a period when our judgments are dictated by our feelings, and we only esteem that which we happen to like. Oh, happy, happy time of our youth, that flies so fast and that we waste

* The union of the Genoese States to the French Empire.

so recklessly! How sweet are its illusions and how far from me already! *Mon ami*, what thanks do I not owe you! Without you, without the happiness I derive from you, I think I could not resist the gloom and melancholy of life's disappointments.

You must try to put up with the extreme dulness of my letters just now. I know nothing, I see nobody, my life is as monotonous as possible, and yet in this dearth of all news you wish me to write to you every day. I must therefore write my thoughts, and you must be patient with their occasional sadness. I am not always able to control it, and I give way to feelings of melancholy, especially when unexpected trials are added to those of my everyday life. Your return only can dispel them; they cannot then master me, for their place will be taken by the sweetest emotions of joy.

I do not know whether I told you that the success of the "Templiers" had aroused all our tragic geniuses, excepting only Lemercier, whose line is decidedly epic poetry. He is writing on the most extraordinary subject. The scene is laid in the infernal regions, and the devils, by way of amusement, are acting plays in which they represent the various scenes of life. There will, no doubt, be something diabolic in the style, and I fear the whole will not be as clever as the devil.*

* "La Panhypocrisiade," a poem by Lemercier, which was not published until 1817, entirely justifies Madame de Rémusat in the opinion given in the above letter. Lemercier, it is well

Sunday.

I finished my evening, yesterday, with the "Templiers," which my mother had not yet seen. She was delighted, and we both shed tears, not of tenderness, but those that are excited by greatness of soul. The interest aroused by the piece is so great that its defects are not noticed until after the performance is over. Meanwhile one admires, one is moved, and any fault is overlooked. It is now going to be published, and will consequently have to pass a severe ordeal. It still attracts great crowds; the house was full last night, and the applause continual. There is one line which is always seized upon. Philip is speaking of the King of England, and says—

"La terreur de mon nom le poursuit dans sons île."

Saint-Prix is splendid in the part of the Grand Master, the principal and best-written character in the play; Talma * also does well, but his acting is somewhat injured by his state of health. He is ill and suffers from frequent nervous attacks. " Madame de Sévigné " has improved a little, but it will never be anything more than an indifferent play, proving, however, that the author has the ability for writing another on a better subject.

known, was succeeded at the French Academy by M. Victor Hugo, whom he had preceded on the path of literary reform, and whom he afterwards opposed as a greater reformer than himself.

* Talma took the part of Marigny. At a subsequent period, after the death or retirement of Saint-Prix, he acted the part of the Grand Master with the greatest success.

I have seen a most beautiful house this morning, belonging to Mr. Crawfurd.* He has bought the Hotel de Monaco, and furnished it superbly— the most splendid carpets and hangings, a quantity of china, and, more than all, the finest collection of portraits of celebrities, both men and women, from the time of Henry II. to our own days. All Louis XIV.'s century by Mignard! You can imagine my mother's delight with pictures of Madame de Sévigné and Madame de Grignan, Madame de Montespan and Madame de la Vallière. I spent nearly two hours in admiring all these fine things, though I felt sorry to think they will eventually find their way to the heirs of this wealthy individual in England; I was annoyed, too, I must confess, to see such a collection in the possession of an Englishman. However, we wandered about as if in an enchanted palace, without meeting a soul. The former owner has given it up to strangers; his wife, Madame Sullivan,† the mother of Madame d'Orsay, keeps herself out of the way. Visitors come and go and examine everything, and nobody interferes. Mr. Crawfurd is one of the richest of rich Englishmen. He has lost over here a hundred thousand francs of income (£4000) and does not even feel it. He spent a million on this new house in a period of two years,

* Mr. Crawfurd, a friend of Talleyrand's, was a clever man, who published several works in French for private circulation.

† Madame Sullivan was, as stated above, the mother of Madame d'Orsay, whose son, Count d'Orsay, was famous, thirty years ago, for the elegance of his dress. He married the daughter of the Earl of Blessington.

without the slightest difficulty. He likes living in
Paris, is hospitable, spends his money liberally,
and enjoys life. I do not require so large a fortune
to be happy, and I think we could lead a pleasant
life at less cost. Here is an opportunity for a fine
panegyric of moderation in fortune, but I could
say nothing new, and although the older I grow
the more I lean to a simple and quiet life, I
could amuse you by telling you what I have felt in
scenes of dazzling splendour and magnificence.
On the whole, I think I dread such splendour as
much as life in a hut.

You tell me that the Empress is good enough to
say that I do not write to her sufficiently often.
It is because I fear to be intrusive. I picture her
to myself so occupied, so agitated, and so overwhelmed, that I fear my letters might arrive at
some inconvenient moment. I will write to her,
however, in a few days, and will send my letter
through you, as I am uncertain as to where she
may be.

---

## XL.

TO M. DE RÉMUSAT AT MILAN.

Paris, Friday, 9 Messidor, Year XIII.
(June 28, 1805.)

We have been greatly shocked by the almost
sudden death of poor Neny. He was struck with
apoplexy on Sunday evening; in two hours he

completely lost the power of speech and movement, and after lingering for thirty-six hours, he expired, quite unconscious of everything. The suddenness with which death strikes us suggests many reflections to a dreamer like me. What trouble, what anxiety we give ourselves, in order to reach death at last! A little pleasure, more or less, and all is over! Where now are all the trifling vanities, which yet had such power to wound us? I do not include the feelings of the heart which adorn our life, and afford us comfort at its end. If in eternity we retain any remembrance of this life, it must surely be of our love for a tender, dear, and faithful friend to whom we have been indebted for all our happiness. And then perhaps, if we are permitted to make a prayer, it is that we may continue to enjoy that same happiness.

Poor Madame Dupuis * is in great grief. Her son has just died of malignant fever, after a long and painful illness. On her return from Plombières, whither she had accompanied Princess Joseph,† she found the child dangerously ill. He seemed to have waited for her in order to die, for she lost him a very few days afterwards. But I have written enough about death; I will try, if I can, to throw off the melancholy into which these sad events have cast me. A letter from you just now would do me great good, for I find it difficult to bear up against depression.

* She was a Creole, from Bourbon, and wife of the Intendant of Finance.
† Joseph Bonaparte.

Paris is duller than ever. Nobody is here; the theatres, not being attractive in hot weather, are empty ; nor can we enjoy the season, for it rains unceasingly, and we have the fire lighted every day. My mother and I are much together; we read or converse, and the order and regularity with which my days are passed, makes them glide by so quickly as to convince me that the right way to get through one's time is to spend it according to a fixed rule. I am sorrowful at being so far from you, but, strictly speaking, I am not dull; I read and think and muse, and the latter occupation affords me pleasure. You would laugh could you know with what plans, what wishes, and even with what delusions, my imagination fills up the void around me. Sometimes I build castles in the air of every kind : at others I hold conversations with interesting people ; I imagine speeches for my interlocutors, which I answer; I narrate and descant, and all this with my arms folded, in an easy-chair, or in my bed, waiting for sleep, which does not come so easily as of yore. Do not think, however, that I amuse myself with mere empty dreaming. There is something serious and reasonable in my reveries. I moralize, I argue, I strengthen within myself the principles in which I was brought up, and which have been confirmed by the happiness that you have bestowed on me. I replace the fond illusions of my youth with truths from which I endeavour to get all the consolation possible. Although I have learnt, by an experience I did not seek, to distrust human nature, I nevertheless try not to mistake my true friends. To conclude : I tell myself that real wisdom is not to be found in heart-breaking suspicion, but that to preserve one's own heart pure, and to allow one's self to be deceived with a certain facility, is perhaps the best way of obtaining all the happiness this world affords.

---

## XLI.

### TO M. DE RÉMUSAT AT MILAN.

Paris, Monday, 12 Messidor, Year XIII.
(July 1, 1805.)

I am writing to you in the midst of constant interruption. Since early this morning I have a stream of visitors to console me in my solitude.* I dare not close my door against them, for friends and kinsfolk, knowing that my mother has left me, seem to have agreed to meet each other here ; and yet the real way to make myself forget the slow lapse of time is to spend it in conversing with you. When writing to you, I regret nothing but your absence. I am thinking therefore, by way of consolation in my retirement, of always keeping on my desk a letter to you partly written, to which I can add a few words when I feel more sorrowful than usual. You may be sure, too,

* Madame de Vergennes and her grandson were at Auvers, Seine-et-Oise, staying with Madame Chéron.

that my book of sermons will not be neglected. The grand answer to unbelievers is the need of religion which we are always brought to feel by sorrow and trials. For my own part, I know that religion has given me comfort that I could have found in no other way; and yet I am but little advanced on the path, and I even feel that I should never wish to advance so far as to prefer anything to the dear and beloved friend of my heart.

What are you now doing? How I dread that you may be suffering from heat and fatigue! How your migratory life must tire you ; mind and body in constant movement, only the heart in repose! For, notwithstanding all that our returned travellers have told me of the beauty of Italian eyes, I cannot for one moment doubt that you have always turned away at once from their glances, rather than fail in those vows of fidelity to me, from which I will, on no pretext whatever, relieve you. I must not, however, include Corvisart among the admirers of the ladies of Milan. He took with him the *ennui* with which his life is everywhere burdened, and he came back dissatisfied with all he had seen. M. de Tournon appeared to me better pleased,* and I suspect he employed his time better than our Esculapius. He rather amused me by his account of the busily idle life

* M. Camille de Tournon-Simiane, Chamberlain to the Emperor, Prefect of Rome, and subsequently Prefect of Bordeaux, was born in 1778. He published some statistical works on Rome (2 vols. in 8vo, Paris, 1831), and died in 1833.

you are leading just now. He declares that he is quite convinced pleasure does not abide in palaces. I believe it, alas! but I feel how easily it might dwell with us, if we could abandon ourselves to the delicious sentiments on which you, as it were, nourished my youth. Were those golden and swiftly passing days the happiest that I shall ever know? I greatly fear so. I know not whether it is that our years, as they accumulate, bringing with them an involuntary knowledge of the truth, fill us also with dread of the future, or whether I possess a secret presentiment of the fate that awaits us, but in any case I own to a fear that we shall never again enjoy a peaceful existence. Far from being prodigal of my time and my happiness, as I used to be five or six years ago, I am becoming miserly over them. I grieve for the loss of either; I begin to perceive that if we suffer the present to escape us, it is irretrievably lost, and I suffer acutely, for instance, at the thought that I am perhaps destined often to be deprived of your dear presence.

I saw yesterday two of our friends who are far more fortunate than we, Mollien * and his wife. They have bought a small country house in which they reside. Every morning the husband goes to

* M. Mollien was not as yet at the head of the Treasury; he directed the Caisse d'Amortissement. He was born in 1758, and died in 1850. His wife, who was an amiable and superior woman, died, aged more than ninety, in 1880. To the last she clung to the memory of her husband and of those early times, so peaceful for her, while for others they were so disturbed. She was Lady-in-Waiting to Queen Marie Amélie.

the Caisse d'Amortissement, where he is employed, and labours honourably for his master and his country. At five o'clock he comes home to dinner, and passes the evening with his family. He has invested all his money in this little property; there are seventeen acres of land, which he amuses himself in laying out, and on which he counts every bit of timber. He is contented with his lot; talked at length with me on the subject, and he wishes for nothing beyond. His salary is sufficient for his wants, the Emperor trusts him, he is respected by worthy people, and he smiles in private at the fear of him which certain ambitious enemies feel, and at the dislike they choose to cultivate, whereas had they taken the trouble to know him, they would see he is too moderate a man to be in any way a dangerous rival. I listened to his account of his position, of his devotion to the Emperor, of his simple, quiet tastes, with the more pleasure that I discerned some likeness to you in his description of himself, and this similarity, flattering to both, lent a great charm to his conversation. Both he and his wife seemed pleased at my visit, and I promised to go there again with you.

## XLII.

### TO M. DE RÉMUSAT AT MILAN.

Paris, Tuesday, 13 Messidor, Year XIII.
(July 2, 1805.)

I went yesterday to Romainville. I had given offence by my neglect; it was my first visit there since you left me, and Madame de Montesson* scolded me for not taking advantage of my liberty to go a little more into society. This is a very general reproach, and I feel it is deserved, yet I have no wish to correct my failings in that respect. What I like most, when you are away, is to divide my time between my mother and my son. . . .

To return to Madame de Montesson. I found her looking ill and trying to amuse herself by superintending improvements in her house. She is so changed, and the contrast is so great between her appearance and the elegance and luxury surrounding her, I could not help being struck by it. It was as if she were adorning her grave. You see that I am still somewhat inclined to melancholy thoughts caused by solitude and separation from you; and I do not reject them, for they are not really saddening except when the effect of a sorrow for which there is no remedy; when they have hope for a companion there is a

---

* Madame de Montesson died a few months later, on February 6, 1806. She was half-sister to Madame de Genlis.

H

charm about them, to which I willingly abandon myself.

I have already told you, I think, that I have taken up Roman history, which I had not looked at since I was a girl of fifteen. It used to delight my youthful imagination, and I like it still but in a different way. Alas! *mon ami*, I have grown old.* I feel no enthusiasm, as formerly, for those austere republicans; our own troubles have opened my eyes to their ostentatious virtues. I admire something I read by Saint-Evremond on this subject. He gives an excellent explanation of the rustic simplicity of the early inhabitants of Rome, which he contends was not virtue, but simply ignorance of any other mode of life. " In spite of what posterity has tried to make us believe," he says, " their valour was nothing but ferocity, and obstinacy, with them, took the place of knowledge. Far from being urged on by a sense of superiority, the Romans, in the early days of their Republic, were but dishonest neighbours, who by main force cultivated the fields of others."† However, I do not expect that you will find in the Italy of to-day any trace of those early Roman manners, whether they were the outcome of virtue or of ignorance, and nothing less than the presence of a great man like our master would suffice, I believe, to rouse

---

* She was then twenty-five years of age.

† The above quotation contains the matter, but not the exact words of Saint-Evremond in his " Réflexions sur les Divers Génies du Peuple Romain dans les Divers Temps de la République," p. 176. His work is very little read at present, which is to be regretted.

the nation from the lethargy in which she is steeped, and which made Duclos always say, *the Italians of Rome.* To such a mind as yours it must be a curious and interesting study to watch the point to which his glory will succeed in arousing them. While he creates new peoples, so to speak, during his triumphant progress, France herself must be a striking spectacle to all beholders. Her navy, formed in two years, after a destructive revolution, and at the present moment taking the offensive against an enemy that has long carelessly despised it; her tranquillity in the absénce of her ruler; and, lastly, her government that has not suffered in any part of its administration during this long absence! All these things are sufficient to excite surprise and admiration, and to kindle the imagination of the ardent. I own that I am not yet too old for enthusiasm of this kind. . . .

## XLIII.

### TO M. DE RÉMUSAT AT MILAN.

Paris, Wednesday Morning, 14 Messidor, Year XIII.
(July 3, 1805.)

. . . Pray tell the Empress that I saw at Guérin's a portrait of her that only requires two sittings more, and is an admirable likeness and painting. It is really charming. It gives all the delicacy of her features and the expression of her eyes; in fact, it is perfection, and I wish it were mine. Thank her also for the kindness with which she receives my letters. Of course I should like to have a few lines from her, but I do not presume to expect it. Herbaut,* whom I have just seen, tells me she is going direct to Plombières. Shall we join her there? Would you be free?

I saw Mademoiselle Contat yesterday; she had written so often and pressed me so much to receive her, that I thought I could not continue to refuse. She told me that Talma's illness is taking the form of such violent nervous attacks that sometimes he is not quite himself. If this be true, the poor Comédie Française will be in a bad way. At the present time there is absolutely no money taken; the best pieces fail to attract. It is not the fault of the actors, for their repertory is good, and they all act; but the weather is warm and the small theatres are crowded. The latter constantly give pieces which excite curiosity, either by their extravagance or, what is worse, their indecency, and Racine and Molière are forsaken for the coarse farces of the Boulevards. I saw some of them last week with mamma, and we had great difficulty in obtaining places for "Le Revenant de Bérézule," and "La Guerrière des Sept Montagnes."† Poor Mahérault is quite paralyzed,

* Herbaut, valet and hairdresser to the Empress, made his fortune as a fashionable mercer.

† The melodrama, "Le Revenant de Bérézule," was brought out at the Ambigu, on 7 Messidor, Year XIII. (June 26, 1806). The ostensible author was M. François, and the real author, Madame de Bawr, narrates in her Memoirs that the piece failed

because your actors all complain that they are not earning anything. "Les Templiers" would bring in some money, but Talma's illness has put a stop to it. Thus, you are longed for and expected ; they come every day to inquire about your return, and perhaps when they have seen you and given you no end of trouble they will be no better pleased, for such are comedians— I was going to say, such are men.

## XLIV.

### TO M. DE RÉMUSAT AT MILAN.

Paris, Friday, 16 Messidor, Year XIII.
(July 5, 1805.)

I resume my journal, *cher ami*. I was unable to continue writing it yesterday, although I was for the greater part of the day at home. After beginning the morning as usual by thinking of you, I next went out to buy the chairs for your room. I have now arranged them and your books also, so all is ready to receive you. I made haste to prepare the room, as if by so doing I could hasten your return. At any rate, it made me think of it, and thus almost enjoy it beforehand. Afterwards I amused myself by putting my papers, as I call

so utterly, that, having made her escape at the end of the first act, she could still, from the Boulevards, hear the hisses. No doubt it was improved afterwards. " La Guerrière des Sept Montagnes," or " La Laitière des Bords du Rhin," is also a melodrama.

them, in order, and by reading over the effusions of my childhood, to which in early days I attached so much importance, and which have acquired it since, from the happiness of the time to which they carry me back. This interesting reading and my sweet reveries whiled away the time for me until two o'clock, and then Madame de Ganay arrived, with whom I had a pleasant talk. She is nice and seems friendly; I like her extremely. Afterwards I saw Corvisart, who annoyed me about my health, and pleased me by the good opinion of you which he is always ready to express.

I dined alone; but did not pass a solitary evening, for Madame Devaines, M. Siméon, Abbé Morellet, Gallois, my sister, MM. de Lacretelle, Desfaucherets,* and Raynouard came in rather early. The latter, to whom I had written a note of thanks for the two copies of his play that he had sent me, had asked my permission to be introduced to me. His slight Provençal accent delights me; he is simple in manner and well bred. He speaks modestly of his success, and gratefully of the kindness of the public. He is not blind to the faults of his piece, and desires very much to obtain for it the approbation of the Emperor,† to whom

---

* M. de Lacretelle, junior, the friend of Madame d'Houdetôt, was a member of the French Academy. M. Desfaucherets, author of the comedy called " Le Mariage Secret."

† He did not obtain this approbation, if we may believe the " Memoirs de M. de Beausset." " It is probable," said the Emperor, " that if M. Geoffroy's paper had not said so much against the piece, others would have said less for it."

he says he is indebted for valuable criticism on the occasion when it was read to his Majesty by Fontanes.

He recited some beautiful lines from his "États de Blois," which, however, he is in no hurry to produce, fearing that after his recent triumph very much will be expected of him. He is quite ready to cede his rights to other authors; for instance, to Legouvé, who has just finished his tragedy, "La Mort de Henri Quatre," to which he attaches great importance. On the whole, I am pleased with M. Raynouard. We read together Geoffroy's last attack on him and M. de Lalande. He says he is under an obligation to Geoffroy's paper for censure, which has given him celebrity, and he is determined never to reply to it, because Fontenelle was greatly admired for his silence under similar provocation; his enemies being driven at last to entitle their pamphlets "Réponse au Silence de M. de Fontenelle."

I have finished "Saint-Evremond," which I like very much. I am now reading "La Décadence des Romains," and I think with M. Bertrand, that Montesquieu has made great use of this early author, who is not now sufficiently read. Their opinions are often the same, and expressed sometimes in identical language. What I like least, as the result of these studies of mine, are the Romans themselves—the turbulent, irritable Romans. Notwithstanding the courage and tenacity of their Senate, whose conduct through whole centuries I cannot help admiring, my opinion is—

and it is shared fortunately by many others—that a monarchy is the best form of government for a nation, and I have a womanly inclination even for a little despotism. When I have finished Montesquieu I shall take up Tacitus, if you give me enough time. Had I leisure I would try it in Latin, in which I beg to inform you that I am improving. Charles's Latin lessons are of great use to me, and I am present at them as much for my own sake as for his. I feel that it would be my favourite study, perhaps because of the beauty of the language in itself, or because I have a natural turn for that kind of work, or—and this is the most likely—because it recalls a time when you first taught me, and there was a charm in every pursuit that brought us together.

I have just been interrupted by M. Dudemaine,* who came to take leave; he goes into Provence on Monday, and hopes to see the Emperor there, because he has been told that a petition was to be addressed to his Majesty, praying him to visit that part of the country. I dare not hope that he may be disappointed, for I am half a Provençale myself, and it seems that our province needs sorely a visit from its master. People say he is displeased with the Prefect; but does mankind ever speak well of those in authority over them? and does not their pride almost always lead them to revenge themselves on those who rule them by censure?

* M. Dudemaine was son-in-law to Madame de Foresta, my grandfather's half-sister.

## XLV.

TO M. DE RÉMUSAT AT MILAN.

Paris, Saturday, 17 Messidor, Year XIII.
(July 6, 1805.)

I am beginning to care less for my desk, and the anticipation of a far higher pleasure rather spoils that of writing. Is it possible that I shall soon see you again? The very thought is a delight to my poor heart, so saddened by your long absence. I rejoice over it more than I can express. Time no longer hangs heavily, the house no longer is gloomy; it will soon be your abode, and I begin to take pleasure in it once more.

After this little outpouring, I take up my journal again, which cannot be very lively reading for you, but amuses me to write. Yesterday, after finishing my letter, I gave a very nice little dinner to Mesdames de Ganay, Sannoise, Nansouty, and M. Bertrand. After dinner they went to the Opera, and I stayed at home with the Abbé Morellet, who had come in to see me, and with M. Pasquier. I took a little walk with these two gentlemen, and so ended the day. I went to breakfast this morning with Mesdames de Sainte-Aldegonde, who are no others than Mesdemoiselles d'Aumont;* they

---

* Mesdemoiselles d'Aumont were two sisters, who had a great friendship for my grandmother. She had succeeded in obtaining the restoration of their property as *émigrés*, as has been told in the Memoirs. They were married on the same day, to two brothers. One of these was a deputy under the Restoration.

were both married a few days ago. I enclose a
letter which they beg you to present to the
Empress. They do not forget what they owe to her
Majesty, and they are both happy and grateful.
This is very nice and also very rare. There was
nothing very noteworthy in the remainder of the
day. I dined alone, and then showed myself at
the Archchancellor's; he has resumed his receptions after a serious illness. The crowd was
immense; people just came for a moment and
then disappeared. I met Madame de Lucchesini;
she told me she had frequently seen you, that the
Empress looked lovely at the coronation, and that
the Emperor has grown stout. She also told me
about the fêtes, which, she said, were splendid. I
finished my evening at the Français. "Le Philosophe sans le savoir" was admirably acted, but
nobody there to see it. Your actors are in despair
at this desertion of their theatre, and Talma's
illness is a crowning misfortune. He is a little
better, but in a state of depression and melancholy
that requires attention, and his comrades want
him, ill or well, to act with them. I was greatly
pleased at seeing "Le Philosophe" again, though
it made me cry.

You will find us all here together on your return,
but when are you coming? The Archchancellor
told me the Emperor had said nothing on the
subject. On the other hand, M. de Fleurien * has
gone to Fontainebleau. Are you going to Mar-

---

* M. de Fleurien, formerly a naval officer, was Intendant of
the Emperor's household.

seilles ? Will our master take that additional journey ? What activity ! what strength ! I think Boileau's line might be applied to him :

" Le ciel met sur le trône un prince infatigable."

Sunday Evening.

I will begin my letter while waiting for your Bouffons, who are to be presented to me this morning by Picard, and to sing something for me. Their public performances will begin soon, but they wished me to see them first, and I very willingly consented.

I received this morning a letter from Deschamps, which the Empress was so good as to direct him to write to me. She kindly says that she would write herself but for her grief at this painful separation from her son. I can sympathize with her. There is no heartfelt sorrow that I cannot compassionate. Poor mothers and wives too often pay for your vanities with their tears, but, if I may say so without offence, those acute feelings procure them a joy of which you can form no idea ; and this seems to me so precious an advantage, that in spite of all the drawbacks of a woman's position, in spite even of the delicacy of my health, which I owe probably to my sex, I would not exchange it for yours. What is the reason of this preference, *mon cher ami?* I leave it for you to guess. Ask your own heart, and you will soon be answered.

I am going to dine with the elder Madame De-vaines, and afterwards to pay a few visits. I am

taking advantage of my liberty, for on Wednesday
my little schoolboy comes back to me, and then
I shall have but very few leisure moments. My
mother writes to me that his improved health
convinces her more than ever that he ought to
spend a part of every year in the country, to
strengthen his constitution. I have several ideas
on the subject which I will confide to you. I
don't think they will be difficult to carry out.
But I hear our musicians arriving ; so adieu, until
after the concert.

Sunday Evening.

I am quite tired out with listening and talking to so many persons, whom I could barely
understand. Your Bouffons, however, met with
approval from the amateurs who came here to
listen to them. However, we made some criticisms ;
none, however, on their appearance. The ladies
are all pretty, very pretty. La Crespy—for I must
call her as she calls herself—is very nice-looking,
and her voice is, I think, very fine. Madame
Megliorruchi's is worn, and she sings out of tune.
Mademoiselle Salucchi has a beautiful voice, but
does not know how to use it. The *bouffon*, I
think, will make us regret Martinelli, but you
know that particular style is not adapted for a
room. There is one superb bass, and another
rather the worse for wear, but good nevertheless.
Nozzari is best of all, but he complains of being
the only tenor.* We hear there will be another

* The Italian Opera had been opened in Paris, at the Olympic
Theatre, Rue de la Victoire, in 1801, under the management of

beautiful female voice. I have now given you my opinion, which perhaps you did not want. You are a judge of beauty, *monsieur*, and will be congratulated, when you arrive, on the pretty faces you have picked up on your travels. Whereupon I kiss you and say adieu. I am now going to Madame Devaines'. All the morning I have been talking the most wretched Italian, which, however, delighted the poor foreigners, who do not know a word of French.

---

## XLVI.

### TO M. DE RÉMUSAT AT MILAN.

Paris, Monday Morning, 19 Messidor, Year XIII.
(July 8, 1805.)

. . . I must tell you that I am delighted with Montesquieu. I had never read the " Décadence "

Mademoiselle Montansier, who in 1802 removed it to the Salle Favart. In 1804 Picard was appointed manager of the Opera, under the direction of the First Chamberlain, and established it at the Salle Louvois, where his company acted together with the Comédiens Français. It was there that the tenor Garcia, father of Mesdames Malibran and Viardot, made his first appearance in 1808. It is not easy to find in the annals of the theatre, or old *almanacks*, the names of the singers mentioned above. I find, however, in the Revue des Comédiens, 1808, a grand panegyric of La Crespy, commencing thus : " Is this Venus, or Minerva, or Madame Crespy advancing towards us? What a beautiful head ! What fine arms ! What grace ! What elegance ! What a noble deportment ! . . . How can any one say, after this, that this adorable Italian has not a good method, etc., etc." Mademoiselle Salucchi was a graceful and intelligent singer.

steadily before, but this time I read it at leisure and with profit. I wished for you, however, first because I like you to share in all my pleasures and pursuits, and next because you could have explained certain things to me, and set me right on others; it would have been a help. Only that I know your time is fully occupied, I would tell you all that struck me most in the book. It must be an excellent guide for those who want to write or *make* a history. The author seems to have been in the secret of every political movement, he points out so accurately the hidden springs of each. One thing struck me very much; on several occasions he seems to have foreseen and explained our Revolution. If we read him attentively, we can understand all our misfortunes and all our triumphs as well. "There can be no State," he says, "so threatening to others as the State involved in the horrors of a civil war. Every man becomes a soldier, and when peace is made within it, such a State has great advantages over others whose subjects are mostly mere citizens." *
What think you of this? But I should copy the whole book, if I were to write you all that struck me. I am so pleased with the "Décadence," that I feel inclined to try the "Esprit des Lois;" but would it be too difficult? I shall wait for you to decide.

I went to Suresnes this morning to breakfast with Madame de Vaudémont. She has a charming

* "Considerations sur les Causes de la Grandeur des Romains et de leur Décadence," chapter xi.

place there; one would never think the village was near. Everything is very simple and in good taste ; the garden is full of flowers, the air is scented, there is a lawn, and a lovely view ; in fact, I was charmed and envious. It would suit us exactly ! It is but a mile from St. Cloud, and quite near Paris, and then it is a tiny place, and just fit for us. I should never wish for anything better.

On returning I called to take leave of Madame de Ganay, who goes away to-morrow. I shall miss her very much. Both my mother and I like her. During her stay here, she had become intimate, I don't know how, with Madame de Fontanes, who often spoke to her of you. Among other things, she told her that Fontanes thought very highly of your keen and sound judgment, and that you were highly informed and yet agreeable. Only that I fear to offend your modesty, I should say that he estimates you rightly, and that, for my own part, I must admit (and this without laying myself open to a charge of partiality) that the more I see of society, and the more I listen to others, the more also do I appreciate you. By-the-by, somebody asked me yesterday if you were ambitious ? The question surprised me at first ; not that I should have found any difficulty in replying, but because experience, which I am gaining in spite of myself, warns me always to seek for the motive of questions before answering them. Alas ! the time is past when I believed them all to proceed from good-natured interest !

## XLVII.

### TO M. DE RÉMUSAT AT STRASBURG.*

Paris, Saturday, 26 Fructidor, Year XIII.
(September 13, 1805.)

I intended writing to you yesterday, but I was tired out, and lay down all day. To-day I am perfectly well. You may believe me, for in an hour's time I shall be starting for St. Cloud, and you know I never stir unless my health allows of it. I received a short letter from you on Thursday, which would have deeply grieved me, only that by the time it reached me, I hoped your mind was set at ease. It is true that I was ill after you left me, but not so ill as you imagine, and I should not now say a word about it but for your affectionate inquiries. I am quite well; pray do not be anxious and add unnecessary pain to the grief of separation.

I spent Thursday evening at St. Cloud. There was a performance in the theatre of two pieces by the Opéra Comique. It was a little languid, but in

---

* The Emperor, who had returned to Paris from Genoa, in July, 1805, went again at the beginning of August, to Boulogne, in order to be present at the departure of the army. War had just been declared. He returned shortly afterwards to Malmaison, and prepared to set out for Germany (where he gained the victory of Austerlitz), and his First Chamberlain received orders to proceed to Strasburg and prepare for the arrival of the Emperor and Empress. The latter was to remain at Strasburg during the war, while the Emperor and part of his household went to the front.

other respects amusing, and the Emperor seemed pleased. After the play he went to his own apartments, and I remained for nearly an hour with the Empress and a few other persons, among whom was our new companion, Madame de Canisy,* who had been appointed that morning. She is extremely pretty.

Her Majesty told me that the " Femmes Savantes " would probably be performed in a short time. The actors have been warned, so the piece is ready. Mahérault, who called on me this morning, is my informant. He is taking the Tivoli baths, and this prevents him from writing to you as often as he would like. He asked me to tell you that he had proposed to punish Mademoiselle Georges, but that the committee opposed it, as she is not altogether in the wrong, and that they had decided on a fine, with the proviso that, if you thought fit, severer measures should be resorted to. Mahérault says the word *prison* struck terror into them all. He is always wishing for you, for he feels too unwell to rule with a strong hand. The actors are complaining of Mademoiselle Raucourt, who is still in the country and never acts. Your commissioner will write you particulars of all this in a few days. But as delay is the darling sin of the majority of mankind, Desfaucherets has

* Madame de Canisy had shortly before become the wife of her cousin, Equerry to the Emperor. She was remarkably lovely, and retained traces of beauty to the end of her life. Under the Restoration, she married M. de Calaincourt, Duc de Vicenza. She died in 1876.

I

not yet drawn up his statement; he sends me continual excuses and completes nothing. I scolded him both on your account and my own, and he assures me that you shall soon have it.

We are in very low spirits here. Alice spends her time crying because Nansouty has joined the army, and my own regrets are silenced by her grief. Moreover, our friends the Chérons leave Paris tomorrow, and my mother will miss them greatly. Our winter will be a dull one; the future is so misty that we dare rely on nothing, and we are again in the state of uncertainty from which we were just beginning to emerge. It is a curious fact, but the uneasiness and anxiety I cannot help feeling under the circumstances, disappear when I find myself in the presence of him who nevertheless is their cause. On Thursday night, at the St. Cloud theatre, when I beheld the calm countenance of the Emperor, I felt tranquillized and assured of peace and of our future. When he first entered his box, he looked grave but not anxious. Towards the end he often laughed, and I felt tempted to thank him for his gaiety, and to augur well from the hopes it permitted me to entertain.

If you care for a piece of news, I may tell you that Count Rumford has come back, and all the members of Madame Lavoisier's * circle have fled at his approach. As they know not where to go, I have taken pity on them without one reproach for their assiduity elsewhere. A coquette com-

* Count Rumford, a German, born in America, was paying his addresses to Madame Lavoisier, whom he afterwards married.

plains ; a lover suffers ; a friend alone can always enjoy without a drawback the pleasures of the present moment.

Did I give you the names of the Ladies-in-Waiting who go to Strasburg ? I cannot recollect. Writing so frequently, I fear to repeat myself; there. is so little for me to tell ! I seldom go out ; I see few persons, and always the same few, and they always say just the same things. When alone, I read ; that is my great resource. During your stay in Italy, I used to write to you on Roman history ; now the history of France, which I have just taken up, will be my subject. It is not an edifying one. Our proud and boastful nation has always been as inconsistent, and frequently as unjust and as cruel as others. The following reflection occurred to me : judging from the excesses into which she has plunged, France is less adapted than other nations for liberal self-government. I ventured on airing this opinion before our old friend,* but you should have heard him lecture me on my hankering after despotism ! " He was not surprised, however—all women have a leaning that way." This reminds me that one evening, when with two other ladies I was playing at cards with the Emperor, and he had been amusing himself with some of the small gossip of which feminine conversations usually consist, he said laughingly, " *Nous autres femmes*," and I was greatly inclined to answer, " *Nous autres rois*." But how I am gossiping ! Adieu. I am now

* This old friend must be the Abbé Morellet.

going to St. Cloud, and will resume my letter when I get back.

Sunday Morning.

*Bon jour, mon ami.* I begin my day, as usual, by thinking of you, and I allow myself the pleasure, besides, of telling you so directly I wake. I went to St. Cloud yesterday. The Empress, who as usual was kindness itself, expressed a wish to see me oftener. I asked her permission to stay a few days with her, to which she consented with a readiness that went straight to my heart. To-morrow, therefore, I shall take up my abode in that royal palace, which, between ourselves, seems to me gloomier than ever. I know not how it is, but each day seems to increase the general reserve and suspicion. People seem half afraid of conversing even on the most trivial subjects ; there seems to be a prevailing want of harmony, and yet, could all hearts be opened, I feel sure that the senti-ments of each would be extraordinarily alike. For my own part, I glide quietly on my way, without pretensions of any kind, and as I stand in no one's path, I am treated with great civility, and I think I am not disliked. Only that I have a real affec-tion for the Empress, I confess I should have found it hard to leave my mother and children while you are away, but I owe her so much love and gratitude, and I have no opportunity of show-ing them except by attending on her. I must not complain, therefore, since my actions are nearly always regulated by my affections.

# XLVIII.

### TO M. DE RÉMUSAT AT STRASBURG.

St. Cloud, Tuesday, 30 Fructidor, Year XIII.
(September 17, 1805.)

I am writing to you from St. Cloud. I arrived here yesterday evening, and now I am far from all those I love best. My mother was rather depressed at my leaving her, for she will be quite alone. Our friends the Chérons are on their way to Poitiers. You can imagine how she will miss them and what a deprivation it is for Charles; they were both quite sorrowful at losing me. But the Empress is so kind to me; and then, as she herself is on the point of departure, I was anxious to spend a few days with her. She is delighted at the return of Princess Louis.* Both mother and daughter wept with joy on meeting; they have been truly happy together, which is rare in their high station, and perhaps not very frequent in a lower rank of life.

Prince Louis strikes me as being thinner and feeble; his little son is a fine child.† They left us at eight o'clock, and we remained, a party of ladies only, until it was time to retire. As you may imagine, the conversation was not very lively. It turned partly on the neglect with which we are

---

* Princess Louis Bonaparte, or Queen Hortense.
† This was the eldest son of Queen Hortense. He died of croup in Holland.

treated by you gentlemen of the Emperor's household, and we asked ourselves, but of course without obtaining any satisfactory answer, why you are not more attentive to us.   Afterwards the Emperor sent for the Empress and we withdrew. I saw M. de Caulaincourt for a moment and gave him your message.   He thinks the Court will depart on the 1st or 2nd of the month, so you will soon see their Majesties, and we shall be reduced to solitude again.

Immediately on waking this morning I threw open my shutters, and the first person I saw was the Emperor walking in the park.   He is the first to rise and the last to retire, always ready and active.   May Heaven protect and watch over him! You may be sure that this will be the subject of my morning prayer.

You are very good to tell me about your Alsatian family ; I quite love the kind people who know how to appreciate you.   Your assurances of affection give me such pleasure !   I rely with entire confidence on their sincerity !   Oh, *mon ami*, how sweet it is to have such a feeling !   Our mutual affection seems like a haven of rest amid the storms of life ; it will soothe all the sorrows that we are perhaps destined to endure, and will add to all our joys.

My mother begs you to thank Madame Dietrich * for her remembrance; she says she found her a

---

* Madame Dietrich was the widow, I believe, of the Mayor of Strasburg, who had perished in the Revolution, and the mother of Madame Scipion Périer and Madame de Sahune.

charming woman, and retains a great regard for her. Adieu for the present. I must dress and go down to the Empress; I shall return to my letter afterwards.

Wednesday.

I was unable to resume my letter yesterday; not that I had much other occupation, but you know how the time slips by here, and although it is not actually employed in any way, still it is not at one's own disposal. In the morning the Empress received a great number of persons as usual, and while she was giving audiences and hearing petitions and complaints of all kinds, I sat at work in a corner of the room, thinking of you, my dearest, and of the devoted affection that makes my life happy and dear to me. Madame de S—— was by my side, and, without malice, I could perhaps tell of what or of *whom* she was thinking; for, between ourselves, she makes no attempt to conceal the object of her thoughts nor the pleasure they give her. She is very often here, and says *openly* that their Majesties take great pleasure in her society and in her conversation. This I can easily believe; but by proclaiming the fact she excites a good deal of jealousy. She forgets that the world seldom forgives, especially in a woman, any triumph of which she appears in the least conscious.

Everything is being got ready here for immediate departure, and you will soon be in the midst of bustle, and I in profound quiet. How dull and sad I shall be until the day of your return!

How uninteresting everything is when you are away!

I have been acting as First Chamberlain this morning. The Emperor has commanded the "Menteur" for to-morrow at St. Cloud. I wrote immediately to Mahérault; I gave orders about the scenery; in fact, you would be pleased with all the pains I have taken with the performance. I should like his Majesty to recognize your zeal in the perfection of the piece, and to feel that you and I are in partnership in our desire to please him.

My mother writes that her little favourite is perfectly well. I saw her for a moment last night at the Opéra, whither I accompanied the Empress. "Don Giovanni" was performed, but, notwithstanding the beauty of the music, was not a great success. Parisians follow the fashion in affecting to admire Mozart, but they are not sufficient musicians to appreciate his genius. I must admit also that the opera was not particularly well rendered. The Emperor was not present—he waited to hear the verdict; perhaps he will go on Friday to take leave of the Parisians.

Adieu. I must now rise and find my way downstairs. I am expecting my poor Alix, who is full of all sorts of anxiety; you can understand why. What vexations and crosses there are in life! On the other hand, what blessings and delights when the journey is made with you!

## XLIX.

### TO M. DE RÉMUSAT AT STRASBURG.

**St. Cloud, Tuesday, 1st Complementary, Year XIII.**
**(September 18, 1805.)**

Since yesterday I have been most anxious to tell you of several things that I have heard, but was afraid of trusting *to the post;* Hébert,[*] however, is just starting, and I shall send my letter by him. Again it is the Comédie that is in question. Yesterday, Monday, before coming to St. Cloud, I had Desfaucherets to dine with me, and he gave me the following history :—Last Friday Mesdemoiselles Duchesnois, Volnais, and Bourgoin betook themselves to St. Cloud, where the Empress received them. The first lady asked for her holiday, the second for a more important *rôle,* and the third for I know not what. They complained also of you. The Empress listened to everything with her usual kindness, and protested against injustice. She sent for Auguste de Talleyrand,[†] and ordered him to give the young ladies a holiday and a *rôle.* Auguste, who was quite taken aback, said he had no power to do this, and that he could only venture on it if her Majesty

[*] The Emperor's valet.

[†] M. Auguste de Talleyrand, cousin to M. de Talleyrand, was one of the Chamberlains and had the care of the Opéra Comique. He also undertook the First Chamberlain's duties in the absence of the latter. Under the Restoration he was minister in Switzerland.

would give express commands to that effect. As she did not think proper to commit herself so far, she dismissed the young ladies with many promises. You may imagine the bad effect of this at the theatre. Auguste de Talleyrand, on his way up to his own quarters, told the whole story to Campenon,* adding that he did not know what offence you had given at the theatre, but that the Emperor had said things were getting on very badly there. Desfaucherets also told me that Campenon receives threatening anonymous letters every day; he is warned to expect a thrashing, and is told that your intentions are well known (I do not know how), and that it is not to be endured that a man like himself, who thinks poorly of actors, should be allowed to govern them. Lastly, Dazincourt paid him a visit of congratulation and abused Mahérault. I considered that you ought to be informed of all this. You would do well to come to some arrangement, for everything is greatly disorganized here. As for me, I will do my best to shield you during the short remaining stay of their Majesties, and if I hear anything further, I shall contrive some way of letting you know.

*Mon ami*, I wish also to speak to you about M. de Nansouty. Caulaincourt told me that the Emperor had stated publicly that he had received

* M. Campenon, a literary man and subsequently a member of the French Academy, was, either then or shortly afterwards, Imperial Commissioner of the Opéra Comique. He filled Mahérault's place at the Théâtre Français during his illness, and there was some intention of keeping him there permanently.

his resignation. I mentioned this to Prince Louis, who seemed to take a great interest in the matter. He blames Nansouty, however, for taking such a step, but will try to smooth matters over. I may not hear anything more of it here, but you will probably know, being on the spot, and will keep me informed.*

I am so hurried, as Hébert is starting, that I must conclude my letter. Moreover, these vexatious incidents are depressing, and I feel almost unable to write on other subjects. You in your wisdom will act as you think fit, while I, in my love for you, can only distress myself. Adieu. I have been here at St. Cloud since yesterday evening. They talk to me of you there, but I would rather talk of you with Charles.

---

## L.

### TO M. DE RÉMUSAT AT STRASBURG.

Thursday, 2nd Complementary, Year XIII.
(September 19, 1805.)

I am in a state of nervousness such as you have often experienced on days of performance at the Comédie. I hope all will go well this evening, and please the Emperor; if not, I shall be terribly

* M. de Nansouty had been appointed Chamberlain to the Empress, a very insignificant post, which he resigned, without, however, falling into disgrace with the Emperor, who made him his First Equerry.

disappointed. A circumstance has happened at the Comédie, with regard to this performance, for which I am partly to blame. About a year ago I saw Fleury act the *Menteur*, and Dugazon the *Valet*, so I wrote to Mahérault asking him for those two actors. Dazincourt * flew into a violent passion, and wrote to me, saying that you had divided the part of the *Valet* into two, and that the *Menteur* was one of his parts. He said that if the Emperor commanded it he would obey, but that he should at the same time send in his resignation. As his Majesty had said nothing about the actors, I wrote to Mahérault that I did not claim the slightest right to alter the distribution of the parts, and that therefore M. Dazincourt must act. This is my most serious misadventure at present.

Since I am on the subject of the *tripot*, I must tell you that the three actresses who were received by the Empress have since made a great boast of their visit to her. I mentioned this to her Majesty, who commanded me to tell you that what she said to them has been greatly exaggerated ; that, far from promising leave of absence to Mademoiselle Duchesnois, she had replied that since you, who are her director, had refused her application, there must be good reasons for not granting it. But all the additions made to her words by these young ladies have convinced her that she will do well not to admit them in future. When she arrives

* Dazincourt's reputation as an actor was inferior to that of Dugazon, his colleague.

at Strasburg you will be able, much better than I, to explain your reasons for refusing leave of absence. *Believe me*, it is of pressing importance that you should contrive a favourable opportunity of discussing all that I wrote to you by Hébert.

My mind has been set quite at ease on the subject about which I wrote the other day. My brother-in-law's affair seems to be arranged. What Caulaincourt told me was merely a hearsay. Nansouty was told, on the contrary, that fighting was at hand, and that he must remain, and that on his return matters should be settled differently. Alix came here yesterday morning. The Empress kept her to dinner and treated her with the greatest kindness. At five o'clock we walked out with the Emperor. It was the first time I had spoken with him since my arrival. He inquired very kindly after you, and asked Alix after her husband in a way that quite reassured her. After our walk came dinner, and in the evening we sang and danced with Princess Louis. The Empress was in a state of enchantment with her grandson, who had been behaving very prettily to his uncle. He is really a sweet child, prattling all sorts of pretty little speeches without appearing to have learned them. He has the kind heart of his mother, whom I can never praise too much. She seems to me to grow every day in wisdom and in grace ; she combines great simplicity of manner with perfect dignity, and an enlightened judgment with an unfailing indulgence. Princess Borghèse is here, rather better in health, but still extremely weak. She looks lovely in her deep mourning; her abiding grief, and the sorrowful thoughts it occasions her, have given a certain melancholy grace to her demeanour which is not unattractive. She is very affable, and I, in particular, can only congratulate myself on her behaviour towards me.

I had news of our children yesterday; they are perfectly well. I am going to write to Charles; if you have any message for him send it me quickly. Adieu for to-day. I will not close my letter until to-morrow, so as to give you an account of the play to-night. Auguste de Talleyrand is in the country; M. de Viry * and I are managing everything.

Friday Morning.

The play went off well; the Emperor was pleased, and the *Menteur* was acted to perfection. Until seven o'clock I was on thorns, as you used to be. When dinner was over I went to the theatre to give a Chamberlain's eye to everything. All the actors had arrived, except Madame Talma.† Six o'clock came, then seven, and no Madame

---

* M. de Viry was a Piedmontese and one of the Emperor's Chamberlains. He was made a senator shortly afterwards.

† This was Talma's second wife, Mademoiselle Vanhove, a daughter of Monvel's. She had been divorced from her first husband, M. Petit. She appeared first in tragedy, and, it seems, acted very effectively. Afterwards she acted the principal parts in comedy, and succeeded equally well. She was even thought to surpass Mademoiselle Contat in parts requiring simplicity, truth, and modesty, rather than coquetry and display. After Talma's death, she married the Vicomte de Chalot.

Talma. I was as distressed as a certain friend of mine on similar occasions, especially as the Emperor wanted the play early in order to hold a council afterwards. At last, at half-past seven, she made her appearance, accompanied by her husband, whom I had to quiet down. They had come in a hackney coach, the horses *walking*, and Talma exciting himself to such a degree that he was ill on arriving, and could not have acted if wanted. But all went well, and you would have been satisfied. Talma told me that the Minister of Police had spoken to the Emperor on his behalf, and that his Majesty had replied that he had intended speaking to you on the subject of the theatre and of Talma, but that you were gone, and that he would do so later. I believe this will be the last performance, and that the departure of the Court is close at hand. My heart aches when I think of it; there will be sad leave-takings. Five of your Chamberlains will join you. The Empress does not know whom she is to take with her. She wishes to start with the Emperor, but no preparations are being made in her household. I am beginning to make mine for my quiet retreat. By the way, would you believe that our ten thousand francs are not yet paid? I am beginning to despair, and I don't know how I shall pay my debts. If all our endeavours are vain, you must make a last effort at Strasburg.

I had the pleasure of presenting your son to the Empress yesterday. She thought him greatly improved, and predicted that he will be a very handsome man. I felt a little proud, I must confess, of my fine boy, as I was leading him about from room to room. He kissed her Majesty's hand very prettily; you know how graceful he is; and the rest of the day he rambled about in the gardens and park. Both he and I grumbled at having no letters from you for the last five days. You cannot say the same of me, for you must have received several.

## LI.

### TO M. DE RÉMUSAT AT STRASBURG.

Saturday, 4th Complementary, Year XIII.
(September 21, 1805.)

I come to you, *mon ami*, quite tired out with my morning; I feel the need of communion with a heart that can understand mine, and of mingling a little affection with the day's work. From ten o'clock this morning the Empress has been receiving such a number of people that I have not been able to see her for one moment. I have passed the whole time among strange faces that interested me but little. Among others, I saw Madame de Coigny* for the first time. She

---

* The Marquise de Coigny (Mademoiselle de Conflans) the mother of Madame Sebastiani, was a clever woman of the old-fashioned type. My father had met her in his youth and remembered her rather affected and sharp sayings. She had a great reputation for wit, but a coarse voice, which made people say that there was only one against her—her own.

completely bewildered me by her flow of words
and screeching voice. She did me the honour of
addressing most of her conversation to me, but
can have no high idea of my intelligence, for I
was so astonished at her style of behaviour that
I felt no inclination to reply. I do not know how
the Empress can listen patiently to so many
persons. It would be quite beyond my power, and
I am always filled with admiration at the un-
wearied kindness with which she receives the
petitions of the last as well as of the first comers.

Meanwhile the Emperor is working with super-
human assiduity. Sometimes, when overtired, he
goes to bed at seven or eight o'clock and is up
again at eleven. It is reported here that on
Monday he goes to the Senate, and will start immediately afterwards. *Mon ami*, what a journey!
How anxious it makes me! I feel as if with him
all the repose and happiness we were beginning
to enjoy will depart. May Heaven watch over
him! You know that when I am in trouble I
have recourse to religion, which alone comforts
me. Whatever you may, all of you, say against
it, this inclination to turn towards God when our
soul is sorrowful, is one of the best gifts of His
goodness, and a strong proof of His existence in
a world that is full of troubles. To return to mine:
when I question the depths of my heart, I find
they are caused first by my separation from you,
and by my position, which is so contrary to all my
feelings and inclinations and individuality. Thinking thus, I am disposed to look at the dark side

K

of everything, and I should not be surprised at any additional sorrow, nor even a fresh calamity. *Mon ami*, your presence would banish all these feelings, and your words of love and affection would sustain me under the misfortunes with which perhaps we are threatened. To us women, the tender emotions of the heart are all that is of importance in our lives, while to most men they are only an occasional solace. This remark, however, which has slipped somehow from my pen, is far from being applicable to you, and in whatever position we may be placed in the future, our mutual affection will sustain us in affliction, or double all our joy. . . .

I have just been receiving Mademoiselle Volnais.* The Empress is overwhelmed with her visits. The young lady informed me that you had advised her to obtain a powerful patron or patroness, and that if I were to write to you that she was befriended by her Majesty, you would accede to her request with respect to the Comédie. I could not understand her long rigmarole ; she says that Mademoiselle Bourgoin is extremely insolent, and makes

* Mademoiselle Volnais was a descendant of Placide, the tight-rope dancer. She came out at the Comédie Française in 1800, and retired from the stage in 1822. She was celebrated for her beauty, and was considered a superior actress in quiet or tender characters, both of tragedy and comedy. She returned to the stage in 1833, undertaking successfully the part of *la Mère coupable.* Mademoiselle Bourgoin, her especial rival, acted also a great variety of parts, or, as it used to be called at the time, wore with equal ease the sock or the buskin—we should express it at the present day, "She wore either mask."

her life wretched. I promised, as I always do, to write to you, and I have kept my word.

I have received a letter from you; it is very sweet and a little sad; it just suits my mood. How well you describe what I have been feeling for the last month, and how true it is that it will alternately brighten and dim the recollections of the past! You say you are dull too? Although my affection is gratified by the regrets you do not hide from me, I yet feel ill at ease when I think that you are melancholy. I have long wished that when we are perforce separated, I could keep all the suffering for my own share. The Emperor was asking after you the day before yesterday, and whether you had mentioned the pretty Alsatian women to me?

We see very little of his Majesty. Ever since I came here on Monday he has been unceasingly at work; I have only seen him twice. One might well say of him, as of the King of Prussia: "Here is a king who does not spare himself!"

---

## LII.

TO M. DE RÉMUSAT AT STRASBURG.

Paris, Sunday, 5 Complémentaire, Year XIII.
(September 22, 1805.)

M. de Caulaincourt is good enough to take charge of this letter. He will see you in a very few days. Just now, at the moment of the

Emperor's departure, I feel more sorrowful than ever that I may not join you, for it is no use deceiving one's self, and I think it will be long before we meet again.

I hope at least that you will not be seized with M. de Luçay's martial ardour; it made me tremble yesterday. You must know that in order to satisfy a large number of the nobility who wish to serve, but whom there would be a difficulty in placing in the army, the Emperor has invented a guard of honour, to which any one with a certain amount of fortune will be eligible. This corps, which is commanded by M. de Ségur, will escort his Majesty. M. de Bouillé has joined it, and so has César de Choiseul.\* M. de Luçay came yesterday to ask me whether I did not think it was the Emperor's intention that all his household should enter this corps, and what I was going to advise you to do? I cannot describe to you my feelings when he asked me this question; I really believe my hair stood on end, and I felt a sharp pain at my heart. I replied, however, that had you been under thirty years of age, whatever might have been my own feelings, I certainly should have advised you to join, but that, although you were still young, I did not think you sufficiently so to change your calling in life, especially being a married man and the

---

\* This M. de Bouillé died blind, leaving a son, the Marquis Réné de Bouillé, who was ambassador in Spain under M. Thiers' Government. César de Choiseul-Beaupré was aide-de-camp to M. de Nansouty, to whom he was distantly related. His widow married the Prince de Polignac.

father of a family. On this I left him and wept
in solitude, quite unable to restrain myself; I was
so upset, that I found myself speaking aloud to
you as if you could hear me. I regret now what
I wrote to you yesterday. Do not, my beloved,
add fresh troubles to the sorrow of separation. I
suffer, but I will not murmur at your absence since
you are doing your duty. Follow your Emperor;
serve him at the post to which he has appointed
you; but think of me also, for for further anxieties
courage fails me. . . .

Monday Morning.

The Emperor is going to the Senate, and has
asked for his gala coat and his diamonds. You
have taken away the keys, so the locks had to be
forced. He will take his departure to-morrow, it
seems. There is a gloom over everything here,
and I have no courage to speak to any one except
Caulaincourt. To him and to his friendship I
have confided my fears and anxieties, and he promised to watch over you with a kindliness that
touched me to the heart. In the name of all the
happiness of my life, I implore you to take care
of your health, and be certain of one thing—if you
were ill, no matter in what part of the world, or
what might be my own state of health, I should
instantly go to you. . . .

If you mention the Comédie Française to the
Empress, be sure to tell her that it was not I, but
Mahérault, who wrote to you about the conse-
quences of her good nature to those actresses, and

speak only of the message he sent you through me. She has been extremely kind ; I lament her absence too. Life is pleasant in her company and one's *heart* feels satisfied. I am now going to rejoin my poor mother, who has to spend a winter with two very sorrowful and tiresome daughters. She says, in one of her letters, that she will never forgive herself for having brought up two such devoted wives.

I enclose the memorandum on the theatres.* It seems to me to be well drawn up. Read it, *mon ami*, and use it as soon as possible, for it is important to put a stop to the daily increasing confusion. Adieu ; in a few hours the Emperor's departure will have taken place, and I shall be on my way to Paris. I hope you will write to me on the Emperor's arrival, and tell me how he receives you. I am going to embrace your children and find comfort in their society.

---

## LIII.

### TO M. DE RÉMUSAT AT STRASBURG.

Paris, Tuesday, 2 Vendémiaire, Year XIV.
(September 2, 1805.)

I am at home once more with the dear children. I feel better here; everything recalls your presence

---

* This was a memorandum which my grandfather had requested Desfaucherets to send him, with the intention of laying before the Emperor his views of the reforms required in that department.

and seems to draw us nearer together. I left St. Cloud yesterday with a heavy heart, and I could see my own feelings reflected in every counte-- nance. I could not restrain my tears on taking leave of the Empress. I told her how ardently I desired every blessing for the Emperor, and then I had to come away in tears. Oh, what a moment! and what will it bring forth in the future!

Paris seems to me rather disturbed just now. The Parisians are depressed by the war and by the absence of those who keep up luxury and expenditure. The conscription, the levying of troops, the guard of honour, and the National Guard occupy every one's thoughts, as you may imagine. I saw Louis de Vergennes this morning; he is delighted with the decree,* because he gets into uniform again. Only for his children, I think he would apply to re-enter the army; for he is greatly inclined to do so, I assure you. He is a patriotic Frenchman, and has a thoroughly grateful disposition.

Madame de Vannoise thanks you for your kind- ness to her son, and makes the following request on his behalf:—M. de Vannoise wrote to Constance, and told her to say to her brother that he should ask you to present him to the Emperor as the son of a man who, by virtue of his military rank, had a seat in the King's carriages. His mother

---

* This first trial of a guard of honour came to nothing. Louis de Vergennes was the second son of the Minister of that name.

rightly thinks this an insufficient reason, and that he is not yet of rank sufficient to claim such an honour. But that she may not seem to be acting in opposition to her husband, you must speak to the young man on the subject, and then write to me, and I will tell Constance. Do not forget.

I saw a courier this morning who told me you were in good health. May you remain so; for you will need health for your travels. I think that perhaps you may find it necessary to make a circuit in this direction, unless you can find time to make up your accounts while at Strasburg. We are now at the end of the year, and Osmont says that M. de Talleyrand is quite at sea about the accounts, and that you only can give him the information he requires.

While on the subject of money, I must tell you that I have not received my ten thousand francs. I mentioned it to the Empress, telling her how straitened were my means, and what a deluge of bills was pouring in on me; she promised she would mention it, but has not done so. Madame de la Rochefoucauld * has written to M. de Talleyrand, in her own name and ours, and the Grand Chamberlain answered that he would speedily settle the matter. Nevertheless, it is not settled; we all of us beg that you will attend to it, and, for my own part, I am so worried that, if it altogether

* Madame Alexandre de la Rochefoucauld was Lady of Honour to the Empress.

fails, I must sell my shawls and other belongings to pay for my Court dresses.*

We are going to lead a very quiet life with two or three friends that you know of. I feel that far from wishing to increase my circle, I shall rather narrow it, so as to avoid hearing all the false rumours that will be circulated, and which, although against reason, one tries in vain to disbelieve. I have already been kindly informed that the Russians had already passed through Vienna, and have left that city. I imposed silence on all, and then I stated positively that I should only believe what I read in the *Moniteur.* How I should love that paper if it would give me some news of the First Chamberlain! While speaking of the First Chamberlain, I must tell him that I believe he has some real friends at the palace, who gladly speak well of him; among others, M. de Viry, General Caffarelli, M. de Canisy, who is an excellent creature for all his madcap ways, and some more besides. They have all established a right to my affection, and M. de Caulaincourt, to whom I was saying this, assured me that in that case he ought to be in the front rank of my friends; and I believe him. Our service is all arranged for the next two months. The Empress settled it herself.

* The salaries of the Court officials were paid with an irregularity and delay that are almost unintelligible at the present day. The alternations between splendour and poverty in which people then passed their lives, are worthy of note, and although I have suppressed many details of family or monetary affairs, I have thought it advisable to retain a few instances of this curious state of things.

I shall be in waiting in December and January, the same weeks, I believe, as Madame de Brignolé,* and Mesdames Ney† and Marescot are down for the same months as I. By that time I think her Majesty will have returned to Paris, where she will be less lonely than at Strasburg after the Emperor has left her. If not, I shall be obliged to give up my turn of service, since I could not travel so far. In that case, you know beforehand what will be my occupations, and you will probably find a very learned wife and son on your return, for we shall study very hard. I shall try to find time between Greek and Latin to read a little history with Charles. If you approve, he shall take fencing lessons once or twice a week, so as to learn to hold himself well. I could afford this the more easily, because, being under no obligation as to dress, I could save the money to pay for them. Yet, notwithstanding my intended economy, I see plainly that our necessary expenses will reach a high amount, and that we are living beyond our means. The war is raising the price of everything. Tradesmen make use of any pretext for raising their prices, but since I have taken to housekeeping I have never known them find a reason for lowering them. . . .

---

* Madame de Brignolé was a Genoese. She is the mother of that Brignolé who was Sardinian ambassador in France, and of the Duchesse de Dalberg.

† Madame Ney was Mademoiselle Auguié, daughter of one of Marie Antoinette's dressers.

## LIV.

TO M. DE RÉMUSAT AT STRASBURG.

Paris, 4 Vendémiaire, Year XIV.
(September 26, 1805.)

I received a letter from you yesterday, by which I see how busy you are, for it is very short. I imagine you must have become more and more pressed with work, until the arrival of their Majesties brought it to a climax. I presume they are now at Strasburg, and that M. de Caulaincourt has given you my little packet of letters. You will tell me if they have been of any use to you, and tell me especially how you yourself are getting on. I am really in a state of suspense about you which is distressing. M. de Talleyrand told me yesterday that he thought you would have orders to accompany the Emperor, and that I must send you plenty of flannel. But, seriously, are you in want of any winter outfit, and what shall I send you? I hope you have been rewarded for all the trouble you have had at Strasburg, by their Majesties' approval of your arrangements. The Empress was told beforehand that her apartments could not be made very comfortable, but she was so anxious to accompany the Emperor that she would not be baulked by any personal inconvenience. Alas! I can sympathize with her! The greatest of evils is to be separated from those we love.

Paris is profoundly gloomy. Everybody remains at home in a state of anxiety and suspense; the theatres are deserted; people groan and await in silence the beginning of great events. The moderation of the Emperor's speech is greatly praised; people desire his success, some sincerely, others from interested motives; for he bears the proud title, as Abbé Morellet used to say, of the *Necessary Man*.

As for me, I am going to live in great solitude. My poor sister comes to see me every day; she is full of anxiety and weeps continually. Why are you both such good husbands, and are not we very foolish that we cannot exist without you? Alix fancies you will have greater facilities than herself for forwarding her letters to M. de Nansouty, because there is no post to Pirmasenz.* Answer me about this.

Your Grand Chamberlain wants you to amuse him with a play at Strasburg, and intends to speak to you on the subject. I was quite gratified at his reception of me. I had occasion to speak with him about something that he will tell you and that I wrote to you by M. de Caulaincourt. It relates to Sobek's mistress.† I wanted him to quiet her; he had already done so. He said he should tell you that I am very fond of you, and I replied that on that head you had nothing further to learn. He spoke in his usual style

---

* A town in Bavaria.

† Sobek's mistress was Madame Devaines, and Sobek was a little dog.

about the inner life at Court ; saying that we were
prudes, and that when we emancipated ourselves,
we should, from not knowing how to be coquettes,
be something worse. I thought it a clever remark,
for it is true that our utter want of occupation and
a little pedantry are more dangerous than might
be expected. But you may feel quite easy about
me, for I am never unoccupied, and my boy leaves
me little leisure for thinking of anything but himself, or, in other words, of you.

We have heard from our friends the Chérons.*
They are delighted with their journey, and not
dissatisfied with their new residence. The house
is very nice, with a beautiful garden. They were
warmly received, and this consoled them a little
for all they have given up. The husband is going
to try to be of use in his district, his wife will be
fêted and courted, and both will be happy. The
Abbé Morellet is resigned to their absence ; he is
pleased at the advantages it seems to promise for
his niece. M. Rumford has come back, and the
house in the Rue d'Anjou is transformed into the
isle of Cyprus, according to mamma's account. All
is perfume and enchantment. The new Adonis has
brought a hautbois player with him from Germany ;
he is stationed in a little hut, and while he draws
forth the most ravishing sounds, the goddess of the
place, lying gracefully extended on a sofa, throws
tender glances at the object of all her thoughts,
and finds a new fire in his eyes with which to en-
kindle her own. People wonder if they are, or

* M. Chéron had just been appointed Prefect of Vienne.

are to be married.   No one can tell, but they seem
happy.   They intend to travel in France all the
winter, which puts the finishing stroke to Bertrand's despair.

## LV.

### TO M. DE RÉMUSAT AT STRASBURG.

Paris, Saturday, 6 Vendémiaire, Year XIV.
(September 28, 1805.)

Whenever I hear of an opportunity of writing, I
feel that I must not neglect it.   Herbault is just
setting off, and he promises to deliver this letter
to you.   I enclose a little note that M. Salembini
has just written at the corner of my table.   It is
an account of the difficulties in which Osmont * is
placed by your absence.   It seems that in order to
get out of them he takes a great deal upon himself
which perhaps you will not approve.   If this be
so, could you not send for him to Strasburg, if you
cannot get away yourself ?

I am in a distressing state of uncertainty.   I am
anxiously waiting to hear from you after the
Emperor's arrival at Strasburg, and I cannot tell
what day to expect a letter.   No doubt you are
full of work ; and then, are you to accompany the
Emperor ?   But for what purpose ?   Day and

---

* Osmont had to discharge part of the duties of the **Grand
Chamberlain**, and consequently the business of the **Court**
theatrical performances devolved partly upon him.

night I wear myself out in conjecture! Sorrowful
thoughts from which there is no issue! I am
profoundly sad. Is it possible that our days of
happiness are over?

I am ashamed that you should see my weakness,
but everything around me conduces to it. There
is great consternation here, and it is increased by
the malevolent. A run on the Bank the last two
days has embarrassed it, and the guard was forced
to disperse the crowds that gathered round the
doors. The conscription irritates people, and the
future alarms them; to escape from it all I am
obliged to shut myself up with two little boys that
you know. They are so happy, so peaceful, so
ignorant of danger, that at last, in their quiet
company, I become calm myself.

As you may imagine, the theatres are losers by
the state of the public mind. They are empty,
and the actors grumble incessantly. If I would
do as they want me, I should see them every
day, to listen to their complaints. Mademoiselle
Volnais wrote to me that the Empress's promise
that she should act by turns with Mademoiselle
Bourgoin has caused her a great deal of annoyance, and that she wanted to tell me about it.
I replied that I could not help it, and that she
had better write to you. She says that you
advised her to apply to me. Mademoiselle Contat
attacks me for the thousand crowns that she says
you promised her. Talma is very grateful. He
is much attached to you, and wishes you could
return here, because, he says, everything is going

to ruin, and nobody obeys Mahérault. However, "Athalie" is in rehearsal; he knows " Manlius," and is learning " Catilina," and he says that if the Comédie chose, they might draw a house, in spite of the dreariness of the times. . . .

## LVI.

### TO M. DE RÉMUSAT AT STRASBURG.

Paris, Monday, 8 Vendémiaire, Year XIV.
(September 30, 1805.)

. . . Our life here is rather dull, as you may imagine. All our friends are either in the country or with the army, and Paris is empty. But our retired life pleases me better than any other just now, for I should have to pay for the pleasure of society by the misery of hearing all the evil rumours that are disseminated, and they are legion. I am too anxious and too agitated to listen to them with the indifference they deserve. In fact, I must admit that I cannot help quarrelling with people who come and repeat to me the absurdities they have heard. The day before yesterday I silenced a person* who, in my own house, was finding fault

* This was M. de Mézy, whom my grandmother does not name on account of the insecurity of the post. This continual apprehension explains the reticence, and many turns of expression throughout the whole correspondence. M. de Mézy was a well-informed man, who had acquired a stock of ideas in England which had made him a Liberal, although he did not always act like one under the Restoration. He had been

with everything and everybody. You would have been astonished—you, who know that I do not like to put myself forward when the company is at all numerous—at the firmness and the comparative calmness with which I said I was surprised that any one should select my house, at such a time as the present, for the repetition of rumours which must be alarming to everybody. You will guess pretty well to whom I thus addressed myself, when I tell you it was to that husband of one of our dearest friends, of whom you often say he has the spirit *sic autem contra*. He was rather surprised at my manner, but held his peace, and my mother thinks I did right.

Another trouble to this good city of Paris is the prevailing scarcity of money. Bank payments were suddenly interrupted, general alarm ensued, and there are now such crowds waiting their turn, that a guard is necessary to keep order. This measure, which makes creditors more than ever pressing, is inconveniencing me very much. By the way, M. Estève * is now with you; he told me again, before leaving Paris, that we could receive our month's pay by sending an application with our own signature to him, yet when Alix wrote to his cashier, he replied that an authorization from M. de Nansouty would be necessary.

at school at Juilly, but was younger than my grandfather. He married Mademoiselle Veron and died a peer of France. His son, who was only known to my generation in his latter days, was an amiable, lively, and well-informed man of the world.

* M. Estève was Treasurer-General to the Crown.

A note from M. Estève to his cashier would be sufficient; please ask him for it, for my sister and myself.

I see two persons every day who are so wretched that I can no longer complain when I think of them. One is our cousin Vannoise, who bemoans by turns her poverty, her daughter, and her sons. The other is poor Madame de Grasse. Her son is very ill, and given over by the doctors.* She nurses him night and day; her means are exhausted, and her courage is failing. If you could possibly obtain some help for her from the Empress, you might tell Deschamps to write and inform Madame de la Rochefoucauld of this. You would be doing a truly kind action. To add to the troubles of the poor woman, it seems to me that she is not on good terms with her hosts, and feels distressed at being indebted to them; when people bestow favours they cannot be too mindful always to seek forgiveness, so to speak, for the services they have rendered. I went once to visit the lady in the house opposite theirs. She is becoming more calm.† She was, at first, for writing tremendous letters, burning her fine clothes, and renouncing the world. " I shall retire to a cottage," she wrote to me. " No," I answered, " you will not; you will stay by your fireside and receive

---

* Gustave de Grasse cheated the doctors, for he did not die until 1858, aged sixty-seven, after a very active and busy life. He suffered, however, from an affection of the liver.

† Madame de Grasse lived in the Rue Royale, at her cousin's, Madame de Sainte-Marguerite, opposite Madame Devaines'.

your friends." Her anger is now appeased, and she is quite determined to preserve a strict silence, which will last as long as may be. I seldom go to her, for, whatever people say, she is no friend of mine.

Joséphine and her husband start for Nice tomorrow. They are going to spend the winter there on account of their child, who is in a sad state.* Our friends the Chérons are settled and in the midst of all the business and bother of provincial etiquette. Norvins is in despair, and calls upon you. If you cannot help him he will die of suppressed ambition. He often comes to see me, more for want of something to do than from inclination; certainly not for my pleasure. What else can I tell you? Abbé Morellet is ageing and sleeps a good deal. Bertrand sighs, Madame Lavoisier is off to Provence, my sister weeps, and my mother rails against conjugal affection. It is not her fault that we do not lead a gayer life. She says it would make us much pleasanter if we did. She is always cheerful, her good spirits are inexhaustible; but for her I should laugh but seldom.

* Joséphine is Madame de Mézy. The child mentioned in the letter died young. He was not the Mézy whom we knew.

## LVII.

Paris, 10 Vendémiaire, Year XIV.
(October 2, 1805.)

I do not hear from you, *mon ami.* I grieve, but I do not complain, for I know that since his Majesty's arrival you have little leisure, so I will be patient, if possible. You can understand, however, that I am doubly anxious, for I am in a painful state of ignorance as to what is to become of you. Are you to follow the Emperor immediately? Where am I to address our letters? Are you still at Strasburg? These questions are always before me, and I cannot decide one of them. So soon as you are able, pray write me one word. I really need it. As for me, who am always writing to you, I have no news to tell. We are all in good health, grandmother, mother, and children ; we are continually talking of you, of this dreadful war, and of the separations it entails. My mother and I begin the day by reading the *Moniteur* at breakfast, and following the march of our troops and of those wretched Austrians on the map. We have already looked a hundred times over at Meiningen and Stockach.* Then Alix makes her appearance and, with a sigh,

---

* Meiningen is the capital of the duchy of Saxe-Meiningen, ten leagues from Gotha. Stockach is near Constance, in the grand-duchy of Baden.

looks for Pirmasenz, although her husband may no longer be there. We all hope and pray for the success of our master, and I confess that I am agitated when I think he is going to risk a life on which the happiness of a generation depends. How I regret that my ill health forbade me to accompany the Empress! I am sure that you at Strasburg, close to the troops and in the midst of the dangers they are about to confront, are less alarmed and anxious than we. No efforts are wanting here to disturb the public peace, and the sudden scarcity of silver is a capital opportunity for arousing alarm, and has not been overlooked by the evil-disposed. A great crowd of people wait their turn at the Bank, and this causes few payments, and of comparatively small sums, to be made. There is a stop to all business; creditors press on every side whom it is impossible to satisfy, and yet it is said that with a little frank good-will, all this confusion would soon come to an end.

This is the latest news I can give you. Do not imagine, however, that the Parisians restrict themselves to this one subject for recreation. Oh, we know how to vary our amusements, and after spending the morning in discussing, rightly or wrongly, the causes of this scarcity of money, the war, and the political system of Europe, we discourse with equal warmth on the " Hullah de Samarcande," * which has just been produced at

* " Gulistan ou le Hullah de Samarcande " is an opera, by Etienne and Dalayrac. It was brought out at the Opéra Comique,

Feydeau, or on Martin's* sudden cold, for which M. de Talleyrand sent him to prison for eighteen hours, and we retire to rest quite satisfied with our judgment on everything, and without troubling ourselves to consider whether it has been a reasonable one. These Parisians of ours, who, in my opinion, are the most agreeable rather than the most estimable part of the nation, have, however, always been the same. You know that in my hours of idleness I have taken up the history of France, and I find them always the same at all the different epochs of which I have read : adventurous, thoughtless, often ungrateful, never taking any trouble themselves, and expecting everything to be done for them. I have just finished the history of the League, and have made myself ready to argue either for or against " Les États de Blois," if it is acted this winter. . . .

Just as I was closing this letter, I received yours, which has relieved my anxiety. César de Choiseul has offered to convey my little packet, and as he is in haste, I have only time for a few words. I shall not write again until I have another letter from you. But if you are to remain

on 8 Vendémiaire, Year XIV. (September 30, 1805). It appears that a Hullah or Hulla is a man who marries, for one day only, a divorced wife, in order to enable the first husband, according to Turkish law, to take her back. Another operetta by M. Lecocq has recently been composed on this delicate subject, " La Jolie Persane."

* Martin, a grandson of the inventor of the Martin blacking, was born in 1768, and died in 1837. He and Elleviou were celebrated singers at the Opéra Comique under the Empire.

at Strasburg, could you not take a trip to Paris? I say nothing about myself, but your presence is needed at the end of the year, and especially at the theatre. Mahérault is in the greatest difficulties about the rent and the retiring pensions; moreover, his authority is set at nought, and nothing goes well.

## LVIII.

### TO M. DE RÉMUSAT AT STRASBURG.

Paris, 15 Vendémiaire, Year XIV.
(October 7, 1805.)

. . . The confidence which you tell me is felt in the troops is quite shared here, even by the people who generally share in nothing, and who, as you know, exist in Paris in large numbers. Whatever private opinions people may have, no one doubts our victory, and this widespread feeling is surely the most flattering and the truest homage that can be paid to our soldiers and their leader. I can understand your admiration, and your thoughts at the sight of those fine troops marching at once to glory and to death. For my own part, if, like you, I beheld armies ready to meet in the field, my first thought would be for the poor mothers and wives, who will have to pay for all this glory with their tears, and who must undoubtedly shed as many over victory as over defeat. I see clearly that I should never make a good ruler, for feeling is too much mingled with all I think and do, and with these fine sentiments I should let my country be invaded and my States disturbed.

You say you are dull at Strasburg? You would be the same in Paris; for it is horribly dull just now, and so empty of news and full of ill nature, that to live without too much vexation and quarrelling, one must do as I do—confine one's self to a very narrow circle, and shut one's door on all the idlers of this great city, who imagine they are increasing their own importance when they are spreading bad news. We are told here that the Empress is likely to return to us, and perhaps, unless better advised, she would do well to spend the winter here, and revive in some degree much that is languishing by reason of the war. I will write to her, since you tell me to do so. The truth is that I did not write for fear of being tiresome; I am so completely ignorant of anything that could amuse her. It is your duty, you know, to enliven and entertain her. Notwithstanding your modesty, you are quite sufficiently agreeable to amuse her if you like, and I should be much inclined to scold you for your shyness, only that while avowing it you use so many kind and loving words, that I must tell you they all went straight to my heart, and are graven there; and that your devoted affection, of which I am constantly receiving the most touching proofs, will always be the true happiness of my life.

## LIX.

TO M. DE RÉMUSAT AT STRASBURG.

Paris, 18 Vendémiaire, Year XIV.
(October 10, 1805.)

. . . *Mon cher ami,* how dull and unoccupied we are in this horrid Paris of ours! Pray tell M. de Talleyrand that it is really pitiable. There is not even the least bit of gossip! In fact, our gravity equals our wisdom. I don't quite know which is the cause and which the effect, but I do know I am horribly dull. The emptiness of this great city is really remarkable; the theatres do not draw, and I scarcely ever go to them, except, however, to the Bouffons, who are improving every day and drawing large audiences. I heard Fertendis * there last Monday for the first time. She has become popular; her voice, although rather thick, is effective, and she sings with expression. She pronounces Italian so well as to make even recitatives delightful. She looks well on the stage, and is greatly applauded. Barilli also is much liked. They acted together in an opera called "La Melomanie." It is pretty and well put on the stage; everybody enjoyed it; I am going to hear it again this evening. I hear

---

* Madame Fertendis was an Italian contralto who came out in Paris in "La Capriciosa pentita." She was the wife of an excellent musician, well known as a performer on the cornetto, which was at that time a new instrument.

it is impossible to persuade the two *prime donne* that they would do well to act together, as each declines to play any but the principal parts. Your authority seems to be needed in this matter.

Halma continues to be quite satisfied with your son; and tells me that he has plenty of ability, but is rather lazy. I am contending with this fault, and I make him work with more steadiness. Tell him to be more industrious. In other respects he is most amiable; his health is excellent; he is even growing fat. His grandmother is untiringly kind to him, and teaches him to act proverbs with her, while I constitute the audience.

## LX.

### TO M. DE RÉMUSAT AT STRASBURG.

Paris, 20 Vendémiaire, Year XIV.
(October 12, 1805.)

. . . I have seen Princess Louis, who is quite well, and her children also. She is dreadfully tired of receiving two hundred persons every Monday, but the company do not suspect it; her manners are so gracious and pleasing. You must tell this to the Empress, when speaking of me, as you do sometimes. I am really afraid of writing to her; I feel so cross and stupid. You only, *mon ami*, can put up with my verbiage, and notwithstanding your indulgence and natural interest in my letters, I fear that sometimes you must find in them a wearisome iteration. How can I help it? I have liberty that I do not want, and then each succeeding day brings me the same occupations and the same thoughts, at the same hours. I read a great deal. I am now in the middle of the "Essai sur les Mœurs," which I like in spite of all my prejudices. I intend, now that I have so much leisure, to go through the whole of Voltaire, so as to know, once for all, what to think about him, and although I have no inclination to let myself be fascinated, yet I begin to find, in spite of myself, that he is more often in the right than I could wish.

## LXI.

### TO M. DE RÉMUSAT AT STRASBURG.

Paris, 22 Vendémiaire, Year XIV.
(October 14, 1805.)

*Mon ami,* what delightful news!* and how we all thank you for writing to us at once! I received your letter last night at eleven o'clock. In another minute I was off. I reach Alix' house, I read it to her, she bursts into tears, I weep also, and all the pain of absence is forgotten. The booming of cannon proclaimed the good news to Paris this morning; it has produced a great effect. Strangers

---

* Either the battle of Wertingen, gained on 17 Vendémiaire, or Marshal Ney's defeat of the Archduke Ferdinand on the 16th.

interrogate and congratulate each other in the
streets; in short, as I have written to the Empress,
for once the Parisians are Frenchmen. I have
written twenty notes already this morning, and
received visits of congratulation. Prince Louis
sent for Alix in order to tell her how well pleased
the Emperor is with her husband, and both the
prince and princess treated her with the greatest
kindness. This was all the more consoling to my
poor sister as she has had no news of her husband
for a long time past. She fears that both his
letters and hers miscarry, and asks you to forward
the one I enclose, if you meet with a good opportunity. But what a splendid victory! How proud
one feels at being French! I could not sleep for
joy. Perhaps you know of other victories by this
time, and while we are rejoicing over this first one,
you have already forgotten it in a second. May
Heaven still protect our brave army and its
glorious leader! We wanted a victory here, for
our wretched Parisians were beginning to grumble.
The solitude of Paris, the state of torpor in which
all business is plunged, and the scarcity of money
that is still prevailing, gave fine opportunities of
fault-finding to the ill-natured, while our foolish
idlers believed everything that they were told. I
was wondering to myself this morning why there
is so little national spirit in the nation and yet
such unity of action and of feeling in the army.
It seems to me that it must be a sentiment of
honour that makes the difference, and that honour
takes the place of public spirit among individuals

who in ordinary times are too happy, too rich, or too careless to interest themselves in anything outside their own particular horizon.

## LXII.

### TO M. DE RÉMUSAT AT STRASBURG.

Paris, 24 Vendémiaire, Year XIV.
(October 16, 1805.)

We are waiting impatiently for news. Our triumphant beginning will, no doubt, be succeeded by still more brilliant victories, and I rely upon you to inform me of them so soon as you know of them yourself. But, amid all this, what is happening to you? M. de Chabrol, whom I met yesterday at the Archchancellor's, told me that at the time he left Strasburg, several of the Chamberlains were preparing to follow the Emperor. Were you one of them? If you are likely to be at a still greater distance, remember that you must warn me in time, on account of my letters, and in order that I may send you what you require; your coat, for instance, if it does not come before you leave Strasburg. I know not whether to wish for or to dread your further journey. There is something agreeable to me in the knowledge that you are still in France, but I tremble at the thought of those gloomy German forests, and almost regret that you did not accompany the Emperor on his journey.

All these feelings make life melancholy and the days long and dreary. The coming winter seems shrouded in a sombre veil when I reflect that it must be passed far away from you, and the thought brings tears to my eyes. The newspapers announce that the Empress will spend the winter at Strasburg. Do you think that is her intention? The general opinion here seems to be that she ought to come back to Paris, where her presence is really required. Everything seems dead; there is no trade, and discontent prevails everywhere; people shut themselves up in their homes; there is no expenditure, no luxury, and every house has become, like mine, a sort of castle in which the owners live in solitude. To complete the picture, the weather is frightful, with such incessant rain we might easily believe ourselves to be in the month of December. The theatres, with the exception of the minor ones, are absolutely deserted. Your poor Comédie exhaust themselves in vain; they play to empty houses. I went yesterday to the "Festin de Pierre," admirably acted by Dugazon and Fleury; there were not fifty persons in the pit. Fleury asked for an interview with me, and I have appointed to-morrow. In those letters of mine that went astray, I asked you for an answer for Mademoiselle Contat.

Mamma is continually begging me to tell you that she never thinks of you now; and I, *mon ami*, I do nothing else at every instant of the day, and each day I love you more. What happiness if I could tell you so with my own lips!

## LXIII.

TO M. DE RÉMUSAT AT STRASBURG.

Wednesday, 24 Vendémiaire, Year XIV.
(October 16, 1805.)

Now that I have attended to all your commissions and that I have leisure to write, and have besides the certainty that my letter will reach you, I must speak to you about your actors of the Comédie Française, whom you are forgetting, but to whom you might write as you are so far away. I suspect that Mahérault does not tell you of all the existing anarchy, because his ill health has greatly weakened him. I saw Fleury this morning. He has a petition, of which I will speak presently, to present to you. We had a long conversation. He much deplores the present condition of the theatre, which he tells me is one of complete disorder. Everybody is master, and no rules are observed. The actors are all away in the country; consequently the doubles have to act, and the receipts are *nil*. Mademoiselle Raucourt has not acted once; while Mademoiselle Fleury * insists on always acting, and people will not pay to see her. On Monday they played " Tan-

* Mademoiselle Fleury was not in any way related to Fleury. She was married to M. Cheffontaine. She had made her first appearance on the stage in 1791 ; she retired in 1807, and died in 1818. She was considered clever. Monvel received his retiring pension shortly after. He died at the age of sixty-seven in 1812.

crède" for the first time since the *début* of
our new actresses. They hoped to draw a good
house. But Mademoiselle Fleury, despite her age
and appearance, took the part of Aménaïde. Her
very name scared people away, and not a single
person went except myself. She looked so old, so
ugly, and acted so badly, that I laughed heartily.
Fleury says that now, at the close of the year,
there are several actors who should be compelled
to take their retiring pension, and thus clear the
way for others. He says that Mademoiselle Fleury
is one of these; that she is worn out, and em-
barrasses him in his distribution of parts, and that
it would be very kind of you to get rid of her,
also of Mouvel and some others. Could you not
write—not to Mahérault, who would not show
your letter—but to the committee, and say that
you are dissatisfied, and that, as your projected
reforms in the management of the Comédie are
stopped by your absence, you expect that at least
the actors will be more than ever zealous; that
those who show themselves most deserving will be
rewarded, and that every personal interest ought
to yield before the necessity of attracting the
public by well-acted plays? These are only sug-
gestions, but it should be a forcible letter. If
you prefer, you might address it to Fleury, and
I would undertake to have it conveyed to him. I
am the more vexed that you did not put an end to
Mahérault's affair before you left Paris. Could
you not write what you shrink from saying to
him? I think you would be very well satisfied

with Campenon, and that, besides, he would be anxious to make a good beginning and do his best for the theatre, which is not likely to flourish this winter. I have dwelt too long perhaps on this subject. But I am annoyed by the sharp comments that are made everywhere, and even in the newspapers, about the mismanagement of the theatre.

To return to Fleury. He is in great need of help; you promised to make up for the leave that he missed taking, and that he will be obliged to claim if you cannot grant him some money. His son * has come back badly wounded from the war, and he says that now, for the first time, he finds himself in urgent need. Pray do not overlook this request. I am much interested in him, and so is Alix, as you know.

Thursday Morning, 25th.

The cannon proclaim a fresh victory, of which the *Moniteur* gives us the particulars. This time it is Marshal Ney, and I see that that poor fellow Lacuée † has been killed. I am very sorry, and sorry also for a poor mother who is here, and who begs you for pity's sake to find out, if possible, the fate of her son. I speak of Madame Fezensac.‡ M. de Nansouty took an interest in

---

* Fleury's son called himself Bénard, his father's real name. He was a sailor, and became an admiral.

† Colonel Lacuée, aide-de-camp to the Emperor, was killed at the battle of Elchingen on 22 Vendémiaire.

‡ Madame de Montesquiou-Fezensac was Madame de Vinti-

the young man, so he may perhaps know if anything has happened to him, and by writing to him
at once, you might obtain an answer so as to give
us news of both. Alix has not heard from her
husband, and is in a most pitiable state. Write to
my brother-in-law, *cher ami*, and tell him to
address his letters to you; be our refuge, in fact,
and watch over us, for we are troubled and anxious.
Keep us informed of everything, for all your news
will be precious.

Before closing my parcel, I must return to the
subject of theatres, and tell you that the Minister
of Police has decreed that no theatre becoming
bankrupt shall open again, nor shall any new ones
be licensed. The Opéra company is in open re-
bellion against M. de Luçay. Rolland, Nourrit,
and Madame Branchu * have sent in their resignation, and his authority is openly defied by the
rest. Pay some attention, I beg of you, to your
own theatre; now is the time, it seems to me, that
it should show better management than the others.

mille's sister. Her son Aimery was that Duke of Fezensac
who wrote his Memoirs and died in 1860.
   * Rolland the actor was Rolland de Courbonne, who died at
a very advanced age, and whose wife held a brilliant *salon*
in Paris, at Rue d'Anjou. Nourrit was the father of Adolphe
Nourrit, who was so celebrated a singer at the Opéra, and who
committed suicide at Naples in 1837. Madame Branchu (Mademoiselle Maillard) had made her first appearance at the Opéra
in 1782. She was more admired for dramatic expression than
for her voice.

## LXIV.

Paris, 25 Vendémiaire, Year XIV.
(October 17, 1805.)

. . . We are passing our time here, thanks to our brilliant military triumphs, in paying visits of congratulation to the princes and princesses. I am going this evening to Madame Louis', and to-morrow to Prince Joseph's, and I shall most willingly offer them the homage which I think they must enjoy. Who, in truth, could sufficiently admire the genius displayed in this wonderful campaign, if the Emperor had not accustomed us, long since, never to be astonished at his exploits? The popular delight is general; malevolence no longer dares to manifest itself, and I must own I take a certain pleasure in watching the embarrassment of those persons who are foolish enough not to rejoice at our national glory. We congratulate one another on our victories, though in point of fact we never doubted them. May they hasten the return of the Emperor! With our friend, Madame de Sévigné, I say from the bottom of my heart, " May God spare him to us ! "

I have just seen Corvisart, who watches over my health with assiduity for which I am grateful. He begs me to thank you from him, for your kind reception of the surgeons he despatched to his Majesty, and says you will like the physician who accompanied them, if he has remained at Strasburg, because he is a man of real ability. Corvisart was present two days ago at an operation for cataract performed on your friend Portalis; it was successfully accomplished on both eyes, and there is every reason to hope that he will recover his sight. Your son asks me to tell you that he is expecting your letter. He is preparing a translation, by way of answer, with which I think you will be pleased. He is improving, and no longer dislikes his Latin lessons so much as formerly; he learns a good deal of Latin by heart, which gives both him and me some trouble, for he repeats his lessons to me. I am glad of the occupation; it occupies both my head and my heart, and when I see him so gay and happy, I arrive at feeling more at ease myself.

The Empress asked me to send her Godwin's novel,* and Deschamps should have received it by this time. I do not think she will like it, for, though clever, it is full of sarcasm, and quite opposed to the disposition of our good patroness. The author sees and paints the worst side of mankind; but, for my own part, and even at the risk of being deceived, I will not fling away that gilded veil through which the Emperor says we look at human nature in our youth. However, there is talent in the book, and it may amuse your leisure.

* This must be " Caleb Williams," Godwin's most celebrated work.

## LXV.

### TO M. DE RÉMUSAT AT STRASBURG.

**Paris, 26 Vendémiaire, Year XIV.**
(October 18, 1805.)

So you have taken it into your head to scold me, though I am always writing to you—five letters, for instance, in the last three days, and if they get lost it is no fault of mine! You are in the wrong, *mon ami*, and you write just like a lazy man, quite proud of his own punctuality. Since you choose to be angry, I will be the same, and will make out a little list of all my grievances, which are better founded than yours. *Mon ami,* you write me very charming letters; you write them often, and they form the happiness of my life; all this is as it should be. But in none of your letters do you answer the questions I am continually putting to you. I know no particulars of the Emperor's stay at Strasburg; I am in ignorance whether you have received the parcel from Desfaucherets, and therefore I cannot give him any message of thanks from you; you say nothing about M. de Caulaincourt, though I am continually inquiring for him; you do not write to my mother, who consequently is not pleased. What else? . . . But I have said enough for once; defend yourself if you can, and to appease me, try to give us frequent news of M. de Nansouty, for his wife receives no letters.

I went yesterday evening to Princess Louis' ; she was glad of our victories, but sorrowful on account of the individual misfortunes which even the most splendid triumphs entail. She is grieved by Lacuée's death, and said pathetically, " When I read the accounts, I am surprised to find that my tears begin to flow, although I am so glad of all our success." Prince Louis frets over his ill health, which compels him to remain here ; he spoke with me for a long time about M. de Nansouty, and was really kind, on this occasion, to the whole family. The quiet little evenings we spend with the dear princess are very· pleasant. She goes out very little, and just receives a few intimate friends ; we all chat quietly together, and yesterday M. de Lavalette, whom I like much, as you know, was there. To-night I am going to Prince Joseph's—he has a reception—and to-morrow probably to Princess Borghèse'. You see I am doing my duty to the whole family. I have also waited on Princess Caroline ; * but if victories continue to succeed each other at this rate, we shall be always running about. How I should like to be again going to and from the Tuileries, with you, and how relieved both heart and head would feel, if I knew the Emperor were resting quietly in his palace, and you in our pretty home ! . . .

* Princess Murat.

## LXVI.

TO M. DE RÉMUSAT AT STRASBURG.

Paris, 27 Vendémiaire, Year XIV.
(October 19, 1805.)

. . . There is nothing in the *Moniteur* to-day, but we are told to expect the news of some great battle this evening ; I am looking for letters from you, and my heart will beat when I receive them. What excitement ! what a life ! Poor creatures that we are, how we struggle on our sandhill, and, too often, hasten the moment when all will be over ! The glory with which we clothe our ardour for mutual destruction is a fine subject for philosophizing, and if anything remained to be said concerning it, I would not spare you, because just now I am deep in philosophy, and, moreover, having plenty of leisure for reading, I have taken up Voltaire, whom I am studying with a delight for which I am inclined to reproach myself. That extraordinary man is too often in the right, and he has so frequently divined things, that I think he must sometimes have alarmed the very being who created him. For my own part, I remain on my guard as much as possible while reading his works, but, between ourselves, in spite of my good intentions and my previous prejudices, I should scarcely resist him, if my heart could find a substitute for that of which he seeks to deprive it. The dry and barren tenets of philo-

sophy must always fail in this, that they only
please the intellect, and sometimes perhaps stagger
our reason, but they can never lessen the bitterness of a single tear—and who is there who is
not called upon to shed many in this sorrowful
world ?

*Mon ami*, if you have any leisure time you
really should spend Wednesday evenings with us.
Wednesday is our " at home " day; my mother
and I decided on it, so that people might be sure
of finding us one evening in the week. How
I should like to see you walk in ! Be assured,
*monsieur*, I would omit nothing to make you
welcome, and that I would willingly push the duties
of hospitality as far as they could possibly go.

I suffer in silence from our separation, for I dare
not speak of my own troubles in the midst of
sorrowful widows and mothers. But if it is heartrending to tremble for the life of those we love,
it is very painful also to be so often and so long
separated from them.

General César Berthier * told me that if you
would write to General Matthieu Dumas, who is
with his brother, you would soon know if anything
had happened to Aimery de Montesquieu, because
it is he who makes out the list of the dead.

* General César Berthier, the brother of the Prince de
Wagram, and very much younger than he, distinguished
himself in the army.  He died at Grosbois in 1819.

## LXVII.

TO M. DE RÉMUSAT AT STRASBURG.

Paris, Monday, 29 Vendémiaire, Year XIV.
(October 21, 1805.)

We are in a state of the greatest anxiety; no news since the 20th! We learn by telegraph every day that you are equally ignorant at Strasburg. What can this silence mean? How alarming it is! Another engagement to follow the two first had been so decisively announced, that we expected it to take place immediately. But now, all is silence; you, even, do not write, and my heart misgives me.* We go every evening to Princess Louis' to wait for news with her. The courier arrives at eleven o'clock without bringing any; we exchange sorrowful glances, and take our leave without trusting ourselves to speak. I was at Neuilly this morning, where I found Princess

* The general longing for news, and for an escape from the tragic situation in which the Emperor was always placing France, made his own admirers even somewhat unjust, for few campaigns can be compared with this one. The Emperor, who had quitted St. Cloud on 2 Vendémiaire, crossed the Danube at Nordlingen on the 14th, seized the bridge over the Lech on the 15th, and fought on the 16th at Werlingen and Aichach. Marshal Soult had entered Augsburg on the 17th, the engagements at Landsberg and Albeck had taken place on the 18th and 20th, and the French had entered Munich. On the 21st the Emperor was on the road to Ulm, and on the 22nd Marshal Ney fought the battle of Elchingen. Ulm surrendered on the 25th, and Austerlitz was won a month afterwards.

Caroline alone and thoughtful. Notwithstanding her efforts to appear unconcerned, she seemed very anxious, and fixing her eyes upon a map, she was unable to see aught but the dangers of the splendid position we were admiring a few days ago. How great is the power of the imagination! how quickly it seizes upon us! how it disturbs our whole machinery! When this letter reaches you, *cher ami*, you will perhaps have received bulletins, and we perhaps shall be more at ease. Meanwhile, what hours, what days do we not pass through! Can we call this living? My poor sister is in a deplorable condition; she weeps continually, and for the last two days believes all that she fears.

*Mon ami*, I have been obliged to lay aside my pen, and I now take it up again to tell you what interrupted me. It was that poor fellow Talma who came to see me, and whose state is such that I was even moved to tears. For some days past, his nervous attacks had returned, and with such violence that he had to give up the idea of acting for a considerable period, for fear of some serious accident. In fact, the cast of the "Templiers" had to be changed, and the play itself injured, in my opinion, by giving Lafond's part to Baptiste, and Talma's to Lafond. I should have preferred the play being withdrawn for the winter, but they would not agree to this. An hour or so ago, Madame Talma arrived, all in tears. She made an appeal to me, and told me that she will lose her husband; that he is becoming insane; that misfortune has driven him out of his senses; that all their furniture has been seized, and that they are without a *sou.* I consoled her to the best of my ability, and asked where was her husband. She replied that he was in a hackney coach outside, not having the courage to present himself. I sent for him, as you may imagine, and he came in, looking a real ghost of tragedy, pale and thin. The first thing he did was to faint; then he wept, cried out, and really frightened me. He showed me a letter he has written to you; you will see the state he is in, and what you can do for him. Meanwhile, I spoke kindly to him, and when he began to come to himself, I advised him to struggle against these seizures, lest he might altogether sink under them. I promised I would ask for a grant from the Minister of Police, if such a thing were possible; I said I would forward his letter to you, and as he told me that he had been obliged to engage to pay away all his future earnings, I asked him to give me an exact and sincere account of his debts, with the names of his creditors and the engagements he had entered into with them, and that I would send it to you. "My husband," I said, "who is now at a distance from the Emperor, will probably find himself unable to give you the considerable sum of money that you require, but if the state of your affairs is explained to him, he may, by making certain promises to your creditors, stop their proceedings against you, and prevent you from entering on any ruinous course of action." I wish you could have seen the poor fellow's looks as he listened to me! It seemed, in truth, as if I were restoring him to life; he wept, and called us both his guardian angels. He is extremely weak, and I fear for his reason if he is not befriended. See what you can do on his behalf, and write either to him or to me on the subject. Be assured that there is no exaggeration in what I have told you, for, in truth, I was not able to restrain my tears. I sent for a score of bottles of Bordeaux, and had them conveyed to his house. . . .

## LXVIII.

### TO M. DE RÉMUSAT AT STRASBURG.

Paris, Thursday, 2 Brumaire, Year XIV.
(October 24, 1805.)

*Mon ami,* you must be satisfied with only a few words from me this morning. I am so agitated and so delighted! * I had been for ten days in such anxiety, that I can still scarcely command myself. However, I have written to the Empress, but I think my letter must have shown signs of the state into which the good news has thrown me. If you knew what evil reports were bruited abroad, and what I suffered from your silence! But let us say no more of this. Your dear letter has made me forget it all. Only I am trembling so much that I can scarcely hold my pen, and I spent all

---

* Evidently the capitulation of Ulm, which took place on 25 Vendémiaire (October 20, 1805).

my little strength in writing, as well as I could,
to our beloved and happy Empress. Tell her of
my heartfelt sympathy with her joy, and that, in
very truth, she has never ceased to be present in
my thoughts since that week in which we knew
of her anxieties. I shared in yours also. . . .

## LXIX.

### TO M. DE RÉMUSAT AT STRASBURG.

Paris, 3 Brumaire, Year XIV.
(October 25, 1805.)

I was so overcome and so agitated yesterday,
with the great news, that I could only write you
a word or two. I am just as happy to-day, but
more tranquil, and I take up my pen to tell you
of everything that had preceded our great joy.
For ten days we had been without couriers,
and for six you had not written, and secret mis-
givings, that I dared not put into words, were
mingled with the great anxiety that I shared with
every one else. I said to myself, " If my husband
knows nothing of the movements of the army, and
therefore can tell me nothing, at least he could write
about his own health and the affection that makes
me so happy." I understand now that you were
anxious like ourselves, and would not tell me so.
As usual, all sorts of evil rumours were circulated
here. There had been a most sanguinary engagement; Prince Murat had been wounded, and several
generals killed! My poor sister wept and knew

not what to believe; added to this, every day I saw poor unhappy Madame de Fezensac, who was in a most pitiable state. Thus, occupying myself in consoling these two poor ladies, without much hope myself, and secretly fretting about you and our future prospects, I spent melancholy days and wretched nights.

Yesterday was a grand day! At six in the morning I ring my bell. I hear that Charles, who had been indisposed the previous day, has had an excellent night and is in good spirits. At seven your letter arrives, and shortly afterwards I receive a note, telling me that Philippe de Ségur has written word that Aimery is in good health. I went to congratulate his grandmother and sisters; * all the family begged me to thank you for your kindness, for which they are most grateful. All this good news arriving at once, moved me very deeply, and your poor wife, as you may imagine, was rather knocked up; but I slept well last night, and am calm this morning. I am dining to-day with Princess Borghèse, and am going afterwards to the "Mariage de Figaro;" for we may as well amuse ourselves a little now that our minds are relieved. The Français has put this play very carefully on the stage. The first performance drew a large house. They hope to make something by it, for this month the receipts have been next to nothing. I am astonished that Mahérault has not written to you, or rather I perceive that

* Madame de la Live was his grandmother, and Mesdames de Vintimille and de Fezensac his sisters.

he has deceived me, for every time that he came here complaining, I used to advise him to tell you, and he invariably said he had done so. I am convinced that a letter from you will be of use, but do not address it to the commissioner, for his influence is worn out. Talma brought me yesterday a list of his debts; they seem terribly heavy. He told me he had omitted nothing, having entire confidence in you. His current expenses do not distress him; he thinks he will be able to defray them, but the amount he owes for rent, and the interest he must pay on his debts, reduce him to a pitiable condition. He met Corvisart here, who encouraged him to bear up against his nervousness in order to overcome it, and who tranquillized him by speaking hopefully of his health.

I wrote a letter to the Empress yesterday; it was perhaps rather incoherent, for my head was aching badly and my hand trembling. Tell her that all of us here were sharers in her anxiety, and afterwards in her joy, and that I could see by the interest she created how much she is beloved. There is great excitement prevailing, moreover. The Emperor's victories have roused every one's enthusiasm; he is called the greatest man that has ever existed, and the campaign the most stupendous. Grandmaison * said, rather happily, the day before yesterday, that it was the Emperor's habit to *improvise* his triumphs.

* Parseval-Grandmaison, a member of the French Academy. He died in 1834.

When the great news was announced at the theatres, they rang with applause and shouts. *Mon ami*, what a splendid sight his Majesty's entry into Paris will be! But when is he coming? and when shall I see you? What mingled feelings will be mine on that happy day! As wife, friend, and Frenchwoman all my desires will be accomplished.

### LXX.

TO M. DE RÉMUSAT AT STRASBURG.

Paris, 5 Brumaire, Year XIV.
(October 27, 1805.)

I saw yesterday a note from M. de Talleyrand to Madame Devaines, in which he says the Empress had been greatly agitated, and afterwards extremely happy. We shared here in all her emotions, and, in truth, such agitation is wearing. You must have had an anxious time, and my mother and I often thought of your melancholy expression and pale countenance. How distressing, my dearest, not to be together on such occasions! There is something pleasing in grieving together, and in the mutual expression of anxiety ending by the sad but tender assurance of an affection which softens every misfortune.

If you care for a piece of news, let me inform you that Madame Lavoisier exists no longer. The Countess Rumford has taken her place. No one knows when this great feat was accomplished, but it seems that nothing is wanting, except, as my mother says, *the Stove.* Count Rumford went yesterday morning to bear the news to Bertrand, Gallois, etc. These gentlemen paid their visit the same evening, intending to offer their congratulations ; but the lady of the house cut them short, saying it was an old affair, and changing the subject, the conversation turned on ordinary topics. The only difference was calling them *Comte, Comtesse.*

I have heard from our friends, the Chérons ; they are beginning to get accustomed to their new life. The husband seems happy, and the wife less melancholy, although she has been obliged to send her son away to school. She asks me to remember her to you, and is, like ourselves, full of exultation and delight. We are expecting to hear next of a victory over the Russians. Madame de Vannoise shudders at the idea, because her son is in Bernadotte's division. M. Dumas* promised my cousin he would make inquiries about her son, and if you would speak with him on the subject, you would be doing a kindness to this poor mother. As she is dining here, she will give me her son's address. Here it is : " Alexander de Vannoise,† Corporal in the 95th Regiment, in Bernadotte's army." She is very unhappy this year ; her affairs

---

\* General Matthieu Dumas, who died in 1837.

† Madame de Vannoise had two sons: Hippolyte, an officer in the artillery, who died in Russia in 1812, and Alexander, at that time a soldier, who died long afterwards.

are in a worse state than ever, and anxiety for her children is killing her. She comes here nearly every day for society and consolation. Mamma made her a little present of firewood, which she accepted so gratefully that it brought tears to my eyes. Meanwhile, her daughter grows lovelier every day. When I take her to the theatre she makes quite a sensation. She is tall, very plump, and, in my opinion, beats all the beauties of the day. Norvins is half inclined to be in love with her, but feels that he is not rich enough, and she thinks him very ugly. By the way, he has quite taken possession here; he comes morning and evening, he entertains mamma and plays with Charles, he does commissions for me, he weeps, or, at least, feels anxious with Alix, and, in fact, makes love to the whole family. He is rather amusing, though not very good style, but, having nothing better, we like him very well. This disgusts Abbé Morellet, whom he worries with bad jokes, and who sighs wearily when he finds him established at our fireside. But it cannot be helped. Paris is so empty now, we must put up with what we can get.

## LXXI.

### TO M. DE RÉMUSAT AT STRASBURG.

Paris, 8 Brumaire, Year XIV.
(October 30, 1805.)

From what you write to me, I see that, among others, you have not received my letter of the 29th, in which I spoke of Talma's visit to me. I told you that he had come to see me, half wild with despair, because his goods had just been seized, and that I could only succeed in calming him by promising I would forward a letter he had written to you, and an exact statement of his debts, as, although I did not think you could afford him any pecuniary assistance during the absence of the Emperor, you might perhaps use your authority to prevent his creditors from taking advantage of his illness, and the confusion of his affairs, to impose hard conditions. I have since forwarded the statement I allude to, but I do not know whether it will reach you. I petitioned the Minister of Police also for a little temporary help, which he promised to grant. Finally, I comforted poor Talma in some degree.

From what you say concerning the theatre, I perceive that another letter of mine has not reached you, in which I mentioned the "Festin de Pierre," which, though admirably acted, did not draw. As to the "Mariage de Figaro," it is quite true that it draws well, and I enjoyed it much.

Do send me your letter for the actors, or come yourself and set them in order.   Your bright idea of asking for leave to come and spend three weeks with me makes my heart beat.   Seriously, apart from affection, which is not counted for much in the affairs of this world, your presence here is necessary.   But when I remember other considerations, I know that you ought to join the Emperor if he remains in Germany, and I say to myself that perhaps your best plan would be to write to M. de Caulaincourt and ask leave to join his Majesty, after staying in Paris as long as necessary to settle the accounts of the year that has just closed.   This piece of advice is the result of an effort that you will appreciate as it deserves ; but you must decide as you feel will be best.

The lines that you send me are very pretty.   I fear it is now a little late for them ; but I will consult Campenon.   He is worried also about his theatre, where Elleviou is terribly missed   It is better attended than the Français, but not so well as to make it pay.

The Opéra only is always crowded, and I cannot think how they can be so much in debt, with such good houses.

## LXXII.

TO M. DE RÉMUSAT AT STRASBURG.

Paris, Saturday, 11 Brumaire, Year XIV.
(November 2, 1805.)

I can quite well sympathize with your dislike of the empty life you are leading at Strasburg, and I understand your wish to be at Paris or Munich. If my feelings make me wish to have you here, I try, on the other hand, to suppress them, because I am conscious that duty calls you to his Majesty's side. Since some civilians are already there, since Auguste de Talleyrand is with him, I feel that you ought to make every effort to be there too, and I try to accustom myself to the thought that you have already preferred your request, and that, valuing the privilege as you do, it will surely be granted. Another reason for bearing bravely the sorrow that I must feel at your prolonged absence, is that I perceive that several persons here are surprised, from different motives, that you are not with the Emperor. I repeat, then, whatever it may cost me, I approve of your zeal, and I consent to the increased distance between us. Write therefore, *cher ami*, entreat, and obtain this favour; I will submit to everything, and, however painful this further separation, I shall have courage for the sacrifice.

I have changed M. de Tournon's money at considerable loss. Madame de la Rochefoucauld, who had intended to start on Saturday, had kindly taken charge of it. But she is ill, and her journey is again delayed; I fear that you may be pressed for it, and I am going to write to M. de Lavalette to ask him how to insure your promptly receiving the four thousand francs, partly in gold, partly in silver. I was obliged to lose thirty-six francs on the notes for a thousand francs, and forty-two on the gold. You see we are far from being at par. It is thought here that there is a good deal of trickery and jobbing on the part of the brokers.

We spent yesterday evening in great state at Prince Joseph's. A *Te Deum* had been sung in the morning, and in the evening there was a grand reception at the Luxembourg. During the concert there were rumours of a fresh victory over the Russians, but the news was not official. We are all expectation. The Princess Joseph is pleasant and kind in her own house, and makes her guests welcome. I am dining to-day at the Arch-chancellor's, and on Monday at Prince Louis's. After that I shall rest a little, for this week of visits and full dress has rather tired me. Madame Devaines says that the Emperor's rapid victories set us paying forced visits, just like his soldiers' forced marches.

I give my son a treat on his fête next Tuesday. M. Desprès is kind enough to bring a conjuror to amuse him, and to write a few verses in his honour.* He is wonderfully well; he asked me

---

* M. Desprès was a writer of vaudevilles. He was at one time Inspector of the University.

yesterday to keep his fête on Monday, which is really St. Charles's Day, and when I explained that I must dine on that day with Prince Louis, "You should write to him," said he, "like some one I have read about, that you would rather eat a carp with your children than go to dinner with the Prince de Condé."

On Sunday and Thursday, to amuse him, he and I act proverbs that we have adapted, or scenes from plays, with Constance and my mother. M. Bertrand, Madame de Vannoise, Madame de Grasse, and Alix form the audience. To-morrow we are going to act the two last scenes of the "Dépit Amoureux;" it makes a kind of proverb, "Like master, like man." Constance acts Lucile, and I Marinette, while Charles, who is the Préville of our company, acts Éraste in the first scene, and then, throwing off his overcoat, is transformed into Gros-Réné. You would be delighted with his intelligent conception of both his parts, and at the rapidity with which he changes from the languishing complaints of the master to the comic reproaches of the valet. How I long for your presence at our theatricals! We will give you some grand performances on your return!

Do not fancy, however, that we spend all our time in amusement. Lessons get on very well too, and I am pleased with the little scholar I am bringing up for you. And I myself do not spend all my time in trifling, as you shall judge on hearing what I have begun to study. I have put history aside in favour of Plato. Yes, indeed, *mon ami*, Plato, that you know I have been longing to read ever since I heard the Emperor talk so much about him. I have borrowed the book, and I am deep in metaphysics! I do not always understand him perfectly, but what I do understand I like, and these dreams of a vivid imagination seem to suit my own. Nevertheless, if I may venture to say so, your old philosophers are somewhat verbose, and occasionally they bring up such a multiplicity of arguments that I forget what they want to prove.

It is thus that I spend my time, and my happiest days are those on which, free from any invitation, I can occupy myself entirely with my home and with everything that reminds me of you. Sometimes, in the midst of my book, or when with the children, I pause to think gratefully of all the happiness I owe you, and of the life that you have rendered so sweet and so easy; and I no longer dare to murmur at the passing clouds that sometimes darken it, for I have to thank Providence for the blessedness of belonging to you.

## LXXIII.

### TO M. DE RÉMUSAT AT STRASBURG.

Paris, 13 Brumaire, Year XIV.
(November 4, 1805.)

If I wanted to fill my letter with messages for you, I could easily do so, for I met a number of persons yesterday at Cambacérès' who desired to be remembered. to you; among others, the host first, then your friend Viry and M. de Ségur. The latter is very much occupied with his guard of honour. He thinks of nothing but fighting, and is continually pressing to get the law passed that is to organize his corps. He says that, if it be delayed much longer, he shall set out and join the Emperor, who will not be very angry, he hopes, with this impromptu journey. He wears himself out with riding on horseback so that he may regain his former strength, and has written a clever letter to the Emperor, in which he says he is the only Frenchman who finds fault with his Majesty's rapidity, because it does not give him time to form his corps. He thought you were at Munich, and in his zeal he charged me to express his hope that you might soon be there. I wish the same, as does every one, if the war lasts; but, nevertheless, I take the liberty of wishing for something else, which would bring the Emperor back to Paris, and suit us all, I think. Don't you think so? . . .

After the dinner at the Archchancellor's, I went to a concert at the Bouffons, where I heard Madame Barilli. She has a pure and high voice, and a good method, but she is very cold, and altogether reminded me of a Mademoiselle Renaud, whom you may perhaps have seen at the old Italian Opera House. She is rather popular, and would do well, I think, in private concerts. I have already mentioned the Bouffons to you in other letters that may have been lost; they are the fashion, and their theatre is well filled.

I forward you a letter from François de Neufchâteau,* which accompanied his book. I answered it as well as I could in your absence, and my cousins paid him a visit of thanks. His history is considered good, though rather flippant. I was congratulated on it yesterday and complimented on my great-uncle. I must read his work, if I can tear myself from my friend Plato, who delights me when I can understand him.

Paris continues to be very dull; people go into society with thoughtful and anxious faces. One thing only is desired: we hope strongly, yet we fear a little; we get through the time without caring how, and yet that future towards which we hasten will certainly not be what we expect.

---

* François de Neufchâteau, senator, member of the French Academy, ex-Minister of the Interior, was born in 1750. He was a poet as well as a historian. The work that he was publishing in the year in which Madame de Rémusat's letter was written, was entitled, "Histoire de l'Occupation de la Bavière par les Autrichiens en 1778 et 1779, contenant les Détails de la Guerre et des Négociations, qui furent terminées par la Paix de Teschen" (Paris, 1805). He had published in the year preceding a "Tableau des Vues que se propose la Politique Anglais dans toutes les Parties du Monde" (Paris, 1804).

# LXXIV.

Paris, 18 Brumaire, Year XIV.
(November 9, 1805.)

At last our correspondence is drawing to a close, and we shall be quits for a few lost letters that need not be regretted, your anxieties, that grieved me so much, and some few little reproofs which, between ourselves, I did not deserve. There are but two packets that I should like you to have received—one containing the list of Talma's debts, of which I will send you a second edition if you wish, and another with a translation by Charles, which would have pleased your fatherly feelings.

Talma came yesterday to show me your letter. He was moved to tears by the " kindness of the reproaches " that he said " it contained." He wants to give up his share of the receipts, and desires that some one should manage his affairs for him. He begs you not to be too angry on the receipt of his *budget*. The melancholy Mahérault pays me a visit now and then. He looks nervous and alarmed; he sighs and asks when you are coming back. When he tells me that the theatre gets on badly in your absence, I always tell him to write to you. But to this he never makes any reply.

What you say of M. de Talleyrand is a relief after the rumours we had heard of his illness and death. I can understand his appreciating you better on seeing more of you. There is one side of his character (not the least worthy) which should harmonize with yours, and I congratulate you on being in his company, because he will do you justice when he knows you better. *Mon ami*, you must admit that I have good reasons not only for loving you as I do, but also for preferring you before every one I know, and on this point my feelings are always approved by my reason. We were talking to Corvisart of you. "You would be too happy," he said to me, "if such a husband as yours were never absent from you, and if your son could grow up without giving any cause for anxiety!" And he is right. Life under such circumstances would be too sweet. How could we make up our minds to quit it!

I agree with you as to your leaving Strasburg, and I admit that you are in the right; in fact, you frequently are, and the older I get the more I perceive that. Do not, however, take advantage of my admission, for you know that with us women, reason herself is not always in the right.

It is quite true that monetary affairs are very uneasy here; and if this lasts it will become a serious matter. Notes for a thousand francs are at ninety francs, and there are even some shop-keepers who will not take them at all. One of them told me that before she received her goods she was obliged to specify whether she would pay in cash or in notes. There is some grumbling, for nobody buys and nobody pays. There are large crowds at the entrance to the Bank, and pickpockets cause constant confusion. It is said that the bankers have met together for the purpose of taking some decision ; that they have written to the provincial towns, Lyons among others, which have declined to help them ; and that the quantity of money required for the army, and the stock-jobbing besides, are the two causes of the scarcity. The fact is that the inconvenience is great, and there is not enough public spirit among the bankers to induce them to sacrifice their private interests to those of the Bank. They have written to the Emperor, but how is it possible to explain everything at such a distance ? and what an annoyance for him, in the midst of his great affairs, to have to attend to details of this kind ! In truth, we do not help him much, and we put on him the whole burden of our well-being.

We have bad news from the Cadiz fleet. The details, which as yet are not given officially, are daily exaggerated ; but after making due allowance, there would seem to have been great rashness on the part of Villeneuve, who insisted on leaving the harbour before the arrival of his successor, and who has managed his dangerous venture very badly. A frightful tempest was raging, and both sides fought with the utmost fury. The admiral was taken prisoner, Nelson killed, they say, and Magon also. There is no doubt about the last. Only twelve of our vessels returned to port, and the *Bucentaure* foundered. If this be true, poor little Parseval * has perished, and

* The battle of Trafalgar was fought on October 2. M. de

perhaps young d'Houdetôt as well. M. de Lina told Alix that all private accounts agreed in praising the courage and skill of the French, but said, at the same time, it was impossible to form quickly and safely into line of battle in such a gale of wind, and against an enemy already in battle order, and, moreover, very skilful. The French were so desperate that, their admiral's flag-ship being taken, in the night the prisoners massacred the English sailors who were guarding them, and succeeded in escaping. But the ship had suffered terribly, and went down in sight of the harbour. I hope that some of these details are exaggerated. You will know sooner than I, and will write me word.

I thank you for your good news. It is indeed a miraculous campaign, and I say, like an excellent country gentleman who wrote to my mother yesterday, "By the side of our Emperor, Cæsar and Alexander would have been but lieutenants." Alix has at last heard from her husband. He had suffered a little from the cold weather and the snow, but is in good health nevertheless. His wife's letters do not reach him. If you could contrive to let him know, either through M. de Talleyrand or M. de Caulaincourt, that she is well,

---

Parseval was not killed, neither was young M. d'Houdetôt, who was destined to become General France d'Houdetôt. He was, however, severely wounded in both knees. He was on board Magon's ship, a friend of his family's who was killed. M. de Parseval-Deschênes rose to the rank of vice-admiral, and died in 1860.

and that Stephen * is more charming than ever, it would be a great kindness. Poor Thierry † travelled fifty miles in vain after the lost letters. Madame de Fezensac has heard from her son ; he is perfectly well, often sleeps on the ground in the open air, but takes no harm, and seems in capital spirits. He writes that the Emperor goes about everywhere, wet and muddy like the rest of them, and that he is positively worshipped by the soldiers. Some young men of our acquaintance, who are there and conducting themselves well, will contrast favourably with all the idlers who, in laying down their sword, seem to have laid down their manhood also. . . .

## LXXV.

### TO M. DE RÉMUSAT AT STRASBURG.

Paris, Tuesday, 21 Brumaire, Year XIV.
(November 12, 1805.)

. . . This morning Charles sneezed, and I politely said, "May you obtain your wish, my son !" "My wish," he said, "is that papa may come home." And, without sneezing, *mon ami*, that is my most ardent wish also. It pervades the whole atmosphere of the house ; mistresses and servants, we all want you back. This is all I have to tell you to-day, for I know of nothing else, and my

---

* Etienne de Nansouty, the general's son.
† M. Thierry was aide-de-camp to General Nansouty.

heart is full of sadness that I do not wish to com-
municate to you. Not that there is anything
fresh ; but the weather is gloomy, people complain
of the scarcity of money, croaking politicians will
have it that Prussia is going to declare against us,
and then this long widowhood, and the solitary
hours far from him I love best, are killing me with
dulness and melancholy. Your empty days at
Strasburg are not worse than mine. How I long
for another year, though perhaps it would be more
sensible for me now not to wish time to fly so
fast ! How painful is the absence of all that
consoles the heart or delights the eyes ! This
great Paris becomes every day more gloomy ; no
one visits, we shut ourselves up that we may not
spend our money. The theatres are absolutely
empty, the shop windows full of things that nobody buys, and *ennui* is the order of the day.
Meanwhile the Emperor is bestowing glory and
success on his army, and the next news will, no
doubt, be dated from Vienna. Would you believe
that sitting here all alone by my fire, and going
over this astonishing campaign, seeing him at the
end of six weeks entering the enemy's capital in
triumph, I feel alarmed for the danger he is perhaps incurring, and lest traitors may be con-
cealed in Vienna. And then, powerless as I am
to do aught but implore God to watch over him,
I exclaim in all sincerity, " May God preserve
him ! "

Madame de Talleyrand had a terrible scare.
Her husband's death was suddenly reported with

considerable appearance of truth. One of her brothers told her of it. You can imagine the state she was in. It was not until two days later that his letters arrived, but we have not discovered what can have given rise to the report.

You must have a great number of ladies at Strasburg. I suppose Madame de la Rochefoucauld made her appearance there on Saturday or Sunday. She was very unwell when she set out on her journey, and I doubt whether travelling can have cured her. I know from her doctor that she is much worse than she herself believes, and that her spirit, rather than her strength, is keeping her up. The unrest of her life is wearing her out, and it is true that a great deal of strength is required to bear the senseless, ceaseless bustle of a Court life. For myself, *mon ami*, I feel that I could not endure anything so opposed to my tastes and temperament, if my affections did not make up for various little annoyances. This, I believe, would always be the case with me; in whatever position I might be placed, my heart must always play a certain part in every important action of my life. Unless this were so, I should grudge the sacrifices imposed on me, and, in spite of the good principles in which I have been brought up, I should not perhaps fulfil all my duties as I ought, although I hope I would still try to accomplish them. Do not, however, draw any evil conclusions from the confession I have unguardedly made. Have you not made those very duties delightful to me? For my part, I find nothing painful in the thought that I owe all and everything to you, even my good qualities.

## LXXVI.

### TO M. DE RÉMUSAT AT STRASBURG.

Paris, 24 Brumaire, Year XIV.
(November 15, 1805.)

There is nothing new here. The crowd has given up the Bank, and assembles now at the doors of the municipalities, to obtain orders for the payment of five-hundred-franc notes; but as nothing is so difficult as to quiet the Parisians respecting their money, the crowd is so dense that to reach the door is impossible; so that, if one is pressed for money, it is better to buy it at once. It is cheaper now. After having reached ten and even eleven per cent., it is now at five, and it is hoped that the good news we are expecting will produce a beneficial effect. The scarcity of money is much talked about, because it inconveniences everybody more or less. For the last month I have become so clever in banking matters, by dint of hearing of bills, discount, etc., that there was no need to apologize for your little dissertation on political economy. Bertrand, to whom I read it, says that you talk like a Secretary for Commercial Affairs? He begged to be affectionately remembered to you; he regrets your absence, and like all our friends, wishes you were back. You are greatly missed at our little Wednesday evenings. You know pretty well the names of all the guests; I have added a few more that accident has brought across my path; among others M. Suard, who seems anxious to meet you again. He dined here yesterday. These evenings of ours are rather pleasant; we say clever things *when we can;* we argue and dispute, as you may imagine, and M. de Norvins' foolish speeches are inexhaustible. By the way, I must tell you that Constance won't hear of him, but if you promise to keep the secret, I may inform you she is rather interested in a certain M. d'Héliand * whom Alix introduced, and whom we like very much. He is an intimate friend of M. de Nansouty's, was brought up at the École Militaire, is a widower and son-in-law to Corvisart's wife. Corvisart presented him to Prince Louis, who promised he would procure him a Receiver-Generalship. If he obtains the post, he will add the salary to an income of ten thousand francs from landed property, and he offers the whole to Con-

---

* M. d'Héliand, who died in 1858, at the age of ninety, did not become Receiver-General, nor did he marry Mademoiselle de Vannoise. He lived a long time in Touraine in great solitude. His son, a playfellow of my father's, also died in 1858. He was in receipt of a retiring pension from the Ministry of Foreign Affairs. Suard, who was born in 1732 and died in 1817, was editor for a long time of the *Journal Étranger* and the *Gazette de France.* His writings have been collected under the title of " Mélanges de Littérature," five vols. octavo. He was always considered to have more talent for conversation, than talent strictly so called.

stance. She seems inclined to accept it, and so does her mother. The Empress will help us, you will also, and Corvisart besides; thus we may succeed. He was rather afraid of a divorced mother-in-law, but the daughter's fine eyes have charmed away all objections, and she considers seven and thirty the ideal age for a bridegroom. You must keep our little secret.

I went to the first performance of "Amalfi," which, notwithstanding all the fuss Picard had made about it, was a complete failure. It is a serious, tiresome opera, and, with the exception of two or three pieces, very mediocre. Your Bouffons are not equal to this kind of opera; they should be satisfied with making us laugh. To repair their mistake they are preparing "Il Finto Sordo." I shall hear Madame Cavanatti on Wednesday, and will report on her to the best of my ability. But if you really want to have good singers here, you must make up your mind to pay them highly, or else, people say, to restore the amateur or the Olympic concerts, which were so good, and did not interfere with the success of the company in '89. There would be a subscription of five or six louis, the singers would improve, and then, by engaging Marchesi, Catalani, Crescentini, etc., Paris would soon possess the finest possible school of music. There is a very good company in Vienna just now, who may perhaps come to us as trophies of our conquest. I wish it may be so, for Italian music is all the fashion, and it would be a good opportunity for calling it *French music.*

## LXXVIII.

### TO M. DE RÉMUSAT AT VIENNA.

Friday, 8 Frimaire, Year XIV.
(November 29, 1805.)

Oh, *mon ami*, what a separation! how my heart is aching!* Your two loving and sad letters arrived together; I must have guessed what they contained, for I was greatly moved, and not with delight, in opening them. I burst into tears as I read, and I am weeping still. I blame myself for letting you see my misery, for it will grieve you, but I cannot restrain it, and I feel it can only increase until the day that I shall hear from you of your safe arrival in Vienna. How I regret now that I considered my health so much and did not accompany the Empress! The journey could not do me more harm than the anxiety that will cling to me night and day. . . .

Sunday, 10 Frimaire.

Forgive me for telling you of my sufferings. It is almost against my will that I write of them, but my heart and my head are full of but one idea. However, I am less agitated than at first. I have been making inquiries about the roads, and I am told they are quite safe for travelling. But I

* The Emperor had entered Vienna on 22 Brumaire (November 13), and his First Chamberlain followed him thither with the regalia that he had already conveyed to Milan, and which included part of the crown jewels.

know I shall be easier when I hear you are with the Emperor. A superstitious feeling that I cannot explain, but which is deeply implanted in me, gives me a conviction that the superior Power who guards him, watches also over those about him, and that no misfortune can happen near his person. This feeling, which was strong before, is now strengthened by many proofs, and, however valiant our troops, I do not doubt for an instant that it is to him we owe all our recent glory.

You can easily picture to yourself the great sensation produced by our victories and our entry into Vienna. There had been extreme uneasiness here. Evil rumours, as usual, were in circulation, and were too easily believed. At last the cannon was heard, and our incredible success became known. The very streets were joyful, and there was a *French* feeling about it all, which struck me, because, unfortunately, that is not very usual among Parisians. After due enjoyment of the news, the caballing has begun again, and for the last week politics have been the order of the day. I should never end if I were to repeat to you all that is said. Everybody rearranges Europe according to his own idea, destroys empires or builds them up, makes peace or carries on the war, without troubling himself much as to the eventual results of his policy; and it does not need much discernment to perceive in each individual the small opposing interests that suggest these various arrangements. The Empress's journey gave rise to rumours of peace, while yours makes people say that the coronation ornaments are being taken to Vienna; in one drawing-room I hear of a King of Poland, in another of a King of Bavaria, and so on. Then somebody comes to see me, asks me questions, and when I am quite tired of interrogations that I have good reasons for not answering, because I really know nothing, I say, "Why don't you leave it all to our ruler, and enjoy at your leisure the prosperity that his activity procures for you?" . . .

## LXXIX.

### TO M. DE RÉMUSAT AT VIENNA.

Paris, 13 Frimaire, Year XIV.
(December 4, 1805.)

*Mon ami*, I passed the day before yesterday alone with my mother. No visits, no more letters from Strasburg! To make up for these privations we had devoted our evening to reading a little, to talking of you, of our children, of their future prospects, and slightly against our neighbour; for you know there must always be a little gossip to enliven women, and even men, I think. After that we went to bed, and I fell asleep, thinking as usual of your absence, and also of your journey. This morning, at seven, I was awoke with a start by the courier. He seemed to make more noise than ordinary; at any rate, he rang a great peal! All my household were instantly on the alert,

and ran into my room, exclaiming, joyfully,
" Peace is made ! " I still doubted; I restrained
their delight, in which I did not immediately join,
but hastened to seek further information. At last
I learned that the announcement has been made
at the theatres that proposals of peace have been
made by the Emperor of Austria, and that nego-
tiations are in progress. You may imagine the
general delight ! You know how soon our Parisians
will let themselves hope, just as easily as they give
way to despair, and on this occasion they are
eager to believe in that which they wish. They
are shouting " Peace ! " * People tell each other
the news in the streets ; they embrace : the
Emperor is coming back ; they inquire what route
he will take, that they may be there to receive
him ! . . .

I am going to-day to the Luxembourg. It will
be my first time of going out since you began your
journey. I have been a litle unwell, and as, unfortunately, the absence of the Empress leaves me
at full liberty, I make use of it to nurse myself
when I feel out of sorts, and, both from prudence
and from inclination, I remain at my own fireside.
This solitude, which I like, is also very useful to
my finances, which are straitened, as you know,
and notwithstanding the economy with which I
endeavour to manage all things, life in this Paris
of ours is so dear that I spend more than I can
afford. . . .

* All this rejoicing was caused by false news. Peace was not
made until later.

Matthieu Molé is bringing out a book, his first attempt; nothing more, in fact, than a short essay on politics and metaphysics, which women will be forbidden to read and very few men will appreciate.* It is to be accompanied by three extracts from newspapers, by MM. de Fontanes, de Bonald, and Lacretelle. Molé does not own to the authorship of the work, but it is well known, and he is quite puffed up. If it amuses him, what does it matter, as Werther says, so long as one is happy, whether one is threading peas or beans? As for me, who am threading nothing at present, I am endeavouring with all my might to dispel the *ennui* that devours me. However, I am in better spirits, as you may perceive, than when I wrote to you last. I revive at the hope of peace; my heart is no longer so heavy when I pass the Tuileries. I looked at the palace to-day, and told myself it was being made ready for the Emperor, and I shed tears of joy. When I know that he is there, and that I see you again in my little room, I shall have nothing to wish for.

* M. Molé published his book, which is alluded to in the Memoirs.

## LXXX.

### TO M. DE RÉMUSAT AT VIENNA.

Paris, Wednesday, 20 Frimaire, Year XIV.
(December 11, 1805.)

*Mon ami*, yesterday evening at seven o'clock Princess Louis sent for me in haste. I went to her immediately in a state of some alarm; for you know one is generally more disposed to expect bad news than good. On reaching her house, I found the princess quite agitated, weeping and laughing by turns. Her first words, like her first impressions, were of the danger to which the Emperor had exposed himself. "He commanded in person," she exclaimed, "and completely defeated the two Emperors!"* And we had known nothing about it! You can understand that on hearing this, I too began to tremble. However, I gathered up my strength to hear particulars of the great day. I was in dread about M. de Nansouty, but was reassured by seeing that his name does not appear on Prince Murat's list of wounded. After having heard all there was to tell, I made my escape and came running back to my mother to tell her the glorious news; then to Madame Devaines', where I began my story over again; then to everybody I could think of, and lastly to Madame d'Houdetôt's, where I found quite a crowd of people. I had scarcely uttered a few

* The battle of Austerlitz on 11 Frimaire (December 2, 1805).

words, ere I was surrounded, questioned, obliged
to recommence my story twenty times over, and
according as I spoke, astonishment and admiration
increased. It was midnight when at last I returned
home, worn out with emotion and fatigue, incapable of speaking another word, and of any other
feeling but that with which I naturally turn towards you, who must have experienced the same
agitation and delight as I.

But only imagine, *mon ami*, we knew nothing,
and were calmly awaiting the conclusion of peace
and the return of the Emperor. Both had been
so positively announced, that nothing less than
such a wonderful victory as this, in place of his
ardently desired return, could have produced an
effect here. People were already beginning to
wonder at the eight days' silence. The French
are rather like women, exacting and impatient.
It is true that the Emperor has spoiled us in this
campaign, and certainly never was lover more
eager to obey the wishes of his mistress, than
was his Majesty to fulfil ours. " You wish for a
rapid march ? " " Well, then, here is an army
that was at Boulogne, and which in three weeks'
time shall be in Germany." " You want a strong-
hold taken ? " " Ulm has capitulated." " You
are not satisfied ? you want more victories ? "
" Here they are ; here is Vienna that you wished
for, and lastly a pitched battle, in order that no
kind of triumph may be wanting to you ! " - To
all this we must add a number of noble and
generous deeds, and words full of grandeur and

goodness, so that our hearts are gladdened by this victory in addition to the national pride with which it fills us.

I am expecting a letter from you within the next few days, to tell me of your arrival at Vienna, and give us the details that we wish for and yet dread. It is impossible that this victory can have been attained without unavoidable sacrifices, and we have so many friends in the army who must have been exposed to danger! Perfect joy is not for this world, and it is we poor women who, for the most part, pay the share due to sorrow. It really seems as if, in the distribution of parts, you had allotted to us that of lamenting the misfortunes which you cause, just as the ancients appointed official mourners in some of their funeral ceremonies. However, I do not blame you for such a division. I love all the emotions to which we are predisposed, and although they sometimes cause us the keenest grief, they procure us enjoyments which richly repay us for everything.

Do not expect me to write to you on any other subject. I can think of nothing but this victory. Yesterday evening, in the midst of all our delight, we made the remark that it would be impossible to bear much longer the feverish agitation in which we have been kept for two months. It wears out, and indeed it spoils, the rest of one's life. How can one, after such violent emotions, resume the daily tasks of life, and return to the circle of narrow ideas which are generated and destroyed, almost at the same time, by the life of society? When peace is made, what can we talk of in those drawing-rooms, where we now discuss such great subjects? How shall we be able to resume our frivolous conversations? The Emperor does not know how he educates us, and what energy he gives to our minds by this succession of miraculous events. Men will be in no difficulty, but you have so arranged matters for us, that we shall not know what to do with the enthusiasm that women can seldom display with impunity, or without making themselves ridiculous.

I have just been interrupted by Charles Lebrun,* who had the kindness to come and see me. He related everything, and my admiration is increased on hearing the particulars. What a splendid story it will be! I wish I had the talent to write it! M. Lebrun did not see M. Nansouty after the battle; but he says that had anything happened to him, he would be sure to know it. I hope you will give us some news of him, and also of yourself, *mon ami.* I hope that you are at Vienna, but I do not know. Oh, if peace only follows on so many victories, I assure you I shall become a *dévote;* gratitude will put the finishing touch to my conversion.

Adieu. I think I love you more than ever when I am happy. It is true that I used to say the

* Charles Lebrun, aide-de-camp to the Emperor, was the son of the Duc de Plaisance. He was subsequently a deputy, then a senator under the Second Empire, and Grand Chancellor of the Legion of Honour. He died in 1859.

same thing when in my melancholy moods. The truth is that my love for you mingles with my every feeling, to embellish or console.

---

## LXXXI.

### TO M. DE RÉMUSAT AT VIENNA.

Paris, Monday, 27 Frimaire, Year XIV.
(December 18, 1805.)

Is it possible that we shall soon meet again? The Emperor's return is announced in all quarters, and I find it difficult to resist belief in what I wish for so much. If he comes, I venture to answer for it, he will be received with the greatest enthusiasm. You cannot imagine the state of excitement in Paris. His praises are echoed on all sides, and persons whom we knew to be most opposed to him, are obliged to yield, and to say with the Emperor of Russia, " He is predestined! " On Saturday evening I accompanied Princess Louis to the theatres, to hear the bulletins read. They were full, for the cannon had announced in the morning that there was something new, and the people listened, sympathized, and applauded with shouts that I never could have imagined. Meanwhile I was crying my heart out. I was so agitated that I believe, had the Emperor suddenly appeared, I should have thrown myself into his arms, though afterwards I must have asked pardon at his feet. I went out to supper afterwards. I was questioned, of course, but I knew the bulletin by heart and repeated it continually, and I felt proud, and at the same time moved, while repeating to certain persons its simple and penetrating words with a feeling of *ownership* which can be better understood than described. . . .

## LXXXII.

### TO M. DE RÉMUSAT AT VIENNA.

Paris, 8 Nivôse, Year XIV.
(December 29, 1805.)

Every one here is still talking of the Emperor's return, yet, I know not why, I dare not hope for it so soon. In your last letters you say nothing of it; the newspapers are full of little alarming paragraphs, and then, as the Parisians can never remain long of the same mind, they are beginning to spread fresh doubts as to peace. May the English be accursed if they contrive further complications, and may the evil they try to do us recoil on their own heads! I am not surprised at your emotion on again meeting the Emperor. I understood and almost felt it. I think he will be pleased with the Parisians on his return. It is true that he will be able to say with Tancred—

" Mon triomphe est parfait, sans doute il m'est bien dû." *

---

* This line is not accurately quoted in the text, and it is a mistake to attribute it to Tancred, who says nothing like it, for

I wrote to Mahérault on the subject of your letter, but as he is really very unwell, and has not strength to transact any business, I sent for some of the actors of the Comédie, and suggested to them to exert themselves a little. They seemed full of " Gaston et Bayard,"* and, after a re-perusal of the work, I am quite of their opinion. The play, although a middling one, is full of appropriate allusions in almost every line. Moreover, it is national. The part of Bayard is a fine one; on the whole, I think it a good selection, and Desfaucherets is altogether of my opinion. They are studying it, therefore, and will study " Manlius "† afterwards, so as to act it in January. Duval‡ has written a very pretty play, which has been accepted, and will also be put on the stage; and then (pray answer all this immediately) this is what is going on. The Opera is preparing a fête which, between ourselves, I think rather extraordinary. They purpose putting the Tuileries and the Carrousel

he is unfortunate all through. But at the beginning of scene 5 of Act 3, Amenaïde exclaims—

> "Mon bonheur est au comble ! helas ! il m'est bien dû."

* The tragedy of " Gaston et Bayard " in five acts, in verse, by M. de Belloy, who was born in 1727 and died in 1775, had been performed for the first time in 1771.

† The tragedy of " Manlius," by Antoine Arnault, who was born in 1766 and died in 1836, had been performed during the Revolution.

‡ This comedy of Duval's is one of the best he ever wrote. It was called at that time, " Une Étourderie de Charles II." It has since been performed under the title of " La Jeunesse de Henri IV."

and the Emperor himself on the stage ; that is to
say, an actor representing him will make his
triumphant entry, his car drawn by the populace
of Paris. This fête is under the management of
M. Esménard ; * yet, if I dared, I would say that it
would be better. to produce a play in which, the
application being less obvious, the public might
voluntarily seize on the allusions. Praise in the
other case seems to savour of flattery. At any rate
Bouilly is now writing a piece in which Mademoiselle Contat is to act. It is on the subject of
the recovered colours. They came to ask me
whether, in my opinion, the piece could be represented at your theatre. I was puzzled, or rather,
I was not, for I said I could not give an opinion on
the matter. What do you think of it ? If the
subject were suitably treated, would you give permission ? Would the Emperor allow it ? Answer
me as soon as possible.

While on the subject of theatres, let me tell
you about another. A few days ago I saw Legouvé's† tragedy, "La Mort de Henri Quatre,"
and was highly pleased with it. I was greatly

---

* Esménard, born in 1770, died in 1816, had just published
his poem of "La Navigation." He was successively a journalist,
the head of the Bureau des Théâtres, Secretary of the Government of La Martinique, Consul at St. Thomas, and didactic poet.
He was exiled in 1811, notwithstanding his production of
"Trajan" at the Opera, in honour of the Emperor's return.

† M. Gabriel Legouvé, who was born in 1764 and died in
1813, was the author of "La Mort d'Abel," of "Etéocle," and of
"La Mort de Henri Quatre," and of a poem on the merit of
women. He was father to M. Ernest Legouvé, who, like himself,
was a most distinguished member of the French Academy.

prejudiced against the work, but my prejudices yielded to the tears I shed. The *rôle* of Henri Quatre is really noble and pathetic, that of Marie is deeply impassioned, and Sully's is very fine. What I particularly liked was a speech of the King's, in which he reveals his designs against Austria—it is an exact history of this last campaign. The conspirator Epernon is well drawn ; he takes advantage of a momentary weakness of the Queen, who is ambitious and jealous in the extreme, to obtain from her a kind of consent, which she promptly retracts ; so that, although guilty, she is not altogether odious. All the traditionary speeches of Henry IV. are given, even to the *poule au pot ;* his last conversation with Sully is repeated, word for word. In short, I was moved to tears, and I think that, despite a few faults, it is a remarkable work, and so admirably contrived that its allusions are invariably comprehensible, without being dragged in, and that it would be impossible, while applauding Henry IV., not to think instantly of the Emperor. Legouvé is most anxious that you should read his work, and I venture to hope you will be of my opinion.

I have written you quite a long account of the theatres, but I have not yet finished. I must also tell you of a performance that took place on Saturday at Madame Pastoret's. The play represented was " L'Avocat Patelin," * and the actors were our children. It was quite a success. Gus-

---

* " L'Avocat Patelin " is a comedy by Breys and Palaprat, taken from an old farce of the Middle Ages.

tave did remarkably well as the *avocat*, and Charles as *Agnelet.* You would have been delighted, and would have shared our maternal emotions. This kind of amusement is very good for Charles; it makes him speak up and clearly, and then it amuses him, and that—may I say it?—is so much gained on the *enemy*.

Next Wednesday will be New Year's Day, and I shall pass it in sadness away from you. Paris is not gay, in spite of the return of January, and the tradesmen dare not give way to the flights of their imagination. As for myself, I am disposed to grumble, because at this time of year I feel more than ever the insufficiency of my means for all the presents I should like to make, and I have the greatest difficulty in adapting my New Year's gifts to the state of my finances. I can recollect when the coming of this time of the year was a great delight to me, but that is already a pleasure of the past, as are so many others that end with our youth. Happy are we if we retain the feelings of our hearts in undiminished strength !

---

## LXXXIII.

TO M. DE RÉMUSAT AT VIENNA.

Paris, Tuesday, 10 Nivôse, Year XIV.
(December 31, 1805.)

*Mon ami,* I wish you a happy New Year, and I wish that you may pass it with me, in order that

mine may be happy also.  My heart is very heavy
that you should be so far away; I had hoped for
your presence at this season, and I am greatly
depressed. . . .

The children are well, and I hope Charles will
get through the winter without any drawbacks; he
looks in excellent condition.  I am busied with his
dress to-day, because he has received an invitation,
in due form, from Prince Napoleon,* to a little
fête, beginning at six o'clock.  There are to be
marionettes, a magic lantern, and a lottery of
toys.

After this entertainment, which, as you may
suppose, will be over at an early hour, I intend
to pay a few visits, and I shall probably pass my
week in that tiresome occupation.  I must relinquish the laziness which your absence and the
want of occupation have rendered dear to me. . . .

Eleven p.m.

I left my letter this morning to attend to my
New Year's gifts.  I received very pretty presents
from my mother, my sister, and a few friends,
and had therefore to reciprocate.  I made a handsome present to Corvisart, and gifts to all my
household, so that this 1st of January has cost me
dear, and at the same time I am full of regret that
I could not give something to all those whom I
love.  This is why I sorrowfully repeat the usual
burden of my song, "We shall never be rich, for
we spend more than we have."

---

* Queen Hortense's eldest son, who died a few months later.

I went afterwards to the Princess Louis's, before her usual reception hour. She had organized a little fête at six o'clock. It was a very pretty party, full of the childish gaiety which is unclouded only at that age when it cannot be appreciated, and your son was thought very handsome; he behaved nicely, and I was quite pleased. I had feared lest his superiority of age should make him unwilling to yield the first place to the little princes in all the games, and had given him a little lecture accordingly. He quite understood the situation, and his manners were a pretty mixture of deference and ease. There was a magic lantern, marionettes, a little supper, and a most successful lottery for playthings. Then my son and I took our leave, and I came home to my mother. Just at present she is at supper at Madame Devaines', and I, in my dressing-gown by the fire, am writing to my heart's beloved, and assuring him, at this season, of the love that is the very happiness of my life. Oh, *mon ami*, this, which makes absence so painful, is also a very great delight, and for nothing in the world would I give up the emotions now filling my heart, unless, indeed, for those I should feel if I could now hold you in my arms. Time is flying, youth will soon escape me, but I shall let it go without dread and almost without regret, because you have convinced me that I shall always be equally dear to you. When I cast a glance over that portion of my life that we have already traversed together; when I say to myself, " What! ten years already ! "

I always feel inclined to add, "Yes, ten years of happiness are gone; but, thanks to the dearest of husbands, all that remain to me will be happy too, because happiness, when built up on heartfelt affection, is independent of the caprices of fortune."

It is painful to me to quit this subject, in order to tell you of other matters, and if I yielded to my own inclination, I should amuse myself by seeking new ways of assuring you of my affection, and of my gratitude towards the guide, the support, the charm, the delight of my whole life; but I must, for a moment, leave all this. I assure you that, if you are likely to remain absent much longer, you must take some steps about the administration of the Théâtre, for Mahérault can no longer manage it. The poor man is in a pitiable state; he can scarcely drag himself along, his speech is greatly affected, and there is a corpse-like odour about him which is horrible. The doctors do not expect he will live long enough to get to some watering-place when the season begins. How can he in such a state attend to the actors? They are left to themselves and everything is in a state of confusion. Discord prevents any variety in the repertory; Mademoiselle Contat will neither act herself nor let others act; Mademoiselle Raucourt does not appear; Talma says he is still weak and ill; there are no receipts except when the "Templiers," which always draws, is given. Four or five tragedies have been accepted. Some of these are said to be good, but they cannot be produced, as their turn does not come until after that of some pieces that, either from weakness or want of judgment, had been accepted, and which for the last eight months nobody will act or even study; and so everything is at a standstill. A kind of deputation came to me the day before yesterday, inquiring for the date of your return as that of the end of all their woes, and complaining that it is impossible for Mahérault to manage the Théâtre. They all beg that, if possible, you will tell the Emperor of the state to which they are reduced by the number of minor theatres in Paris, and really they have no hope but in what you may be able to say. I doubt whether the Emperor, in the midst of his great occupations, can find time to look into their grievances; but I can foresee that you will have enough to do on your return in setting all this machinery in order. I pointed out to them that this year ought not to be judged by ordinary rules, for it was only natural that the theatres should have suffered greatly from the general depression; that the only way of meeting their ill fortune would have been to redouble their exertions; and that at the present time, in order to conciliate His Majesty, they should prepare some amusement for him on his return, and carefully revise their repertory, immediately on his arrival. I ventured to tell Mahérault to say, as if from you, that "Antiochus Épiphane" must be played within a fortnight. It is a terribly stupid piece, that has stopped everything for the last nine months. They promised me to push forward "Gaston," which has been authorized by the police, at the same rate;

also "Manlius et Catalina," Duval's charming
comedy, and another comedy, I don't know what,
in five acts. You see what I have done; but as I
dare not put myself too forward, I cannot answer
for it that there will be no difficulties, and I,
like your actors, wish for you with my whole soul.
The other theatres are not more flourishing. The
Opera has made ten or fifteen thousand francs
less than the Porte St. Martin. For two months
there has been no division of profits at the Feydeau, and the Bouffons are in great need of the
recruits you are procuring for them. "La Prin-
cipessa d'Amalfi" and the "Finto Sordo" were
failures, and did them harm. You see that it is in
the order of things that amusements should not
flourish in your absence. But Paris is only waiting for her master's return to be brilliant, and I
to be happy. The newsmongers would have it
that he arrived last night at the Tuileries, and
were looking for him through the windows. I dare
not again ask you what you either do not know or
may not tell. I long for you; I hope that you
will come, but I dare not expect you; I pray to
God; I try to be brave and to make a virtue of
necessity; but I have made little progress in this
direction, and I am sometimes so discouraged and
impatient, that I should be angry with myself only
that I find relief in solitary tears.

## LXXXIV.

TO M. DE RÉMUSAT AT VIENNA.*

Paris, Monday, January 6, 1806.†

You, who know me so well and so completely share my every feeling, can easily imagine my emotion on reading the words, "*I shall soon see you again.*" I have read them over a hundred times; their sweet sound rings in my ears, following me everywhere, blending with all my thoughts, and giving joy to the hours that are still to be passed away from you. At last happiness is returning to me! What a delight to see the Emperor again, and how keenly will it be felt in Paris! The splendid campaign, the glorious peace, his Majesty's prompt return—all are wonderful, and to me, who love to trace the workings of Providence in the events of life, it is delightful to see the hand of God in all these things. And yet, my dearest, when you are restored to me, when once more I shall hold you in my arms, I shall

---

* The new year, 1806, opens on the same state of affairs as that which existed at the end of 1805. The Peace of Presburg had been made on December 26th. But on January 1st the Emperor was still in Germany, at Munich. He did not return to Paris until the 24th of the same month.

† By a Senatus-Consultum of 21 Fructidor, Year XIII. (September 8, 1805), the decrees of the Convention respecting the Republican calendar had been repealed, and the Gregorian calendar resumed, dating from January 1, 1806.

whisper to you that this painful separation has
been cheered by many sweet emotions; that your
loving punctuality in writing to me, the deep
affection expressed in all your letters, nay, even
the tears they made me shed—all these things
possessed a charm which I shall never forget, and
which binds us only the more closely together.
I hold the first place in your heart; you tell me
so continually! I believe it, I shall always believe
it, and in this lies my happiness. But you too
may feel assured that I can never love aught else
as I love you, the friend, the guide, the joy of
my life; and I have the advantage over you that
these were the first feelings of my heart.

The return of the Emperor will be the signal for
some splendid fêtes. The Opera is preparing,
and so is the city. I hope the performances will
be in a truly national spirit. One of them, and
it will perhaps be most gratifying to his Majesty,
is a comedy which we are going to perform in
his family circle, if I may use the expression.
Princess Louis has kindly given me a part to act
with her. I am deeply touched at such goodness,
though my affection at least deserved it. It is
a very nice *rôle;* there are phrases in it that I
like, because they express my own feelings, and
if timidity and emotion do not hinder me, I think
I shall act it pretty well. The princess will act
as she always does. The piece is clever, so I think
I can answer for its success. But I am unable to
say as much for your Français. Mahérault is in
such a state that he can do nothing; he tries his

best, but he is very ill, and your Comédie people
take advantage of your absence and his illness.
I have done my best, but you alone can remedy
all the existing confusion and disorganization.
It would be to their own interest to make more
effort, but on that stage, as on a larger one, the
actors prefer grumbling at fate and indulging
their vanity, which is ruining them. They
quarrel, abuse each other, and hinder everything.
I tremble at the complaints, the demands, and
the discontent you will have to encounter on your
return.

Meanwhile I have strongly insisted on " Gaston,"
" Manlius," and " Catilina " being put on the
stage this month. I enclose a programme that
was brought me by Dazincourt. He and his colleagues desire that the Emperor should be fêted
by the Théâtre Français also. Lebrun * under-
takes the ode. Just read over the programme,
and write a line if you approve of it, or send it
back. I am ignorant whether actors can rightly
take upon themselves thus to applaud in public
the sovereign of the nation. You are a better
judge than I, and you will decide the point.

I am busy this morning with preparations for
a fête of another kind, of the success of which I
do not feel so sure. Duval has requested permis-

---

* Lebrun, who was called *Lebrun Pindare*, born in 1729, died
in 1807, was at that time greatly celebrated as a lyric poet, and
with more reason as a writer of epigrams. His hundred and
forty odes are forgotten, but a few of his six hundred epigrams
have survived him.

sion to read me a play that he has written for the
Français, and which is said to be very clever. I
have invited about thirty persons to hear it, who
may give me more trouble than my guests of
yesterday, although they will probably not upset
my chairs and tables. But talking of guests, you
will soon return, and I must give you an account
of some new acquaintances that I have made,
partly by my own wish, and partly because your
wife's Wednesdays are beginning to be talked of,
and people seek for introductions to me. First
of all Fontanes, for whom you know I have a
weakness ; Monge, who has long had a weakness
for me ; Carrion-Nisas, whom I find amusing, and
cannot resist because he speaks so highly of you ;
Norvins, who makes us laugh ; your friend M.
Camille Tournon, who is extremely pleasant ; M.
Petitôt, with whom we have renewed our acquaintance ; * Legouvé occasionally ; a little man named
M. de Lagarde, who is husband to Mademoiselle
Rilliet, and is agreeable besides. These are the only
names I remember at present. I can see from
here the little sarcastic smile I know so well—" So
my wife is setting up as a *bel esprit!*" By no
means, monsieur ; but I let any one else who
likes be clever, and when my friends choose to
come, they meet my mother—who is a strong at-

* Monge, a member of the Institute and a senator, was, as
every one knows, the inventor of Descriptive Geometry. He died
in 1818, aged sixty-seven. Carrion-Nisas, an ex-tribune, was an
officer in a cavalry regiment, and a writer of tragedies ; born
in 1767, died in 1842. Petitôt, Inspector-General of the
University, and also a tragic poet.

traction to my salon—a good fire, tea, and philosophers. I listen with equal pleasure to Fontanes' preaching and Morellet's sarcasms, and as tolerance is not the fashionable virtue at present with either party, the tolerance of my salon procures me friends.

But all this would be much better if I had more money; for, begging pardon of idealists, the metal that is so greatly despised and yet so sought after forms more than half the attractions of a hostess, and if to all my own I could add the very superior ones of a good table, I should be really celebrated, and might double the number of my friends. Such a life is, between ourselves, that which would please me best. My health is not good enough for the bustle of the world, and complete repose of body, with some emotion for the heart, and exercise for the brain, would suit me exactly. But I hope you will scarcely have time to read all this rubbish. You are now on your road home, I hope and think, and in five or six days perhaps. . . . Adieu. I am expecting you, and this expectation is itself a happiness. .

## LXXXV.

Paris, January 10, 1806.

So your homeward journey is again deferred. I went yesterday to Princess Louis's, to rehearse the little play we are going to perform before the Emperor. I was in high spirits; I had received your Munich letter, and everything seemed to announce your speedy return, when Madame Maret made her appearance with a letter from her husband, telling her of Prince Eugène's marriage,* and of the return of the Court at the end of the month. *Mon ami*, tears filled my eyes, and I came back sorrowfully to my solitude, which for the last few days had been made so bright by the hope of seeing you. Princess Louis is grieved by her absence from her brother's wedding. She told me with tears of the obstacles that had prevented her from going to Munich. She hides her grief courageously, but is distressed, and if her brother does not come to Paris for a while she will be perfectly miserable.

Meanwhile we continue the preparations for our fêtes. The Opera will be brilliant, and the Comédie Française is also at work, and will put " Gaston," " Maulius," and " Catilina " on the

---

* Prince Eugène de Beauharnais, Archchancellor of State and Viceroy of Italy, married Princess Augusta Amelia, daughter of the King of Bavaria.

stage in a month's time. But, unfortunately, Mademoiselle Fleury has seized upon the best parts in each play, which will both delay and spoil them. It would be necessary that you should give orders for the distribution of parts. Mademoiselle Duchesnois was willing to act in "Gaston," but Mahérault is ill, and I have no authority. Bouilly has written a play in one act on the anecdote of the recovered colours, which has been accepted; it is said to be clever. Finally, we too are acting plays. While awaiting the return of the Court, we are rehearsing day and night, with an extraordinary mingling of sentiment and nonsense. We shed tears when we think how great will be our emotion, and we laugh at the difficulty your Chamberlains find in singing in tune. Monsieur d'Aubusson especially is excessively amusing; his voice is absolutely false, but he insists on singing, quarrels with Grasset, whom he wants to accompany him by striking all his notes *first*, and then, after a great fuss, he begins again, and is no nearer the tune than before. Happily the actors' feelings are more in harmony than their voices, and that unison will cover a multitude of sins.

I have just received a most extraordinary letter from Madame de S——. She says that she has been informed that the Emperor is coming back, but that the Empress will remain at Munich; that her husband importunes her to come to Paris, as he desires she should show special devotion to the Emperor. She adds that she has manifold reasons for wishing to remain in retirement, and begs me

to write her a letter advising her to do so, such
as she can show to him. She says M. de S——
will probably be annoyed with me for giving her
such advice, but that she is in extreme need of it.
I replied, telling her simply of the delay in the
Emperor's return, and ended my letter by expressing a great wish to see her again. I can understand why her husband wishes to put her forward.
She is his best qualification, and his surest road
to success.

I dined at Fontanes' the day before yesterday.
The Archchancellor was there and a number of
legislators. I complimented the President on a
charming article of his in the *Journal des Débats*,
praising Mathieu's book.* We had some conversation about the speech he has to make on the
opening of the Corps Législatif. He confided to
me that his subject frightened him, that it would
be impossible to pronounce a panegyric worthy of
the occasion, and that he shrank from coming to
any decision. I quite believe him, for to praise
duly is more difficult than people think, and I fear
that our writers will prove their inferiority in that
respect.

I am requested to ask you to make inquiries
at Munich about Count Rumford. I heard such
an extraordinary account of him that I am
curious to know the truth. It would seem, if I
may believe my informant, that this "man of

* M. de Fontanes, the President of the Corps Législatif, had
written an article on M. Molé, who was generally known in
society at that time by his Christian name of *Mathieu.*

science " is a mere philosophic charlatan, without fortune or position, and mixed up with several unpleasant stories. In fact, he is said to have no recommendation but that of being subject every five or six months to a certain malady that shall be nameless, but which has apparently not frightened the (pretty) widow of five and forty. My mother wants you to get full particulars, and desires me to tell you that since the wedding a recipe for economical marriages has been discovered. They are called *Rumford marriages.**

---

## LXXXVI.

### TO M. DE RÉMUSAT AT MAYENCE.†

Auteuil, September 25, 1806.

So it is my turn now to give you household news, and yours to leave home! What a melan-

---

* The allusion here is to cheap soups and Rumford stoves. The rumours then prevalent regarding that learned man may have been exaggerated. The marriage, however, ended in a separation, as may be seen in the Memoirs, and Count Rumford was obliged to leave Paris and reside in Germany, on an allowance made by his wife. He died long before she did.

† There is, as the reader will perceive, an interval of six months between this letter and the preceding one. My grandmother had passed part of the summer of 1806 at Caûterets, while her husband, children, mother and sister, and Madame de Grasse and her son, had taken up their abode in a hired house at Auteuil. The letters she wrote during her stay in the Pyrenees have not been preserved. She came to Auteuil from Caûterets at the end of August or beginning of September, and very few

choly way of spending one's time, and I could say a great deal on the subject if I had not made up my mind to dismiss it altogether. We must bow our heads in submission, and hope for better things in the future—for a time of repose that will have cost us dear, but that will console me, as I have already told you, for the loss of youth. If only your health does not suffer from this new journey! That anxiety is always before me. It seems to me that you were scarcely strong enough for all the trouble and cares that must fall upon you. Can you have undertaken a task beyond your strength? Have you a second time tried to battle against illness? You know what it cost you once before. These are the anxious thoughts that pursue me since your departure, without counting bad roads and all the rest of it, so that all my days are passed in gloom.

I went yesterday to take leave at St. Cloud. I found every one sad and silent; people were coming and going, and I looked on at their preparations and thought of you. I had breakfasted on the previous day with the Empress. In the midst of all the confusion at the palace, I contrived to catch M. de Talleyrand for a moment. He spoke of you, and thinks it *well* that you have gone; tried to prove to me that I ought to be

days afterwards, the departure of the Emperor again separated her from her husband, who left Paris for Mayence on September 21st or 22nd. The Emperor set out on the 25th to undertake the Prussian campaign, which was not concluded until July, 1807.

delighted; says you must take care of yourself, and is pleased at the thought of finding you there; in fact, he thoroughly likes you. I thanked him; but, although I was glad, tears filled my eyes. Alas! *mon ami*, of how little account are the feelings of the heart in the business of life, and yet our true happiness is derived from affection alone! As I pen these words I feel I must think of my children in order to be able to endure the burden that oppresses me. After parting from M. de Talley-rand, I saw Fouché, who was very kind, too, according to his own fashion, and then the Grand Equerry,* who spoke of you. This sad but precious subject of conversation was the only one on which I could speak, yet it made me weep, and most of the persons who were there would have been unable to enter into my feelings. I do not understand why, under such circumstances, people fancy themselves obliged to look pleased at what distresses them. Of course, we must do our duty, but who could require us to rejoice at being separated?

The Emperor began his journey last night; the Empress seeming happy at the prospect of seeing her daughter. She told me she was glad to think you would be there. I must confess I was two or three times greatly tempted to ask leave to join her, but my discretion held me back. . . .

Mademoiselle de Luçay was married this morning; after the ceremony, they left Paris for St.

* M. de Caulaincourt.

Gratien. M. de Luçay said that he hoped it was of good augury for his daughter, since it was a place that had witnessed many happy marriages.* The name of St. Gratien and all the memories it includes impressed me in the midst of that splendid salon. We passed many happy days in that little place, and I never thought it so ugly. M. de Luçay calls it a *kennel*, but I think we were very comfortable there—what say you?

The impression at Court yesterday was that the Emperor's return would be speedy, and that of Paris is that we shall have no war. We can all rely on the activity and skill of the Emperor, but I do wish they were not so often called upon. If my new-born religious feeling did not forbid me to curse my neighbour, I think I should devote much imprecation to the King of Prussia. . . .

## LXXXVII.

### TO M. DE RÉMUSAT AT MAYENCE.

Auteuil, Sunday, September 28, 1806.

I am still without a word from you, and, although I am well aware that it is almost impossible I

---

* M. de Luçay was Chamberlain to the Emperor. His daughter married Philippe de Ségur, son of M. de Ségur, member of the French Academy, and himself married to Mademoiselle Daguesseau. General Philippe de Ségur, member of the French Academy, died in 1873.

could have received a letter as yet, still I am full of sadness and anxiety. . . .

My thoughts are of you in this quiet little Auteuil, which I should like better if we could live in greater solitude; but I must admit that my mother is right, and that it is unfair of Paris idlers to come and disturb us at every hour of the day. We are overwhelmed with visitors, and we must escape to Paris in order to live more to ourselves and with greater economy. However strange it may seem, it is nevertheless true that I shall not be able to carry out my intended reforms until my return home. However, as Charles is benefiting by the fine weather and country air, we purpose remaining here until October 15th. Then I shall disclose my new regulations, on which I am now hard at work. I am full of admiration, I assure you, for those who undertake to lessen abuses in the financial department of a nation; for, though I began only three days ago to wage war on those that have crept into my little kingdom, I already feel sick of the complaints, quarrelling, and grumblings that come before me, and I am often tempted to wish that I were rich enough to let myself be robbed without noticing it. But as this is far from being the case, I make up my mind to severity, and am becoming a regular Barbé Marbois.*

I saw Louis de Vergennes this morning. He

---

\* Barbé Marbois was Minister of the Treasury. He fell into disgrace with the Emperor in this same year (1806). Under the Restoration he was First President of the Cour des Comptes.

begged me to ask you to find out whether it is. true that the Emperor intends to increase the number of his orderlies; and if so, whether it would be possible for you to present an urgent application on behalf of his son, who is longing to serve in the army, and you can imagine how gladly he would serve under the very eyes of his Majesty. If you could obtain this favour for him, he would be deeply grateful.

Yesterday morning, at nine o'clock, who should walk into our little salon, booted, curled, and brushed up, but the Minister of Finance.* He had been riding a fine Arab, the gift of the Emperor, in the Bois de Boulogne. I wanted him to make me a present of his horse, but he could not agree to that. He was very pleasant, and promised to find a place for M. de Pradine. Alix was rather comforted by his visit; for he still hopes that the King of Prussia may act with common sense, and the Queen with prudence. Many wagers are laid among our acquaintances on this subject, but there is only one opinion as to our success.

If you hear anything of M. de Nansouty, pray let us know. His poor wife is very unhappy. Really we are *too good* as wives, and it is very foolish to be so attached to the absent. But why are both of you such kind and good husbands? I

---

* M. Gaudin, the Minister of Finance, retained the costume of the *ancien régime*. He wore his hair powdered à *l'oiseau royal*, and always rode with high boots, a three-cornered hat, and an equerry by his side. He was an old friend of Madame de Vergennes. There were, at that period, two Financial Ministers, one of whom was called Minister of the Treasury.

met one yesterday who takes no such pride in conjugal fidelity. It was the young Maître des Requêtes. He paid us a long visit, and made himself very agreeable; but, between ourselves, I was rather shocked at the double meaning of the conversation that took place on the subject that is now engrossing him. People make things easier for him by pretending only to see the ridiculous side; but is not this excusing the wrong-doing? This world is a strange place, and even the best-conducted women—— But I will not conclude my remark, and I leave it to be finished by your upright and conjugal mind.

Your boys are in good health. Charles was in the salon this morning, and his grandmother is enchanted with his clever remarks. I am trying to get him to work harder, and although he does not like it, I must give him due praise for his docility and obedience. There is a sweetness in his disposition which he inherits from *I know whom,* and which I hope he will not lose in the world. Adieu; I hear more visitors, and must lay aside my letter. My friends come to congratulate me on my return from Caûterets, but I cannot receive them as gaily as at first; they should have come then, for my joy has not endured, my sorrow has quickly returned. Such is life.

## LXXXVIII.

### TO M. DE RÉMUSAT AT MAYENCE.

Auteuil, October 4, 1806.

. . . I imagine, as I am writing this, that you are
enjoying perfect tranquillity, and that the Emperor
has already left Mayence. We find it absolutely
impossible to believe in war; new bets are made
every day, and couriers constantly arrive, whom
nobody sees, but of whom every one is talking.
What I like about Auteuil is that we only get the
truth here, and are not told of false reports until
they have been contradicted. Alix has heard from
her husband; he has not yet marched, and seems
to know nothing, or perhaps chooses to say
nothing; she goes back to Paris on Saturday.
Our friends are teasing us to return, but we
shall remain here until the 15th, and the fine
weather and Charles's good pleasure shall decide
the day of departure. The season is still quite
beautiful—may it be the same at Mayence! Take
advantage of it to walk about; see a good deal of
M. de Talleyrand, who is such a capital talker, and
who promised me to take care of you. Enjoy
yourself, in fact, as much as you can, and in the
midst of it all write as often as possible to your
poor Claire.

Friday.

Everything I have heard since yesterday tends
to prove you must never again jump out of a

carriage when it is going fast. M. de Kerkado was killed by so doing; M. de Léon,* severely hurt; in·fact, I shudder at all the accidents I have heard of. Take pity on me and care of yourself, I implore you. I saw Madame de Vannoise and M. Lemercier yesterday evening. The latter is greatly occupied with his "Faux Bonhomme," and is made anxious by Fleury's illness, which continues. Out of regard for him, he will not take his part from him, and he does well, for this sustains Fleury's hopefulness, which is especially desirable. Constance de Vannoise seems reconciled to her lot. The bridegroom is absent; she is busy with dresses and finery, and thinks marriage all that is pleasant. Madame de Vannoise, on the contrary, trembles and grieves, and finds the thought of separation insupportable.† . . .

I dined yesterday at the Archchancellor's. Several persons asked after you in a fashion that Madame de Sévigné describes and says she used not to take the trouble to reply to, but left the inquirers to their *ignorance* and *indifference*. When you and I are separated, I am so depressed, the least trifle hurts me so much, that I carefully avoid speaking of you to persons who I know feel no real interest in us. Their coldness would hurt and vex me. But I feel a true happiness in meet-

---

* M. de Léon became afterwards Duc de Rohan. He was Chamberlain to the Emperor, and died in 1816. He was father of that duke who was Cardinal-Archbishop of Besançon, and who died in 1833.

† This marriage did not take place.

ing friendly people who question me kindly about you. I got on capitally yesterday with M. de Lavalette, who seems to like you; we had a good deal of conversation during the long dinner at the Archchancellor's. I begged him to come and see me, and I hope he will; I think him most agreeable. . . .

How bright my mother is! how delightful I find her companionship in daily life! The more I know of the world, the more do I admire her character, her evenness of temper, her sweet reasonableness, and unquenchable gaiety. Latterly she has been, as well as I, anxious about your health; but, when she sees me in tears, she forgets herself in order to cheer me, and makes me laugh. I revealed a great truth to her yesterday, viz. that I love her more and more every day. Marriage is a critical moment for mothers and daughters. All the new blessings that then become ours, the disappointment which comes from maternal jealousy, the readiness of husbands to spoil us at first— all contributes to disturbance, to separation, to draw us apart, and at such a moment it is almost impossible that the mother should not be a little unjust, and the best of daughters a little ungrateful. But if both are really kind-hearted and loving, time effaces the little grievances caused or excused by excessive affection. The young wife advances on her life-journey, she looks around her, she encounters disappointment, she needs a true friend, and in whom can she find one if not in her mother? Thus the difficulty ought to end, oftener than it does, with a little indulgence on the one side and some gratitude on the other. . . . But I am interrupted! Crescentini * wants to see me.

Monday.

I was not able to resume my letter all yesterday. After receiving Crescentini, whom I thought changed in appearance, we went to Paris to see "Les Horaces." I was much pleased, first with Corneille, who is an old love of mine, and then with Leclerc,† the new actor. He played the father with spirit and dignity, copying Saint-Prix a little too much perhaps, but he uttered the famous "*qu'il mourût*" in such a way as to produce a great sensation, and was immensely applauded. Your nephew tells me that he is rejected by the Comédie; this is a pity, I think. M. Saint-Eugène seemed to me very second-rate. Mademoiselle Georges has improved, I think, and Mademoiselle Duchesnois acted well as Camille, with the exception of a little drawling occasionally. On the whole, it was a fine performance; I even think that the study of comedy that Lafond has been

---

* Girolamo Crescentini was the Italian singer whom the Emperor detained in Paris, by force, from 1806 to 1812. He was a *soprano* after the fashion of the day. He was born in 1769, and died at Naples in 1846.

† Leclerc was, at the beginning of the present century, a somewhat successful actor at the Théâtre Français, though his style was rather monotonous. He succeeded especially in the *rôle* of the elder Horace, and in that of Mithridates. Saint-Eugène, who played Curiace, has left no great reputation. Lafond played the younger Horace.

obliged to make, has diminished the heaviness of his style. I should not have ventured to rely on my own judgment in this, because " *au sortir des montagnes on n'est pas difficile;* " but this is *your son's* opinion, so there is nothing more to be said.

After the performance, we returned to our little hermitage, and this morning Charles and I have taken a long walk. We began by going through the Bois de Boulogne as far as Boulogne itself, and thence we took the St. Cloud road and the Point du Jour, and returned to Auteuil by the Avenue de Paris. We had great conversation all the time. Your boy asked me questions about the Revolution, and especially about the Emperor. I told him the story of the Italian campaign, of the campaign in Egypt, of the Emperor's return to France, of his wars and victories. He was deeply interested, and when I had ended, he said, " Mamma, that is like one of Plutarch's Lives." I advised him to work hard, so as to be able to write it when grown up, and he was delighted at the idea.

Adieu. I will end my letter with your son's words; I could not improve upon them.

## XC.

### TO M. DE RÉMUSAT AT MAYENCE.

Paris, October 16, 1806.

I left Auteuil yesterday morning, and am alone in our apartment, which recals your presence so vividly, and renews the keen pain of our too frequent separation. While establishing myself in my room and putting everything in order, I came across your letters, and set about arranging them. It pained me to read over those of last year. Alas! *mon ami*, it was the same state of things, the same distance between us, the same anxieties. All these are now renewed, and it is thus that we pass our life. Just then the courier arrived with your letter, which, like all I receive from you, is kind and loving; it moved me, but not so painfully as those I was reading again, and I said to myself, "It is still the same affection." Retain all those feelings which are so necessary to my happiness, and which are infinitely precious to me. The great events of which we are spectators, make time fly so swiftly, that we possess, as it were, a premature experience that ages us beyond our years. We have therefore lost taste for all the frivolous amusements of the world, which turn us aside, without any real solace, from the cares by which we are harassed, and it is, in truth, in the affections of the heart only that we can find consolation and happiness.

These are my sentiments, *mon ami*. The new
sorrows of the present year, your absence, and
Alix's discouragement grieve and absorb me, so
that I feel little inclination for society, and, unless
winter brings some change in things, I foresee
that my life will be one of seclusion. Charles
will be the gainer, and I promise you he shall
work hard; it shall not be my fault if his progress
in Latin and Greek does not surpass yours in
German. I am bestirring myself for fear that
when you return, quite proud of your new accom-
plishment, you may want to impart it to your son.
But I warn you that I will have nothing to do
with German; it is quite enough for me to be-
wilder my brains over crabbed Greek characters,
without toiling over an inharmonious wretched
Teutonic language that I do not care about in
the least.

Meanwhile, before seriously resuming our lessons,
I am going this morning with Charles to Sannois,
and intend remaining there until Sunday. Madame
d'Houdetôt insisted upon this, and mamma thought
I had better take Charles with me. Gustave
is going on as well as possible.* Dubois says
that his leg was properly set; he is not feverish,
will not be lame, it is as favourable a fracture as
can be, but he must remain lying on his back,
without stirring, for a month, and this enforced
inaction, for him especially, is a real illness. It
will be a great privation for Charles to be separated
from his friend, and, in order to make up for it, I

* Gustave de Grasse had broken his leg at Autcuil.

am going to make him acquainted with the Princess de Carignan's son. He is educated at his mother's house, passes the day in the house, and I should rather like him as a companion for my boy, more especially as his tutor is said to be an estimable man.

On arriving here, I heard that Madame de Souza is so seriously ill as to cause some anxiety to her friends. Her husband is at the Hague, but is coming here. He has given up Portugal, and intends settling in Paris. All the old bachelors in the neighbourhood are delighted, and Bertrand will be quite at home. He begs me to give you his kindest remembrances. The stir and animation abroad only increase his love of quiet, and he sticks to his armchair more than ever. He is the only person I have seen as yet, and I expect he will be our most constant guest. All the others have taken flight. Cousin Pasquier is engrossed by his Jews and his commissions, and now that he can only give us a divided attention, we will have nothing more to say to him. Poor Norvins has gone, as you know. You will see him probably, and hear his adventures ; he enters the army at thirty-nine, gives up his family, his friends, and all his habits, and is not sure, after all, that he is doing a wise thing. I told him he would come back to us a *curé!* Notwithstanding my little jest, our parting was pathetic ; he was greatly moved on taking leave of us. His future plans are as heretofore ; he wanted to manifest his zeal, but does not intend to remain always in the army.

He begged that you would name him to the Empress, and hopes to have the honour of being presented to her at Mayence.

---

## XCI.

### TO M. DE RÉMUSAT AT MAYENCE.

Paris, Friday, October 26, 1806.

I wrote to you twice in the course of yesterday, *mon ami;* both my letters will, no doubt, give you pain, but I could not measure my words at first.* I feel quite as much hurt to-day, perhaps even more so, but I am less excited, and will curtail my reproaches. Besides, it is impossible that you should not be conscious of the pain you have inflicted, and if absence has not changed him I love, I am sure that regret will soon follow on the injury he has done me. Oh, my beloved, remember that in such a union as ours, which time only serves to draw closer, the slightest appearance of doubt must wound the sensitiveness inseparable from such an affection as mine for you. After passing ten years and more with no other thought

---

* Letters were constantly lost on the way, and this caused confusion, annoyance, complaints, and suspicions. I have omitted most of those in which these feelings are expressed on mistaken grounds and are disclaimed in the next. I also suppress or shorten those that are only a repetition of letters that are thought to be lost. The reproaches contained in this one are in reply to complaints that would certainly have been very unjust had nothing been lost or delayed.

than you, with your image present in all my life's memories, and in all its future hopes, how can I endure the suspicions revealed by your cruel words? Were I in your place, I should, no doubt, be anxious too, but in a different way, and I should express my anxiety differently. Whatever my sufferings, I could never insult those I love and esteem, and it is thus that you should love me ; nay, I will even say it is thus that I deserve to be loved. Forgive me for returning to the subject, but I suffered so terribly yesterday! To-day I have a grief which is entirely my own ; for I have to complain of you, whom I love exclusively, and whom I fondly thought superior to all the weakness of ordinary men? But I see that you are occasionally all alike, and I am daily more and more convinced that your absence is my greatest misfortune, and your presence, cruel one, the greatest joy of my life.

I am sending this to-day through M. de Talleyrand ; to-morrow I shall write by Deschamps. I shall try every possible means, and then, if my letters are lost, I shall leave house and children and come to you, for I cannot endure the idea of your uneasiness. I suppose that like last year my letters are sent to head-quarters, and yet M. de Lavalette assures me that orders have been given at Mayence for opening the bags there and carefully sorting the letters. And yet you receive none, and you are alarmed and you accuse me, and I sympathize with your grief, which I feel keenly, and suffer from your injustice ! What a life it is !

So full of troubles and difficulties, when it might be passed so peacefully! I feel weary and worn out with mine! And then to the secret sorrow which you inflict are added a thousand alarms about the military engagements that have taken place since the 14th,* of which we know nothing. I am surrounded by weeping mothers, sisters, kinswomen. Alix has not had one moment's peace, and one dares not give way to joy, and admiration of all these miraculous victories, without knowing at what price they have been bought. I was told yesterday that Aimery de Fezensac is wounded. But as this report has not been as yet corroborated, it has been kept from the two mothers. Philippe de Ségur was wounded, but he writes the news himself, and this shows that his wounds must be slight. We hear nothing of my brother-in-law, and we ought to look upon silence as good news, if one were guided by reason on subjects so near and dear. But reason, *mon ami*, is seldom made use of by anxious hearts, and you who used to pride yourself on it, even you—— But I have finished with that subject and will say no more.

---

\* The battle of Jena had been won on October 14, but no particulars had as yet reached Paris.

## XCII.

TO M. DE RÉMUSAT AT MAYENCE.

Paris, October 27, 1806.

I must still be sad and anxious until I know you have received my letters and are at ease about me and Charles. It will not be my fault if none reach Mayence. I send them in every possible way. From what M. de Lavalette tells me, it is at Mayence itself that the mischief lies; you might therefore prevent it, probably, and spare yourself anxiety and me real misery. But let us drop the subject ; by the time you receive this, all misunderstanding will be over.

The arrival of the bulletins quite made up for the long silence that had given rise to many gloomy conjectures. They are as fine pages of history, as have ever been written in any, and that will efface all former achievements. I have also seen several private letters giving miraculous accounts of personal deeds. Such daring, although sometimes rash, is always fortunate, and such coolness in the midst of danger, such wise forethought, such prompt determination evoke feelings of admiration which seem as though they could never be surpassed, and yet are continually renewed. The bulletins were read out at the theatres and produced a great sensation. Talma read them at the Français. He read very well, simply and quickly; for, the principal events once known, the public does not care for military details, or positions in a country they scarcely know. The effect was not so good at Feydeau. Chesnard* read pompously; he put on an affected voice, and made more affected when he came to the list of the killed. As he was naming the colonels, some lady, either a relation or a friend of one of them, uttered a loud shriek and swooned away. This caused a kind of consternation in the house and spoilt the effect. It has been decided, therefore, that in future only extracts from the bulletins shall be read at the theatres, and never the list of the killed.

More wagers are being laid as to peace or war. People must always, as you know, be betting about something. The Emperor's return is spoken of with hope and desire, but I, *mon ami*, can only be silent when I hear of rumours which, if confirmed, would make me happy in so many different ways.

I do not know whether the letters in which I told you of my visit to Sannois have reached you. I stayed there three days. Madame d'Houdetôt was unwell, and she is now suffering from tertian ague, which, together with depression natural at her great age, has much reduced her. She is still young in mind and heart, and, notwithstanding all she has lost, clings fondly to life. "My

* An actor of the Opéra Comique, who came out in 1782, in the part of Julien in "Colinette à la Cour." He was a fine musician, with a good bass voice.

regrets," she said to me, "are memories which embellish my life even now." This is certainly looking on the bright side of things.

If you care to hear about your theatre, I may tell you that it seems well attended, in spite of the war and of the emptiness of Paris. Lafond is an attraction ; he has just been acting the "Misanthrope," rather badly in my opinion. There was something of spitefulness in his anger against mankind that does not belong to the part, and a flavour of melodrama in his passion which, although always acceptable to the public, is unworthy of Molière. I thought him very superior in the "Femmes Savantes;" his natural talents require to be wisely directed. It has been said that Mademoiselle Georges intends to leave the theatre, I do not know why.

---

## XCIII.

### TO M. DE RÉMUSAT AT MAYENCE.

Paris, Tuesday, October 28, 1806.

Frederick * will hand you this letter on his way through Mayence. He is starting for Prussia—

---

* M. Frederick d'Houdetôt was the son of General d'Houdetôt by his first marriage, and grandson of the lady so frequently mentioned in the Letters. He was successively Prefect of Ghent and of Brussels, and peer of France, and was a deputy under the Second Empire. He died without children.

got his orders and had to be ready in twenty-four hours. Is there not something amusing in this spirit of rushing about that has seized upon every-body? _Amusing_, however, is not the right word, for it will be sad enough for the many who are left behind. You will also, perhaps, see M. de Tournon. He came to ask me if I had anything to send by him; but I preferred M. d'Houdetôt. This certainty I do not like to miss. . . .

So you have given up your Electoral College? We cannot understand here how you could do so without permission. My mother feels sure that you have made a mistake, and that probably you omitted writing to Franche Comté to keep your claims in remembrance there. Who takes your place? M. Clément de Ris * asked me this question one day. So you have seen Norvins? What do you think of his wild proceeding? Is it not absurd to enter the army at close upon forty, in order to obtain a place in the Government or the magistracy, for which he pressed with unshrinking urgency? . . .

You see how our circle is gradually thinning. We shall scarcely have any one left but M. de Nouy, who was here this evening, and who is pleasant enough, only that he is so deaf that he hears nothing, and cannot talk, on account of his asthma. Bertrand will not "join," I fancy, but Madame de Souza and the _economical household_ absorb him entirely. Gallois is lost to us, and never stirs

* M. Clément de Ris was a senator. He was subsequently peer of France, and died in 1827.

from a certain fireside that you know. Abbé Morellet is growing old. M. Pasquier can seldom escape from the cares of State, which require his attention, and from his surroundings ; and our salon is deserted, which does not grieve me much. But even were I more dull than I am, I should think it natural to look for happiness first, and then for pleasure, from your ever-longed-for return. We are told to hope for it soon. I cannot believe it, and am much more disposed to fear that you too will be summoned to Prussia. This would be additional sorrow for me, and I dare not dwell on it. . . .

## XCIV.

### TO M. DE RÉMUSAT AT MAYENCE.

Paris, November 1, 1806.

*Mon ami*, I have seen your tailor, who says it will take a week to embroider the coat, and, however I may hurry him, I do not think we can get it sooner; but I will do my very best. It will be too bad if you have to set out for Prussia ; however, I should apply to M. de Lavalette, who would know where to send it to you. But can you not see my face as I write the words, "*If you have to set out for Prussia!*" I confess that I am upset at the idea. Distance ought to be indifferent when once we are parted. But, in truth, it is an aggravation of absence, and the difficulties of correspondence alone are enough to make me apprehensive of the moment that removes you still farther from me. Heaven grant the speedy return of the Emperor, and that my own private happiness may unite with the general rejoicings! I have heard of you in a letter I received from Norvins. He gives an amusing account of the confusion produced by the clashing of divers opinions in his corps, and of his regret at this loss of time while the Emperor is swiftly marching from victory to victory. If he is still at Mayence, pray remember me to him. I do not know whether I ought to write to him, for I cannot tell where to address my letter. I have just read a clever and interesting one from Eugène de Montesquiou.* He relates his journey to Jena the day before the battle. Having been sent to Prince Hohenlohe, he was detained on various pretexts, and could not succeed in reaching the King. On the morning of the great battle the King sent to say he could not receive him until it was over. Thus he remained an inactive but agitated spectator of the engagement. General Blucher ostentatiously gave orders in his hearing that no Frenchman was to be suffered to escape in the rout that was thought to be inevitable. Towards evening the Prince of Würtemberg arrived at head-quarters with the fugitives from the field of battle. He was so ignorant of the disastrous state of affairs, that

* M. Eugène de Montesquiou was a cousin of Aimery de Montesquiou-Fezensac.

he was intending to take medicine that night. Eugène was just in time to tell him that the effect of the dose would probably be greatly interfered with. His life was afterwards in great danger. Some Prussian soldiers, angered at their defeat, wanted to kill him, and an officer with great difficulty saved his life. Finally, he was allowed to return to our head-quarters, having lost his suite and his horses. On his way he came up with two Frenchmen, and shortly afterwards with eighteen Prussian stragglers, whom the three took prisoners, and marched to the camp in triumph. He says the Emperor was amused at his adventures, and laughed very much at his capture of prisoners. If you already know the story I have told it unnecessarily, but I thought it too good to lose.

We have no direct news from my brother-in-law, but the silence of the *Moniteur* is comforting. Aimery, too, does not write ; however, he is known to be in good health and about to get his lieutenancy. Charles de Flahault wrote to this effect. Thus, all the mothers and wives of my acquaintance are tolerably tranquil at present. I saw M. de Tascher, the senator, yesterday; * he seemed very anxious about his son, of whom he has heard nothing. He is sub-lieutenant in General Soult's division. Perhaps if Deschamps were to write a line as if from the Empress, he might get an answer. I was touched by the poor father's affection and solicitude for his son. . . .

* A kinsman of the Empress. His son was a peer of France.

Madame Simons * is waiting for your permission for the Français to join the other theatres in a performance for the benefit of her father. She has already M. de Luçay's permission for the Salle Favart and Duport. " Manlius " is to be the play, but Talma is waiting for orders from you. Do not delay.

## XCV.

### TO M. DE RÉMUSAT AT MAYENCE.

Paris, November 2, 1806.

We have just received the news of the Emperor's arrival at Berlin,† and Alix has at last got a letter from her husband, written from Potsdam. There is something very remarkable in the marvellous good fortune of the Emperor, which is so constant to him both in great and little things. It is said he arrived at Potsdam on the same day as that on which, a year before, the Emperor

---

* Madame Simons-Candeille, a daughter of Candeille, a former singer and composer of operas, was born in 1767. After coming out at the Opera, she became *sociétaire* of the Comédie Française, which she soon quitted in order to act in plays written by herself—" La Belle Fermière " among others, which had a great success. She was divorced from her first husband, and subsequently married M. Simons, a Belgian merchant, who had come to Paris expressly to prevent his son from marrying an actress, a Mademoiselle Lange. She died in 1834.

† On October 27, 1806.

of Russia had arrived there, and it is no small thing, nor unworthy of record, that both should have slept with the same year in Frederick's palace. We hear that there are rumours of peace in the army. It is also reported here. What is thought at Mayence? . . .

---

## XCVI.

### TO M. DE RÉMUSAT AT MAYENCE.

Paris, November 5, 1806.

I am very sorry to hear what you say about the war. We simple folks had imagined that one lesson would have been enough for the King of Prussia, and that he would have wanted to make peace. Now we must *resolve upon* fresh victories; but my heart is heavy when I think of the Emperor penetrating further into distant countries, and bearing with him the fate of us all. Besides this, what sad separations must be entailed by the continuance of war, and how slowly time will drag along away from you, although life will be passing none the less swiftly! You are not a soldier; your desires are moderate; your tastes are for civil and family life; and yet for five months of this year, and for seven of last year, we have been parted, and I have never been able to accustom myself to the solitude of heart in which your absence leaves me. I think I could feel more resigned if I were the wife of a general. At any rate, I could not reasonably object to the kind of life I lead. Yesterday was Charles' fête day. I shed tears when I gave him my blessing ; it seemed incomplete without yours, which has twice been wanting on this anniversary.

*Mon ami*, my sorrow is renewed every moment. Alone or in society, at home or abroad, you are always present to my mind, and, alas ! I find you nowhere. Whether I am grieving or enjoying myself, I feel that I want to share every thought with you. To-day, for instance, I have longed for you all day. My mother and I have decided on giving no dinners during the month, but every fortnight we shall invite about a dozen persons to spend the evening. On this occasion we have had Madame de Vintimille, MM. Lavalette, Pasquier, Dorion,* Molé, Morellet, Bertrand, and Desfaucherets. There was some good talk ; my mother was in unusually good spirits, quite animated and brilliant ; conversation did not flag for a moment. I must tell you that M. de Lavalette made himself most agreeable, and that he is quite an acquisition. There is delicacy in his wit, modesty in his speech, and straightforwardness in his manner that make him very prepossessing. I was wishing for you among all these pleasant people, and you would have enjoyed the conversation. I could not help thinking, when it was most animated, of a curious feature of our social life. At this moment a number of our fellow-creatures

* M. Dorion wrote two poems, " La Bataille d'Hastings " and " La Chute de Palmyre."

are wearing themselves out in marching and watching, or are fighting unto death, to procure for *us* an opportunity of talking idly at our firesides about all the trifles to which we choose to attach importance. I was struck by the mobility of our impressions and the strange incoherence of our ideas. At first we were all depressed by the news of the prolongation of the war ; its possible chances filled us with alarm ; but by degrees these feelings wore off, and presently, in pursuit of I know not what ideas, we were far away from war and politics, and entirely engrossed in fine-spun dissertations on sentiments and thoughts that one would have imagined could only have been interesting in times of profound peace and entire exemption from real trouble.

We have heard from Aimery; he is well. M. de Nansouty has written also ; he says he is in a state of stupefaction at the total disappearance of an army so fair to the eye, and that he thought so excellent. You remember his old admiration for Prussian cavalry, and you can imagine his satisfaction at having defeated it. His wife is now going to be miserable again, after having been tolerably at ease. Glory is a poor solace for heartache, and the tears of women record the triumphs of masculine pride.

If you have nothing to do, tell us which suffers most from *ennui*, a clever man, a fool, or a brute ? We could arrive at no conclusion this evening on the subject.

## XCVII.

### TO M. DE RÉMUSAT AT MAYENCE.

Paris, November 9, 1806.

I am at my sister's, *mon ami*, and sitting by a good fire, with my desk on my knees, near a little table in a little green room that you know. While I write, Alix is singing, and her sweet voice blends with the emotion that always fill my soul when I am thus communing with you. . . .

Paris is illuminated. The *Te Deum* was sung this morning. Alix was warmly congratulated yesterday at the Archchancellor's, and Princess Caroline was good enough to send her word that the Grand-Duke of Berg speaks highly of her husband. This is the reward of some of her tears, if indeed there can be any compensation for the absence of one we love, except his return. Is it true the Empress is coming back, and, if true, what does it mean? This is the question, and people draw from it either good or evil auguries, according as they are most inclined to fear or hope. In any case, it seems to me she would do well not to desert Paris. Her presence would restore a little life, and do away with the prevalent discontent.

Your reflections on the wonders of this last campaign seem very just. There is something in the Emperor's fortune that confounds ordinary ideas, and is, so to speak, above them. One feels carried away and almost stunned; and yet he seems to be raised so far above circumstances that one has no right to be terrified at the dangers to which he exposes himself, and still less to fix the limit at which he should stop. Yet it makes one's heart heavy to think of the terrible distance which now separates him from us. May God be with him, and preserve him to us ! This is my constant prayer.

While he, with the finest part of the French nation, is marching onwards to glory, we are vegetating here in great monotony. There is very little going on; people are living to themselves and giving no invitations. My mother and I go out very little, but are always "at home" on Mondays and Fridays. Our friends, knowing this, come to us on those days, and we have pleasant talks until ten o'clock, or eleven at latest, when every one retires to rest. Madame de Vintimille, who is very attentive to us this year, seldom fails to come, and makes herself very agreeable. M. Pasquier is her faithful attendant, and ours too. He starts our subjects, discusses, and decides them. Lemercier refines and sometimes obscures; my mother contributes her charming humour; Bertrand and the abbé condemn them for the most part as twaddle, all the more so as this year, I don't know why, we seem to turn naturally to sentimental questions. For instance, we were discussing the day before yesterday which should have the pre-eminence in love—the man or woman who sees faults in the beloved but loves on, or he who is so blind as to take faults for qualities? If you have nothing to do, send us your opinion, and also some *bouts rimés*. By-the-by, what are you doing with your own talents? How is your German getting on? . . .

---

## XCVIII.

### TO M. DE RÉMUSAT AT MAYENCE.

Paris, November 10, 1806.

We have heard a report that Magdeburg* has been taken, and we are expecting official news. We know nothing about the armies, and imagine nothing for ourselves; the general inertia seems to extend even to our thoughts. I think that the German campaign of last year was more stirring, though less miraculous, than this one. It is true that the Emperor has accustomed us to wonders. On speaking of this to Fontanes a few days ago, I asked him what he would contrive to say this time on the Emperor's return, and he owned that he did not think he should be able to find words worthy of such great deeds. "History," he said, "can show us nothing like them; it is no longer possible to read it." I

---

* Magdeburg was taken on November 8. The Emperor had been at Berlin from October 27.

do not agree with him on the latter point, and I confess that I consider it, on the contrary, the most useful reading of the day. Thanks to your son, I am going through a course of ancient history again, and I make numberless comparisons, which are interesting and at the same time instructive. Only it seems to me that we of the present century are, as it were, in the secret of things, and that in searching into past times we are like those persons who, instead of remaining in the pit, look at the play from behind the scenes. We are nearer; we see the machinery, and we do but admire the more, because we must needs, in a nation like ours, make use of some that is considerably rusty. But I must pause, for my subject would lead me far, and I should probably lose my way.

To return to our own circle. I don't know whether the story of Hochet's duel has reached you. He took it into his head to say * in a *feuilleton* that Chazet made a trade of his talents, and, in fact, it is asserted that he lends his name to young writers for a consideration. Chazet asked Hochet for an explanation; they fought, and Chazet received a wound in the chest. He has been spitting blood since. This affair has greatly raised Hochet in the estimation of society;

* M. Hochet, a very agreeable man of letters, was a friend of Madame de Stael's. He died at eighty-six or eighty-seven years of age, in 1857. His adversary in the duel was Alissan de Chazet, a well-known writer, then and subsequently, of vaudevilles, and a *collaborateur* with Désangiers.

but I, who am at times, as you know, a reasonable and reasoning being—I can only regard Hochet as a writer who did not confine himself to purely literary subjects in his *feuilletons,* as he should have done. Some of the Abbé Morellet's friends want him to follow Hochet's example, and to send a challenge to Geoffroy ; but our abbé's eighty winters dispense him from this new style of literary discussion. By the way, he is much changed this winter. Old age has come upon him at last. He is dull and drowsy ; sometimes of an evening Cousin Pasquier's voice rouses him for a moment, but he is not strong enough for argument, and sinks back grumbling into his armchair. . . .

## XCIX.

### TO M. DE RÉMUSAT AT MAYENCE.

Paris, Saturday, November 15, 1806.

There is a great discussion going on at the Academy just now. Maury, who, as you know, is to pronounce the panegyric on Target, insists on being addressed as *Monseigneur* in the reply. The matter makes a great stir. Some say it is against the custom, and that the republic of letters must be maintained. The cardinal declares he will not put his foot in the academic temple unless he is addressed by his title. The amusing part is that D'Alembert formerly wrote a grand letter in support of that very equality, and that it is the philosophers who contend for the *Monseigneur* against the Chéniers, Regnaults, etc. The question is to be referred to the Emperor, and in the midst of all his war triumphs he will be appealed to on this important point. *Vanitas!* But, as you know, vanity is to be found everywhere, even in Christian humility, from which, however, our modern prelates hold themselves discreetly aloof.*

How good it is of you to speak as you do of our boy, and of my care of him! I replace you as well as I can, but he is advancing, and I am no longer sufficient; he requires a masculine hand over him. He is making some progress, and I am taking pains with him, but do not think that I help him so much as I did a year ago. I am quite convinced it is necessary that he should learn to depend on himself, and he now studies alone much more. Only I watch him to see that he works, and keep him in my room, where I know that he wastes no time. As for the taking up of my own, how could it be better employed? What other object should I have in life? Rousseau says somewhere that when women have become mothers, they should forbid themselves the taste for study, and, laying all theories aside, regulate the employment of the day solely with relation to the education of their ·children. I am very far indeed from such perfection, for I have many hours to myself, and waste them on the frivolous

* This discussion is related with fuller details in the Memoirs.

occupations habitual to us women. Albert is growing strong; he talks away, in a language which he has invented for himself, and which is only understood by a select few. His deafness is against him; but I feel sure it will disappear when he gets rid of the eruption, which is so trying to him, and I wait patiently for this. He has a sweet disposition, so affectionate and gentle. Both little fellows are made of right good stuff.

To prove to you, however, that I still find time for serious reading, I must tell you that hearing Montesquieu constantly quoted in our circle, I looked for his works, and the first time I opened them I came upon the following phrase, which seems to me of good omen:—"A conquest may destroy injurious prejudices, and place, if I may venture to say so, a nation under a better genius." I can say nothing better than this. When you are at home, if you have time, I will read Montesquieu again with you. You can explain many things to me, and that will please me much.

---

## C.

### TO M. DE RÉMUSAT AT MAYENCE.

Paris, November 18, 1806.

The quarrel at the Academy is still going on. Cardinal Maury sticks to his *Monseigneur* out of respect to his office, and there is hot discussion.

Would you believe that some persons are so un-reasonable as to want to compel him to wear the green coat instead of his cardinal's robes? This absurdity has made a sensation which will scarcely surprise you, knowing as you do our French ardour about trifles. It is really surprising how we let great and important things slide, and excite ourselves about nothing at all. I am often re-minded of Alcibiades' dog's tail, only just now it would serve not to amuse, but to wake us up. For want of something better to say I may tell you that Lemercier read his comedy " Le Faux Bonhomme " to us two days ago. Fleury's illness delays its performance. Madame de Vintimille, who was eager to hear it, had begged that favour of the author, and he read before a select circle, who pretended to be pleased, but were, as usual, very dissatisfied. There are none of his favourite eccentricities in this last production, but there is a decided want of strength and action, half-drawn characters, tasteless lines; and yet, with all these defects, there are a few pretty portraits, some clever observations on society, and some well-arranged scenes. This is my opinion, but keep it to yourself. He read it admirably. You know how he reads; it is a pleasure to hear him. Mean-while Lafond has taken possession of the stage and draws good houses. He succeeded admirably in " La Métromanie." I was quite delighted with it, and remembered that you had predicted a success in that *rôle* for him. This recollection was with me all the evening. I welcome all such;

they brighten and comfort my loneliness. I cannot say that they make it *gay*, for I always end by weeping in secret. Your *tripot* is not doing badly; it is not deserted, and, notwithstanding the emptiness of Paris and the war, it is better attended than last year. The princesses are said to be reconciled. Things were rather serious for a moment; Mademoiselle Contat seems to have made up her mind to remain.

I much wish to know whether you have heard from M. de Talleyrand, and what is to become of you. We hear all sorts of contradictory reports. The Emperor, it is said, after settling the army in winter quarters, will return to Paris, to ascertain for himself how all is going on, and after a short stay will again leave us. A King of Poland is also mentioned. Now he is Prince Jérôme; again, the Elector of Saxony or Prince Charles. Yesterday it was reported that the Queen of Prussia had poisoned herself in despair, etc. Such are the rumours in Paris. The details given in to-day's bulletins are very remarkable. It looks to me as if there were no more Prussians to fear, and that they have paid dearly for their imprudence. M. Molé has received a most comical letter from Frederick Houdetôt. He writes from Berlin, where he had been for five days at the date of his letter, and had not been able to see anybody. The ministers have not yet received him. He is staying at an inn, not knowing what he is to do, frozen, solitary, and so ignorant of what is going on, that he begs we will keep some *Moniteurs* for him, so that he may be able at a future day to fill up the hiatus. He says that Berlin presents a most peaceable appearance, and that his journey seems to him like a dream. Meanwhile, his cousin here is immersed in the pleasures of contentiousness. . . .

November 18.

I reopen my letter to say that M. Pasquier has just come to tell me that the Archchancellor wrote to the Emperor to ask for auditors. They are to be appointed. Your nephew is anxious to be one of them. If you can write to the Archchancellor, it must be done immediately. I would place the letter in his hands.

Just as I was closing this, Charles brought me in a letter for you. He wrote it quite by himself, and it is very clever. I am really sorry not to send it to you, but I fear it might get lost, and the child has innocently entered into certain domestic details that I should not like to be made known. But as I do not like to disappoint him by saying I cannot send it, will you answer him as if you had received it, and tell him that you are obliged for the news he gives you concerning all of us ; that you are very glad Halma is pleased with him ; that his Latin quotations are good, and his judgment of Philip, King of Macedonia, correct—for he tells you he has just been reading the life of that king in Rollin's History. I will keep his letter for you ; my maternal vanity is delighted with it. In all respects there could not be a more charming child. . . .

## CI.

Paris, November 20, 1806.

For the last few days it has been rumoured that their Majesties are returning, and that the army is settled in winter quarters in the north. How I hope it may be so! How much we need to be roused from the lethargy in which we are plunged by the absence of you all! Princess Caroline, whom I saw yesterday, told me she hopes that we shall see the Emperor back again this winter. I went to her early in the day, and she was good enough to take me all over the handsomest and most elegant house in Paris.* Her State apartments are not yet finished; but part of the ground-floor is furnished most sumptuously, the garden is charming, and when one recollects the ruinous state of the place only a year ago, its sudden metamorphosis seems almost miraculous. The princess leads a very quiet life, receiving but few guests, very rarely giving large dinner-parties, and never going out herself. The Archchancellor alone continues to give great receptions. Talking of the Archchancellor reminds me to say, but with no ill meaning, Madame Devaines has returned from the country, refreshed and rejuvenated. She loves it

* The Palace of the Elysée in the Rue du Faubourg St. Honoré.

more than ever—intends giving up the world, and fashionable dress, and living in the fields. She can only talk of her trees. No more dinner-parties, nor visitings; only nature, the song of birds, delicious shade of trees, and perfect peace—she wants nothing beyond. Some of her friends think she is mistaken, but I am quite of her mind. At her age one must live quietly if one would inspire respect. Madame de Souza is still here, out of health and rather lonely. She is anxious about Charles; not a word about M. de Souza. Madame de Labriche has returned; Madame d'Houdetôt is expected at the end of the month.

Madame Pastoret is full of an individual who has just arrived here and is causing some sensation. Do you remember hearing, about a year ago, that Madame Cottier had met in the Pyrenees a sublime creature—a religious philosopher, who had reached the heights of contemplation, and intended bringing out a book that was to settle all discord, religious and moral? The name of this person is M. Azaïs.* He is here; his book is published, and discussion goes on just as usual, except about his book, which is said to be utterly absurd. His

† Azaïs was born in 1766 and died in 1845. He was at first a Professor at the Prytanée de St. Cyr. He was the author, as everybody knows, of a system of philosophy and physics which explained all the vicissitudes of human destiny by the law of *Compensation*, and the phenomena of nature by the law of *Equilibrium*. He was Inspector of Libraries under the Empire. His first work, "Des Compensations dans les Destinées Humaines," was published in 1806. At a later period he wrote his "Système Universel" and a "Cours de Philosophie Générale," in eight volumes.

principle is that the immortality of good is the explanation of the universe. He proves this truth by the physical system of the world, and is foolish enough to try and upset Newton's theories, etc. Our men of science, who deny all his assertions, have referred him to the theologians, who will have nothing to say to him. He is now patronized by the metaphysicians, and women, or at least a few women, are upholding him, because of their " taste for the unintelligible," as M. de Saint-Lambert used to say. Madame Pastoret, who has a turn that way, has made the acquaintance of M. Azaïs, and has invited me to meet him at breakfast. I shall represent the audience, as you may suppose, and expect to be much amused. Azaïs wants to see the Emperor; he says they are equals in the moral world, and should stand by each other. He is said to be a fine speaker; his imagination is ardent, his manner animated, and his nonsense very clever. . . .

---

## CII.

### TO M. DE RÉMUSAT AT MAYENCE.

Paris, November 24, 1806.

Never have I sat down to my desk to write to you so sorrowfully. My heart aches at what I am about to say, but imperious reason counsels it, and, whatever the cost, I must accustom myself not to oppose reason. I have just received your last letter; it made me weep, and I was as much affected as you in reading your words, "We are parted for a long while." The worst of your position is that you are equally far from the Emperor and from your home. I think, therefore, that if his Majesty prolongs his stay in Prussia, you should make up your mind to ask leave to join him. My tears are falling; I know not how I shall endure such an increase of distance between us, nor the fear of all the accidents you may meet with on your journey, but every one tells me that our interests require this sacrifice, and I submit. I advise it, and I have now done my duty. But, nevertheless, I cannot help saying that every other consideration would vanish in the joy that I should feel, were you to receive orders to come to me. Oh, my beloved, how grievous is this long absence! What a life is mine, passed far from you! What a loss of happy days for which neither rank nor riches can ever compensate!

You are quite right in thinking Paris was startled by that bulletin.* Some few wise persons concede the necessity of finishing the war once for all; but the masses are opposed to it, and, moreover, at present we only feel the misfortunes of war. The Emperor's return had been looked for; it is now no longer expected, and great dis-

---

* The *bulletin* which produced a bad impression was probably the Emperor's *proclamation* to the army, announcing new enterprises and new dangers, and promising fresh laurels. It was written from Potsdam on October 26, 1806.

appointment is experienced. The necessity of the Empress's presence is therefore very strongly felt, and this should be explained to her. It would put a little life into this dead city, and show that she takes some interest in its welfare. For my part, I believe that her return is absolutely necessary. I cannot understand her reasons for wishing to remain at Mayence. Here she would get all the news almost as quickly, and would be quite as quiet; for the moral atmosphere is not gay, and all is dull and depressed.

Cardinal Maury's *Monseigneur* business is not yet over. I was present at a curious but rather ill-timed scene on this subject last Friday. It occurred at Princess Caroline's. She had had a dinner-party of about thirty people, and a reception in the evening. The cardinal and I were both at the dinner. At nine o'clock M. Regnault de Saint-Jean d'Angely makes his appearance (he, as you know, is one of those most opposed to the title). " Monsieur," says the cardinal, " I wish to say a word to you. Let us go into another room." " I must have witnesses," replies Regnault. This annoys the cardinal, among whose virtues, as you know, patience is not included, and he begins to complain. Regnault answers sourly, and the abbé waxes wroth. " I suppose you don't recollect," he says, " that in the Constituent Assembly I treated you more than once like a little boy. If my name were Montmorency I should despise your refusal, but it is my literary merit only that has made me what I am, and if

I gave up the *Monseigneur*, you would be calling me *mon camarade* the next day. Now, this I will not have." He was red and angry, and Regnier in a great passion. Everybody crowded round them, and the princesses, who were at cards in an adjoining room, sent several times to request silence. No one knows how it will all end. There is but one precedent, that of Fontenelle ; he understood academic equality well, and yet he addressed Cardinal Dubois as *Monseigneur* and *your Eminence*. But the new Academicians say that the times are altered. Possibly ; but men are not, say I.

I have just been interrupted by a visit from Lafond, who had asked me for an interview. He appeals to you because his theatrical dresses for the comedy have cost him a large sum. He really deserves some recompense, and if you cannot grant it, at least write him a few words of encouragement and hopefulness. He had a great success in " La Métromanie," and will, no doubt, prove an excellent actor of high comedy. He is going to act " Le Glorieux,"* and he draws houses at your theatre at a time when it is not easy to do so. Talma, too, it is said, is going to try comedy, but I do not believe it. Lafond seemed to doubt, but not to fear his doing so. Mademoiselle Duchesnois has asked me to obtain your leave for her to go and see her mother, and also permission to give a performance at Valenciennes. Pray answer me on this subject. . . .

* A comedy by Destouches.

## CIII.

Paris, Wednesday, November 26, 1806.

I wrote to you yesterday, advising you to ask permission to go to Berlin. I believed myself prepared for this additional trial. I stifled my tears and my sorrow, but all this show of courage has vanished on reading the letter I have just received. The idea of your departure has completely upset me. I think of the immense distance, of the bad roads, and the severe weather! My heart is breaking. You will go; I feel it must be so; and I, your poor wife, must brood over my anxieties by my dull fireside, all alone, with no hope of your speedy return. For, since the Empress also goes, it must be that the Emperor is to be long absent from us, perhaps all the winter. I cannot reconcile myself to this, and my tears are falling as I sit here alone. Sometimes I think I will go to Mayence and ask the Empress's leave to accompany her. And then I banish the idea, because we must not both leave our children. I have been separated from you five months of this year, and seven of last, and who can tell what the future may have in store for me! All my life is in your hands, my beloved! Take care of your health, therefore; do not add to my anxieties; and if you go, write as often as possible, so as to spare me all the misery you can. What can I say to you besides? I have no courage to speak of anything else. Yet I cherish one hope still—hope in the armistice, which you do not mention.. This may, perhaps, change the Emperor's plans, and bring him back to us. If so, the Empress would not go to Berlin ; and to this straw I cling. Moreover, Paris is in real need of her sovereigns, and their further journeyings will have an additionally depressing effect. Charles regets very much that he is not a few years older; for then he says he would go with you ; and I would let my own youth vanish without regret so that I might see that of my son. I think he would not accompany you, for you would stay with me, *cher ami*—with me, who would have desired never to spend one single day out of your dear presence, and am reduced to counting the endless number that begin and end without you !

Adieu. I am too sad to write more, and I blame myself for adding to your regrets. We must submit to what is imposed on you by duty. . . .

---

## CIV.

### TO M. DE RÉMUSAT AT MAYENCE.

Paris, November 29, 1806.

The quarrel is still raging at the Institute. Maury and Regnault are abusing each other.

Neither the one nor the other includes moderation among apostolic virtues or magisterial qualities. The Abbé Morellet, whom I saw the day before yesterday, is greatly displeased with the recent sittings of the Academy, and especially with a proposition made two days ago by Lacuée,* to deliberate on the question whether the Emperor can or cannot decide the great business of the *Monseigneur.* Our abbé considers there is a lack of respect in such a discussion, and I think the remark is just. The point will be decided on Thursday. Meanwhile the cardinal tells everybody that he cares very little for the Institute, and he imports into the dispute, really a very trivial one, a degree of violence which gives him the appearance of being in the wrong. Don't you think it absurd that the Emperor should be disturbed from the great questions that absorb him by all these paltry vanities?

The Empress's departure for Berlin is becoming known here, and is greatly regretted. It is said openly that the Emperor will not return this winter. I still hope that nothing is settled, or how many more days of sadness and *ennui* will have to be endured! I await letters from you with impatience, and try to believe you will not write, " I am going."

Nearly all our friends have returned; Madame

---

* Lacuée de Cesson, who was born in 1752 and died in 1841, had been in the army. His writings are exclusively on the art of war. He belonged to the class of moral and political science, and to the class of languages and literature, viz. to the French Academy, from the year 1803.

d'Houdetôt is expected on Monday. We shall
begin our Wednesdays at once, and you will be
much missed.   You already know how I shall pass
my time ; I shall be much at home, for, in default
of other pleasures, I can enjoy my favourite laziness, which I regard as almost as good a defence
for women as virtue, but not nearly so good as
love.   I am afraid you will not admire this remark.
Fortunately, you are tolerably sure, I think, of
those three safeguards, and you can scarcely object
to my preferring the latter.

---

## CV.

### TO M. DE RÉMUSAT AT MAYENCE.

Paris, December 5, 1806.

I know not what to think of our future.   War is
reviving ; the foreign kings seem struck with blind-
ness.   The measures taken by the Emperor are too
imposing to be judged by the ordinary standards of
human reason.   The worst is that people are not
sufficiently convinced of the insufficiency of their
judgment in times like these, and everybody inves-
tigates, thinks, and concludes according to his own
mind or his own interests.   I admit that this
makes society distasteful to me ; the issues involved
in the coming events of this winter are too great
for me to endure with patience the arguments of
a crowd of idlers who know nothing, and yet are

T

always talking and pronouncing judgment. I
prefer, therefore, to live in retirement with a few
friends who can understand and sympathize with
me. But even when alone, I am not free from
alarm. The Emperor is so far away, and surrounded
with constantly recurring dangers! Will his good
genius always preserve him? Are the troubles of
France quite at an end? And then yourself? How
long will it be before I see you again? Sometimes
I have the courage to wish you were at Berlin; at
others I wish you were not going to leave Mayence;
but I resist this feeling because it is selfish, and
because it is only I who would suffer from the increased distance between us, while you, in attendance on the Emperor, with more occupation and
feeling yourself useful—you would be happier.
There were momentary hopes here of their
Majesties' return, and now the certainty of their
absence has caused something like consternation.
Paris is like a dead body—it has neither life nor
motion; and as the dulness of our life here, and
your absence, reduce me to the *pleasures* of reflection only, I find myself reflecting by my fireside
on the influence—which, though seemingly purely
imaginary at a first glance, is happily very real in fact
—that is exercised by one man over a vast crowd
of beings to all appearance like himself. By what
degrees has this result been brought about in the
social order? This would be a curious and interesting study. But it would be very difficult for
my poor brain to consider the subject for any
length of time, nor should I have sufficient capacity,

even were I in perfect health. Yet how can I avoid serious thought when our interests are all involved in the question? You may imagine the discussions that are held concerning the last decree against trade with England.* Ah! *mon ami*, it is neither pleasant nor easy to govern mankind!

. . . I have not yet met M. Azaïs. You shall have an accurate account of him, since he interests you. The party has been put off on account of my health, and I am glad of it, for I think one must want a clear head to launch into metaphysics. You have probably seen by the newspapers the new resolution that has been taken by the Institute. It now seems that the final decision does rest with the Emperor. Did I tell you Cardinal Maury informed an acquaintance of mine that, having been for a moment tempted to publish his sermons, he had read them over, and then burned them without mercy, as too philosophical?

. . . Adieu; my head is aching, and I must take some rest. I think it is very polite of you to learn German; to my mind, it is for foreigners to learn French. . . .

* This was the Berlin decree that placed the British Isles in a state of blockade, forbade all trade or correspondence with them, and declared all property belonging to British subjects confiscated.

# CVI.

Paris, December 12, 1806.

I could not let Madame de Lagrange * leave Paris without giving her a small packet for you, and as this is a safe opportunity, I send your son's letter, which I did not like to trust to the post. You will see how clever it is; and it is entirely his own. You answered it charmingly, and he has no idea but that you received it long ago. You will tell me what you think of it.†

* Madame de Lagrange was the daughter of Madame de Talhouët, one of the Ladies-in-Waiting.

† It is certainly an abuse of the liberty granted to an editor of private correspondence, to publish the letter of a child of nine years old. Unless, however, I am greatly mistaken, the interest attaching to the development of this youthful mind, which from the first was so remarkable, and which was destined to become so famous, is one of the attractions of this correspondence. The incident also furnishes an additional instance of the terror inspired by the Emperor's police, and the resolution taken by my grandmother not to forward the letter by the ordinary post, affords an explanation of much of her reticence, and also of many expressions which seem out of harmony with her later writings. The following is the letter, which I have already given in a note to the Memoirs :—

" Wednesday.

" I beg your pardon, my dear papa, for not having written to you sooner. Mamma told you probably of Gustave's accident; he is a little better. We are all quite well. I have been to the Musée. The pictures I like best are ' Jeanne de Navarre' and those by Richard. I do not like the ' Deluge' much. M.

I grieve to see by your letters that you are so very dull, and I sometimes think that if this lasts I ought to ask leave to join you, and I might perhaps obtain it. But I will not conceal from you that it would be painful for me in many ways to do this. The greatest difficulty would be the cost, which I am not well able to meet at present; then the children, Charles especially, who requires a stricter supervision than my mother's, and, besides, she very naturally dislikes the post of governess; and, lastly, *my health*, though I do not think it would suffer materially. Therefore, if at any moment you consider my presence desirable, just say the word and I will take the necessary steps. Does the Empress ever mention the subject? You can reply without going into particulars, for we ought to be very prudent in our correspondence, and, if I may say so, I think you are not sufficiently cautious. There are sometimes philosophical sentiments in your letters which might give offence. It is an additional sorrow not to be able even to write to each other freely at such a distance, but we must make up our minds to every

Halma is pleased with me; I work harder than I did at Auteuil. We often go to see my aunt; she is not very gay, because she feels anxious. We hear that the Emperor is everywhere victorious, and that we shall march into Berlin as we did into Vienna. His conquests are worse than those of Alexander or Cyrus. That line of Phèdre may be applied to Paris: *Humiles laborant ubi potentes dissident.* I am now reading in Rollin about Alexander and Demosthenes. I do not like Philip; he is too ambitious. But I love you better than all of them. Adieu, my dear papa.

" CHARLES."

sacrifice, and hope that this one may procure us a long peace. Peace! it is scarcely hoped for here. Discontent and discouragement prevail everywhere; people suffer and complain openly. This campaign does not produce a quarter of the effect of the last. There is neither admiration nor even astonishment; we have become accustomed to miracles; the bulletins receive no applause when read at the theatres; in short, the universal feeling is bad—I might even say it is unjust, for it may happen to the strongest men to be led farther than they wish to go by circumstances, and I cannot believe that a superior mind will seek for glory in war alone. Add to this, the conscription and the last new decree on commerce! All these things are pabulum for our ill-wishers, who judge of them unreasonably, and see nothing but the effects of passion in the measures I speak of. I am far from presuming to judge them, but in spite of all I hear, I must needs admire and rely on the power that is arbiter of the fate of all those I hold dear.

You will write to me as soon as you are able after receiving this letter. I could not resist the opportunity of conversing freely with you. It is sad to spend my life thus in suspense and separation; sometimes even displeased with friends who do not share opinions that I believe to be right because they are moderate. All these things depress, agitate, or disturb me. The future alarms me, and I long for you to restore me to calmness and hope.

## CVII.

Paris, December 14, 1806.

. . . Well, I have at last seen this M. Azaïs, and, after hearing him talk for three hours, I was inclined to say, as Portalis said of La Harpe, that my throat was sore with listening to him. The man is certainly mad, and all the more so that he has missed his age, and in this one will neither obtain the altar he thinks he deserves, nor the persecution for which he is prepared. Picture to yourself a thin and pale individual of about fifty, dreamy and cold in manner, indifferent to all convesation except on his own subject, ignorant of what is taking place in the world. He rouses himself only when a certain chord is struck ; that chord is his system of philosophy. Then he rises from his seat, his countenance brightens, he begins to explain. Nothing can then stop him ; he goes on for two, three, and four hours without a break. He speaks with great facility, his elocution is admirable, and his own conviction intense. To any and every objection he only replies, " You will believe me when you have read my ten volumes," and it is said that in these ten volumes he has explained, or tried to explain, all that the learned have merely discovered. He opposes Newton and all the physicists, he upsets parts of the astronomical system, he regulates the universe according to his own ideas, so as to arrive at his favourite principle and only aim, which is to prove that order and virtue are necessary to the organic system of the world, and that the health of mankind will improve in proportion to the number of their good actions. He asserts that this system of morality thus brought within the reach of every one, will triumphantly take the place of religion, now on the decline, and of the authority of government. While talking, he reveals his belief in a first cause whom he calls the *great proprietor*. Beyond this, he is quite a materialist—holds the soul to be only a collection of ideas; ideas themselves to be but bodies produced in us by the concurrence of I forget what fluids, which form in our brain the image of the object that has struck us.

But I feel I must now take breath. I will return to this extraordinary man on another occasion. I am rather glad, on the whole, to have heard him talk; for, notwithstanding the fragile foundation of his theories, he is so clever in finding proofs, and so fertile in their expression, that he excites interest. Our men of science will have nothing to do with him. He appeals to posterity and to the Emperor, with whom he claims equality in the moral world. The guests at breakfast were Pasquier, Molé, and Dorion; they held their own well in the discussion. Madame Pastoret talked very cleverly. As for me, I could not venture to meddle with such matters, but I made my own private reflections on the curious mania which leads mankind to wander in search of all the mysteries surrounding them, while they fail to understand themselves in almost all the circumstances of life.

---

## CIX.

TO M. DE RÉMUSAT AT MAYENCE.

Paris, December 23, 1806.

The Empress's return is still looked for here, but I do not hope for it, and I think that for the next few months I shall escape the grief of disappointment, for I am not caught in any of the snares laid by hope for others. I wish for you, my dearest, but dare not expect you. Alix heard yesterday from her husband. She had had no news of him for a month, and was in an anxious state. He is in good health, and stationed beyond Posen, far from head-quarters, with which communication is difficult. May Heaven watch over him and bring him back to us!

I met a person yesterday who was at St. Petersburg at the time of the death of Paul I., and who gave me some curious particulars. Poland reminds me of them, because Benningsen,* now in command of the Russians, was the man who struck the first blow. The task was entrusted to

* Count Benningsen, a Russian general, born in 1745, died in 1826.

him, and he took the lead of the conspirators,
who all felt a momentary panic on entering
the apartments of the Czar. Benningsen encouraged them, and knocked down the hussar on
guard at the door. The man's cries warned the
Emperor, who sprang from his bed, and hid behind
a screen. The murderers entered the room, and
not seeing him, wanted to withdraw; their chief
ordered them to remain, searched everywhere, and
at last caught sight of part of the Emperor's
clothing which projected beyond the screen. Seiz-
ing him by the hair, he dragged him to the
middle of the room and struck the first blow
with his dagger; the others then finished him.
And this man is now commanding Alexander's
army! He is a bad man, incapable of the least
generosity, cruel to his enemies and harsh to his
inferiors, and will incite the Russians to all the
excesses they may commit in their retreat. But
since we are marching upon him, his hour is
probably near.

In order to revive Paris a little, the princesses
and the Archchancellor have begun to entertain,
and are giving balls. On Sunday the Archchancellor gave one; there were a good many women,
but very few partners for them, and but for a con-
tingent of pages, who were sent for, I don't know
what would have happened. The princesses are
also going to give fêtes, but none of these things
will be pleasure. I am not even sure whether the
contrast of noise and movement with the mood
of the guests, will not increase the melancholy

caused by the absence of so many beloved ones. For my own part, my heart ached at sight of the Emperor's empty chair, and at the thought of the distance that separates him from us, exposed as he is to so much fatigue and danger; and with such feelings, the sound of gaiety and music inclined me to serious thought, if not to tears. But his return, his return alone can revive us and make us susceptible of pleasure by bestowing on us tranquillity of mind.

I met some of my colleagues at Cambacérès', but only a few; we are all rather scattered. Madame de Serrant is passing the winter at her place in the country; Madame Talhouët, who came to Paris for a passing visit, has just returned home, and can talk only of the delights of rurality; Madame de Luçay never leaves St. Gratien, where M. de Luçay is very happy. His daughter lives with her mother-in-law, Madame de Ségur.* Madame Savary is in an interesting condition, greatly altered, and very much alone. Madame Duchâtel is in the same state. She looks lovely, dances, and goes everywhere. I have seen Madame Brignole; she is a pleasant woman, and I could get on with her, if our terms of waiting fall together. If you care to hear the nonsense that is talked here, I must tell you that people say Madame de la Rochefoucauld is resigning her place, and will be succeeded by Madame de Montmorency; †

---

* Madame de Ségur, wife of the Comte de Ségur, had been Mademoiselle d'Aguesseau. She was, therefore, aunt to Madame Octave de Ségur, her son's wife.

† Mademoiselle de Matignon.

also that the Emperor intends on his return to appoint a *Gouverneur des Princes*, and that your name figures on the list.* I laughed at this last piece of news. However, if this should be the case, as seems so *likely*, pray grant my request and let me be appointed to *give the lessons.* Every day qualifies me better for such a post, and I venture to say you will be satisfied with my zeal.

## CX.

TO M. DE RÉMUSAT AT MAYENCE.

Paris, Thursday, December 25, 1806.

I doubt, *mon ami*, whether my head will be able to hold all that has been stuffed into it lately, and unless we take care, I am really afraid that on your return you will find an office-like air about your salon, and in my mother and me a likeness to *Catau* and *Madelon.* Within the next week, I shall have listened to three tragedies, a comedy in five acts, and an *opéra comique.* All the rest of Paris is asleep, but the literary world is awake, and on account of our position, the smallest scribbler must endeavour to obtain your protection through my intervention. Aignan† has just finished his

* This appointment of tutor to the princes was not made.

† Aignan, born in 1773, died in 1824, a member of the French Academy in 1814, was the writer of some translations and some tragedies. The tragedy mentioned was probably

tragedy, and has asked me to name a day for his reading it; on Friday I am to hear "Les États de Blois;" M. Dorion keeps a comedy in verse in his pocket; Duval has finished an opera called "Joseph," which is highly praised; Madame Simons, still writing, persecutes me. In vain do I make excuses; I must not be uncivil, and I devote myself. Mérotte is amused by this, and we do our best to deceive all the authors who ask so disinterestedly for our *advice.*

The Français is doing pretty well this year. I think it is the best-attended theatre. They are acting "Venceslas" successfully; Talma is very fine in certain parts, but the rest of the play was badly acted. Lafond continues to act in comedy; he did not succeed so well in the "Glorieux" as in the other plays. The public were disappointed, for they had been looking forward to this impersonation. This proves that it is a mistake to suppose an actor will represent cleverly a defect or habit

---

"Brunéhaut ou les Successeurs de Clovis." Raynouard's tragedy of the "États de Blois" was performed before the Court only, in 1810, and was not acted in public until the Restoration. M. Dorion was a poet whom my grandfather had met during his stay at Caûterets. He died in 1829, in his seventy-first year. He wrote no comedies for the theatre, and only published two epic poems, now forgotten, "Palmyre Conquise" and "La Bataille d'Hastings." Alexander Duval, who died in 1842, at the age of eighty, is the well-known author of a great many dramas and comedies. He had been a sailor, a soldier, an engineer, director of the Odéon, and was finally made a member of the French Academy in 1812. The opera of "Joseph" remains in the repertory, probably on account of Méhul's music, though the play is not without interest.

that resembles his own defects or habits. For if he attempts this, he gives way to his natural leaning, exaggerates, and acts badly. Lafond, who is naturally rather stiff, was altogether heavy in " Le Glorieux," and Mademoiselle Duchesnois, whose voice is naturally tender and touching, assumes a monotonous sing-song in parts which are exclusively pathetic.

I saw M. Dorion yesterday ; he told me that M. de Talleyrand and Maret had been upset in their carriage in Poland, but nothing serious had ensued. It seems that the roads are extremely bad and the climate damp. So far, none of our friends in the army have suffered from the hardships of the campaign. By-the-by, have you any news of M. de Caulaincourt ? I have not seen any of his family, nor have I heard anything of them. If you are writing to him, say a word or two from me. I had some thoughts of writing to him myself, but he has enough to do without having to answer letters from me. I will write to M. de Talleyrand so soon as I know the protocol ; but I feel it will be rather a difficult task, and, notwithstanding your favourable judgment, I must admit that I find it difficult to write unless I can rely on the sympathy of my correspondent. I come to a full stop when I reflect that M. de Talleyrand must be perfectly indifferent to the subjects on which I usually write, and which occupy my mind while you are away. He gives an account of his accident to Madame Devaines, and reminds her that last year he wrote to her from Presburg, and this year from Warsaw.

"God knows," he adds, "where I may be next year!" Heaven grant he may be in the Rue d'Anjou! *

---

## CXI.

### TO M. DE RÉMUSAT AT MAYENCE.

Paris, December 28, 1806.

... I am very glad you have received your son's letter, and I think you must be pleased with it; he is going to write to you again to-morrow. He has long meant to do so, but has some difficulty, because of his natural indolence, and also because he is working harder. Halma has thought well to begin mathematics with him; this makes an additional task, and, besides, games are the order of the day. Gustave is quite strong again, and little Carignan † is a great friend of Charles. He brings other little friends in of an evening, and they are

---

* M. de Talleyrand's house was in the Rue d'Anjou St. Honoré.

† The Princess de Carignan, who was supposed to have married M. de Montléard, Auditor of the State Council, resided on the first floor of the house on the Boulevard de la Madeleine. Her son, Charles Albert, was my father's playfellow and about the same age. He was tall, ugly, and awkward, and the butt of his companions. My father and M. de Grasse still laughed sometimes at these recollections when I was a child. None the less, however, was he a chivalrous and patriotic king from 1831 to 1840, and the father of the founder of the kingdom of Italy, the great Victor Emmanuel.

continually at games and exercises. With all this our boy's health is good. He grows fast, is strong, and *not too ugly*. I sometimes remark a tender and intelligent look in his eyes that reminds me of eyes whose expression goes straight to my heart. When shall I see them again, those eyes that tell me I am beloved and happy? And oh! how happy I could be!

We heard "Les États de Blois," at Madame Pastouret's yesterday. Lafond read the play to a numerous company. It was thought rather dull, but well written, and the characters cleverly drawn. The Duc de Guise is very fine, Henri III. well portrayed; there is a capital Crillon, and a leaguer exactly like the Jacobins at the beginning of the Revolution. The part of Henri IV. contains several beautiful and pathetic lines, but he harps too much on his love for the French, and frequently repeats himself. The style is polished and lofty, but somewhat cold; in a word, the play is wanting in action, and it is quite possible that at your theatre it might only meet with what you call a *succès d'estime.*

Mademoiselle Raucourt has returned, and is going to act in "Pyrrhus." After that a play by Lemercier will be produced. . . .

---

The letters of the early part of the year 1807 are almost entirely devoid of general interest. The correspondence is resumed in July of that year, when Madame de Rémusat is at Aix-la-Chapelle, and associating chiefly with the De Lameth family. The Russian campaign had not yet assumed its disastrous character; the battle of Friedland had been fought on the 14th of June, 1807. An important event had occurred in the interval over which we pass, *i.e.* the death of the eldest son of Louis Bonaparte, King of Holland, to whom the Law of Heredity had secured the succession. The child's death, the effect on the Emperor, the Empress, and Queen Hortense, and the influence which it exerted in the matter of the divorce are dwelt upon in the Memoirs at considerable length.

---

## CXXIX.

TO M. DE RÉMUSAT AT PARIS.

Aix-la-Chapelle, July 24, 1807.

I shall now be longing for letters, and suffering from terrible curiosity. It seems strange to be so far removed from these great events and important interests. Lemarrois * passed through this place yesterday on his way to drink the waters at Spa. While changing horses, he sent us a complimentary message; I should have much liked to have seen

* General Lemarrois had just been appointed Governor of Warsaw. He died in 1836.

him and I am rather vexed with him for being in such a hurry. My neighbour here has received a letter from the army in a handwriting she does not know, and without signature, giving her an account of the principal conditions of peace. We easily guessed at the writer. By the time you receive this, I conclude you will be fully informed of everything, so I will not attempt to tell you any news.

I passed yesterday evening at the house of a merchant, who talked a great deal about you. You accompanied the Emperor, he told me, when his Majesty visited the factory belonging to this wealthy and hospitable M. Vermonteu. There are frequent assemblies at the various merchants' houses here, and without giving ourselves the airs of Court ladies, we cannot absent ourselves from them. I behave admirably, playing at cards with great courage. I shall become an expert whist-player. Happily, my mornings are my own, and they do not seem so tedious as I feared they would. . . .

## CXXX.

### TO M. DE RÉMUSAT AT PARIS.

Aix-la-Chapelle, July 26, 1807.

I think by this time the Emperor must be in Paris. I dreamed last night that I saw him, and fell weeping on his neck. What a relief it is to know that he is in Paris, and that peace is made!

We can now look back and see with astonishment how long we have been walking on the edge of a precipice. We are safe at last, and the little speck in the universe, called the earth, is safe too; for everything depends on that one life. A few officers have already made their appearance here, drinking the waters to cure their rheumatism. By-the-by, I was told yesterday that General Loyson, who lost an arm last year, not at Austerlitz, where he was much exposed to danger, but at a shooting party, took it into his head to have it embalmed and fastened by some sort of mechanism to his shoulder. He says he will not relinquish anything given him by nature, and he prefers a dead arm at his side to none at all. Only imagine the effect this pale, cold hand will produce on any one who touches it!

There is another young and strikingly handsome man here, who also lost an arm at Eylau. He makes no attempt at hiding it, but carries his coat-sleeve in a sling, and dances all the more gaily, waltzing, springing, and whirling about. He is noticed and sought after, while perhaps, had he no limb wanting, he would not be looked at. . . .

I like the Lameth family. The mother is a good woman, so is the daughter, and the son-in-law is excellent. They are a united family and seem happy, and I like to witness happiness. Madame de Nicolai's * happiness is the result of a

---

* M. de Nicolai was Madame de Lameth's son-in-law.

love match; that rascally little god is occasionally of some use, and I don't think him altogether out of place in marriage. Are you not of my opinion? The Prefect is agreeable; he has more talent than the others, but is not quite so good-natured. He is, however, most attentive to us. He told me he had met a retired officer at Digne, who is related to you, and who likes you very much. His name is Salves or Salles,* or something. He has heard you much spoken of. How on earth did he discover that you were a very clever and agreeable man? He also talked to me of my father, whom he knew well, and of my mother, who was considered a very superior woman. I do not know where he has not lived. He is tolerably popular here. The people are not very *French* as yet; time and tact are needed for this.

Will you be surprised to hear that I am at the end of the fourth canto of Virgil, at the last letter but one of my novel, and that I have all but finished the chair I am working? Moreover, I am improving on the guitar, and I am a Duc de Laval at whist. It is only in love for you that I can make no progress; yet this does not mean that I am near the end.

I open my letter to give you some news. Is not this impertinent? But now see how well informed we are! This is what is reported here. Prince Jérôme is to be King of Westphalia; Prince Murat, King of Poland, under the protectorate of Russia; the Grand-Duke Constantine, King of Servia and

* M. de Salve-Villedieu.

Montenegro. This is the last news at Aix-la-Chapelle. And I love you very much, which is no news at all. . . .

***

## CXXXIV.

Aix-la-Chapelle, August 14, 1807.

Are you quite aware, *mon ami*, that I start on my homeward journey to-morrow week? Have you sympathized with me in my joy at the preparations I am making for my flitting? In truth, I must give over grumbling either at the few days I still have to remain here, or even at our separation. There is something so sweet in the thought of return, so keenly delightful in the actual home-coming, that I feel tempted to rejoice in the emotions that have preceded it. We shall soon meet again! I shall see my children and all whom I love! I am coming home to you in better health, with heartfelt delight, and with the satisfaction of having borne my exile courageously, and passed it in gaining the advantages that you wished me to derive from it; these thoughts will be my travelling companions, until, in your arms, I shall receive sympathy and reward.

My mother writes me word that "Ésope" was not a success at Court. I am not surprised; although it is a well-written work, I always thought it tiresome. You are now again in the tribulations of pleasure; it is no easy task to have to provide amusement for a master, and especially for a conqueror, who for so long has had glory and good fortune as ministers to his pleasure. I always think that the Emperor must find life at St. Cloud very insipid after such great deeds, and that quite one half of him must be at a loss for occupation. Such spells of languor and *ennui* are the penalty of the great in this world, and are a compensation to small people like ourselves. Talking of great people, I have just read a chapter of Montaigne that I like very much; if you happen to meet with it, pray look through it again. It is entitled " De la Constance," and is full of remarks very applicable to the twenty years that have just expired. " Those who first shake the foundations of a State," he says, "are actually the first to be involved in its overthrow;" and, "The fruit of disturbance is seldom reaped by him who sowed it;" and then " The very best pretext for novelty is dangerous." I pointed out this last maxim to M. de Lameth, who owned that he thought Montaigne was in the right. Do, pray, read the chapter. I feel very happy at the Emperor's kindness to M. de Nansouty. There is something great and grand about his gifts which harmonizes well with the gigantic scale of events. Victory is assuredly the best title-deed. I was half inclined to write my congratulations to M. de Talleyrand, but ignorance of his new titles prevented me. Tell him this, with my compliments. Do you know, I begin to like him very much, because he appreciates you.

## CXXXV.

TO M. DE RÉMUSAT AT PARIS.*

Aix-la-Chapelle, July 12, 1808.

I have arranged my life here, so that time slips pleasantly away. I rise at eight; drink the waters until ten; then I bathe and return to bed, take my breakfast, and dawdle about until noon. I then dress for the day, read, write, and sing until M. Aldini's† arrival. He is kind enough to read Italian with me, and, by the way, is well pleased with my pronunciation. My English master comes next; I engaged him to give myself something to do. We dine at five. In the evening we walk out, receive a few visitors, and by ten o'clock we are all in bed. In this way do I pass my time when far from you as profitably as possible. My companion, who goes out a great deal, often asks me to accompany her, but I decline when it is possible to do so without giving offence; my mourning dispenses me from balls, and my health serves as an excuse for not joining fatiguing excursions. Moreover, Madame de —— is very intimate this year with Madame K——, and that

---

* There is a lapse of nearly a year between this letter and the last, and Madame de Vergennes had died in the interval. Madame de Rémusat had returned to Aix-la-Chapelle, accompanied by Madame de Grasse.

† Count Aldini, Secretary of State for the kingdom of Italy, has left behind him a distinguished reputation.

would not suit me. I fancy both ladies think me very reserved and not very amusing, but if I were to yield to them, I should lose the good effects of my visit here, and it costs me too dear not to wish to *utilize* it, as M. Pasquier would say.

What you say of your own loneliness distresses me; it is a real grief to me to know you are so solitary. On former occasions, alas! my poor mother was with you. I knew that you were together, and thought myself only to be pitied; but absence, of which I know the pain so well, is equally hard on you this year, and thus I suffer not my own sorrow only, but yours as well. Oh, how I should like never to leave you! How sweet life is at your side! How I love you! How happy you make me! How closely you bind me to a life that you render so fair! How can you expect me not to grieve over the separations entailed by my delicate health? I cannot but love my life, when its every moment is gladdened by your love. Be less good to me, and I shall be less anxious; teach me to forget your caresses, since I must be deprived of them; prove to me, at least, that I may reckon on the peaceful future you are preparing for me, and then I can be patient and resigned. Ah! could any one promise me that my life shall last as long as yours, I should be restored to ease and calm; this is the only certainty for which I crave. Ah, my beloved, could we but travel through life together and quit it at the same moment!

If you should be writing to M. de Talleyrand,

remember me to him, and say that I am leading too dull a life to venture on writing to him, but that I beg him not to forget me, and to be grateful for my silence. I have really nothing to say. Life is short here, but its hours are long; one must swallow the waters, hold one's tongue, and get away as soon as possible. And this is what I intend to do, so soon as I get my dismissal.

## CXXXVI.

### TO M. DE RÉMUSAT AT PARIS.

Aix-la-Chapelle, July 15, 1808.

You may be getting through your arrears of work, but you evidently do not include writing to us in the list, for you write very seldom. For the last three days we have had not a word from any one, whether sister, husband, or Gustave—in fact, we are altogether forsaken; and yet we certainly need a little diversion, for our life is very monotonous. The heat is excessive. . . .

My health is really good in this place. I can scarcely attribute the improvement to the waters, for as yet I have taken only three baths, but I think it proceeds from the quietude of my life, and this is an additional proof that I am made for that country life of which we have so often talked. We really must contrive to have a house in the country some day; I long for it more and more, and I think I should delight in rural leisure.

We are far from this, as yet, and you especially, who are about to resume your Court life, if the Emperor * comes back, as is expected. Aldini, who fears he may soon be recalled to Paris, leaves us to-day for Spa. I shall miss him exceedingly; his conversation was both improving and agreeable, we got on capitally in our Italian dialogues, and he was always most kind to me. If you happen to see him, you must express my thanks, and say that I miss him very much. I have met with a pleasant Dutch family here; both husband and wife are good musicians; we sing together, and that fills up my time a little. I employ the rest as best I can. The Prefect often comes to see us. Madame de Grasse has become accustomed to him; she likes him pretty well, but he is the only person to whom she will speak; she dislikes Germans. . . .

To-day is Thursday, and I fancy that while I write, you are at his school with our boy.† He must feel the heat very much in that treeless playground, where I picture you to myself, embracing each other. How I wish the little fellow

---

* The Emperor, who had returned from Italy in January, had started again for Bayonne, whence he returned by way of Toulouse on August 15.

† Notwithstanding what was said further back on the advantages of home education, my father had been sent to school in September, 1807. The Lycée Napoleon had been selected, simply because Madame Pastoret's two eldest sons were there—Amédie, who was older than my father, and already a rhetorician; and Maurice, very much his junior. Amédie Pastoret died about the year 1860. He was a senator under the Second Empire.

were with you! . . . I am quite sure that you see nobody, and that on my return all our friends will be asking me for news of you; consequently I do not ask you to tell me anything about them, but I wait for letters from Alix to give me all the gossip. Madame de Vannoise will be your only visitor, and the only person about whom you will write to me; the unhappy are sure to find you out, but you carefully avoid every one who could merely give you pleasure or pay you court.

In my solitude I meditate on education, and I study books on the subject. I have been reading "Adèle et Theodore," a book that I had not opened since my childhood, and I find there are really excellent things in it. I remarked one paragraph which I must transcribe for you, and you will tell me whether you think it applies to any one : " A child who only likes to converse with those whom he trusts, who is silent in the presence of strangers, who chatters only with his friends and playfellows, and who, besides this, listens with interest to others—*such a child will certainly be extremely clever.*" What does your Excellency say to this ? I think you will first laugh at me, and then think that I am right.

Madame de Lameth said to me yesterday, " You have left your husband among all those actresses —does it not make you feel uneasy ? " " No," I answered. " What, not a bit jealous ? " " No." " And why not ? " " Ah ! why not indeed ? I cannot say—but the fact is, I am not in the least uneasy." And you—can you tell me why ? . . .

## CXXXIX.

Aix-la-Chapelle, July 24, 1808.

If nothing happens to prevent it, I still intend
to leave Aix on the 20th of August—that is to say,
in less than a month; but I hardly dare to dwell
on the thought. It seems more difficult for me
to get away from this place than from any other;
though certainly not because of the pleasure I
take in it. In spite of M. de Lameth's kindness
and attention, life here is wearisome, and the very
things got up for our amusement are, generally
speaking, those that we care for the least. Concerts given by poor fellows who want to profit by
the presence of visitors; music of the dreariest
kind; a third-rate play; drives in the neighbourhood in wretched, jolting carriages; picnics with
people I do not know and do not want to know,
etc., etc., and then those eternal whist-parties!
If I consulted my own feelings I should certainly
stay at home. I have not the strength for long
expeditions, and I am never dull with Madame de
Grasse, who takes care of me and spoils me, and
who sympathizes with my sorrows, my anxieties,
and my affections—in short, with all that burdens
my mind, or fills my heart. . . .

## CXL.

TO M. DE RÉMUSAT AT PARIS.

Aix-la-Chapelle, July 30, 1808.

This evening you will have your son with you; I rejoice over this in my solitude, and quite enjoy these two days, Saturday and Sunday. Next time you will keep him longer with you. . . . Just now I am pretty well. The poor Prefect cannot say so much for himself; his health is in a sad state. He has feverish attacks every day, and suffers much from his liver. He has been confined to his room since the beginning of this week. We go every evening to his sick room to play *quinze.* People may say what they please of him in Paris, but he is an agreeable man, and a good man too. I can say nothing of the past, but I am greatly pleased with what I now see of him. I believe that the fancy we have taken to him has given rise to some satirical comment in the Faubourg St. Honoré.* The cousin has already written to Madame de Grasse, and I believe that

---

* The following note by my father throws some light on this passage:—" M. de Lameth was one of the most unpopular men in our circle of acquaintance, which was in general anti-revolutionary, although strongly imbued with revolutionary ideas. My mother, although full of the prejudices natural to the daughter of one of the victims of 1793, had tendencies to liberalism and impartiality, which rendered her both more indulgent and more just, especially where she recognized ability."

Alix also makes fun of us; but we have made up our minds to brave everything, and, right or wrong, in despite of the critics, to like every one who deserves it or who likes us. However, as this will not pass unnoticed, you may imagine beforehand the disputes that will arise, similar to those of last spring about another favourite of mine.* By the way, do you not write to him? Do you hear nothing of him? Does he not intend to stir from his château? The rumours that arose in another place have reached us here, but I do not believe a word of them. . . .

## CXLI.

### TO M. DE RÉMUSAT AT PARIS.

Aix-la-Chapelle, August 3, 1808.

. . . I have finished reading Voltaire's correspondence; that is to say, I gave it up when I came to the affairs of Calas and Sirvens, which bored me. I am now reading Gulliver, on Madame de Vintimille's recommendation, and after having regarded it formerly as a mere story to amuse children, I am now astounded that any one dared to publish so severe a censure on all human institutions, and especially on the government of the country in which it appeared. If Bertrand has not looked at it lately, I advise him to read it again; it is really an amusing book. Abbé Morellet has good reason

* M. de Talleyrand.

for his attachment to Swift; I discover that he was a very clever man.

I was amused by finding in Voltaire's correspondence all the *débuts* of those old philosophers, whose foolish vanity is now so obsolete. Their mad imprudence in digging the pit into which we fell along with them, makes one heartsick, now that we know into what misfortunes they led us. Ah! how they deceived themselves with their pride and their vain science! In a letter to one of his disciples Voltaire writes, "Let us educate the people, and we shall be of service to every country. Thanks to us, Cromwell could not again succeed in England; Cardinal de Retz could not make us endure barricades." The Revolution has proved how well we can defend ourselves from barricades!

I have a lively letter from Madame Devaines, but she makes too much of what she calls my foolishness and her own common sense. She deserves that some day I should tell her the truth concerning herself; for, after all, she is always mistaking indifference for wisdom, and moderation is easy and of little merit to those who take nothing to heart. She tells me that M. de Talleyrand is very dull at Valençay, and that he has not ceased to regret his nephew. If this be so, I am the more sorry not to be near him. Perhaps you should have proposed going to see him. I am sure a visit from you would have done him good and given him pleasure; I fancy it is a long while since he has seen a human being. If he is unhappy, I should like to write to him; but I fear it is too late, and that my letter would only arrive at the moment of the Emperor's return. On reflection, I will not write, and when I come back, I shall get up a little quarrel with him.

## CXLII.

### TO M. DE RÉMUSAT AT PARIS.

Aix-la-Chapelle, August 12, 1808.

. . . We are beginning to prepare for the Emperor's fête. M. de Lameth, whose health is rather better, is decorating his house, and intends to give us a ball. You, too, will be having some kind of fête, for everything seems to foretell the Emperor's return by that time. I hope that you will then see M. de Talleyrand, and that you will speak to him of me. He ranks among the few whom I shall be glad to meet again.

I have received a long and pleasant letter from M. Bertrand. If we were oftener at a distance from each other, we should carry on a great correspondence. With my love of writing, and the numerous ideas which the most trifling circumstance furnish to his fertile imagination, there would be no end to our letters. He seems quite enchanted with the Comédie Française. He will go nowhere but to the theatre, and it is there that we meet. He says the house is comfortable, the comedy is excellent, the actors perfect, the plays are charming ; it is a passion with him, in fact, with the charm of novelty. If we are left in peace on my return, I should like nothing better than to pass my evenings there with him. But—yes, I *should* like still better my beloved country house, in which I would willingly pass the autumn. This morning two fresh eggs were brought to me; Madame de Grasse and I exclaimed at the same time, "Ah! if we were in our country house, we should have brought in the eggs ourselves from our own poultry yard!" I want you to tell me whether you would advise the purchase of some Spanish sheep. Madame de Grasse insists on our having a flock; do you think this would be a good speculation?

## CXLIII.

### TO M. DE RÉMUSAT AT ERFÜRTH.[*]

Paris, Sunday, September 25, 1808.

. . . I have not much to tell you since your departure; the hours have crept slowly along, with

---

[*] Madame de Rémusat returned to Paris at the latter end of August, and a month afterwards, on September 22, the Emperor started for Erfürth, accompanied by his First Chamberlain, whose task it was to organize in that town those famous performances of the Comédie Française which, it has been said, drew together an *audience of kings* (*un parterre de rois*). Every one knows the insolent speech, " Ce n'est par un *parterre*, mais une *plate-bande.*" It would seem that the Emperor imposed on every one his own indefatigable activity, for between September 28 and October 13—that is, in the course of one fortnight—the following performances were given at Erfürth : "Cinna," "Andromaque," "Britannicus," "Zaire," "Mithridate,"

little of interest.  The theatres do well.  Trajan
has made more than seven thousand francs;
Mademoiselle Leverd has played twice.  Fleury is
said to be ill, and thinking of retiring into the
country.  I went to see "Scarmentado;"* it is a
wretched and tiresome rhapsody.  I do not think
the Odéon will see much of me; one can be almost
as dull at home.

---

## CXLIV.

### TO M. DE RÉMUSAT AT ERFÜRTH.

Paris, Tuesday, September 27, 1808.

. . . I went to Tivoli the day before yesterday,
and was present at the daily dinner to the troops.
It amused me.†  The tables are well supplied; the
soldiers merry, but not noisy.  Women and children walked about among them, and not the
slightest accident occurred; shouts of "Vive l'Em-
pereur" were echoed from one table to another,
and the whole thing had a joyous air.  Charles
much enjoyed the sight, and also the amusements
provided for the soldiers after the dinner.

I also went yesterday to the first performance of

---

"Œdipe," "Iphigénie," "Phèdre," "La Mort de César,"
"Rodogune," "Rhadamiste," "Le Cid," "Manlius," and
"Bajazet."

* A comedy by Lemercier.

† Fêtes and banquets were given successively to the regiments
passing through Paris.

" Ninon." * The piece had a well-deserved success; there is some affectation in the style, but it is pretty and fairly well acted.

These two are almost the only occasions on which I have been out. I am going, this morning, to Malmaison, where they say the Empress is enjoying herself. She is well; I hope it is the same case with you. Tell me about your health. M. Edmond de Périgord, whom you will see, will tell you about mine; he was kind enough to send to my house, and I saw him yesterday at his sister's, just as he was starting. Madame de Vintimille, M. Pasquier, Bertrand, Abbé Morellet, and Picard dined with me on Friday. I don't suppose that you pass your afternoons at Erfürth as we passed that one; it was one long discussion. We ended by the usual argument on La Rochefoucauld and La Bruyère. You know how this always excites Madame de Vintimille; the abbé shouted as if he were but twenty years old, and I as loud as I could; M. Bertrand repeated at intervals, " Allow me! Allow me!" but we would not allow him; Picard laughed, and could certainly have made a scene in a play of it all. The next morning Bertrand came to give me the opinion to which we had not listened. He told me, with respect to La Bruyère, that he had read his works many times in his youth, without daring thoroughly to enjoy the pleasure they gave him. " It seemed to me," he said, " that after his satire of others, I should, as I advanced in the book, find

* " Ninon chez Madame de Sévigné," an *opéra comique* by Dupaty.

satire of myself as well; I dared not think, because I believed that I could not escape him; in short, he seemed to me the *Talleyrand* of writers." . . .

## CXLV.

### TO M. DE RÉMUSAT AT ERFÜRTH.

Paris, September 28, 1808.

. . . I was at Malmaison yesterday; the park is wonderfully improved. The Empress is in better health; she thoroughly enjoys her ownership of the place, walks about all day, in spite of the rain, and seemed to me to be happy and tranquil. She had heard from the Emperor; she thinks you must have arrived yesterday, the Emperor of Russia to-day, and perhaps to-morrow I shall see you all in the *tripot* of the Comédie. If your mind does not give way under all the obligations imposed on you, it must be a very strong one; I always imagine you surrounded by your actors, all talking together. The theatres here are going on pretty well; I am busying myself with "Numa," like the fly in the fable. I have seen Gardel, who answers for the ballets. Paër is rehearsing every other day, and tells me that the opera might be performed by the 25th; Isabey is getting on rapidly with his work.

I have received two letters from the Bishop of Alais. He is very much obliged to the Emperor for selecting him; and he accepts, although fearing he will be unable to perform the requisite functions.

At the present moment he has such an attack of gout that he cannot walk even on crutches; but Fontanes has written to tell him that nothing beyond correspondence will be required of him. He says a great deal in his letters to me about this " Life of Bossuet; " he says four years of reading will be necessary before he can put pen to paper; in fact, he seems afraid of his immense undertaking.*

## CXLVI.

### TO M. DE RÉMUSAT AT ERFÜRTH.

Paris, October 7, 1808.

I passed the whole of yesterday at Malmaison; there were but few persons there. The Empress has got over her stiff neck, but she is depressed by the return of her headaches. The works are being carried on in every direction, and the place is really becoming like fairyland. When from time to time I catch a glimpse of the country, through a window as it were, all my rural desires are revived, and I return to this great city with melancholy feelings. I am expecting Duval to-day. He is to read his comedy† to us. You will think I am

* M. de Bausset, the former Bishop of Alais, had just completed his " Life of Fénélon." He had been appointed Councillor of the University, established in this same year, 1808. His " Histoire de Bossuet " was not published until 1814, and he died in 1824, having received the cardinal's hat in 1817.

† Probably the " Chevalier d'Industrie," a comedy in five acts and in verse, performed in 1809.

always having plays read to me; and, in truth, this is the third. I hope after this to be quiet. As I have made it known that I shall scarcely ever go out in the evening, my drawing-room is more crowded than it was at first; the few idlers who are neither in the country, nor with the army, nor yet on their travels, come to meet each other by my fireside. There was excellent company here the day before yesterday : M. Delambre, M. Cuvier, Mademoiselle de Meulan, M. Bertrand, and Madame Devaines, who talked rather loud, but who nevertheless made herself pleasant. I like M. Delambre very much ; he is the essence of kindness and simplicity. I think that Cuvier is what would be called a cleverer man ; his conversation has more point and pungency, but he is rather sarcastic. We talked a great deal about the " Lycées." They are dismayed at the amount of work that has to be done, and at all the obstacles in the way, and say they ought to educate the professors before entrusting pupils to them.

Nothing but departure is talked of here; the officers are going off, and leave-taking has begun again. We shall find it difficult to enliven Paris this winter, unless the rapidity with which the Emperor always outstrips our human foresight causes everything to be over before the bad weather sets in. As you may imagine, there is much said here concerning the recent capitulation; it is considered a fine thing and honourable to our arms. Many details are added, of which I do not believe one word. This is another of the annoyances of life in the capital just now. In the country one sees the newspapers only, and one hears the bare facts, while here one must be constantly on one's guard against gossip invented either in an idle or a malicious spirit.

I scarcely count on letters from you, and I see plainly that I am right. Your valet writes about you to Laure ; I know you are well, and that is enough for me. He says you are continually at work, overwhelmed with petitions, with visitors, with letters, and with lists, and that he cannot conceive how you hold out. I trust that at any rate all the trouble you take will be rewarded by success, and that the plays will succeed and your own services be appreciated. I hear that the theatre at Erfürth was a very bad one and in great disorder. Your southern vivacity must have found full scope for action ; and I, just now, am very far from the vortex in which you are plunged, for I have never been more quiet or more lazy. This physical repose suits my health, and would be of still further benefit did it reach to my poor brain ; you have not the leisure to listen to all the thoughts that pass through my mind, and sometimes distress me in my solitude. Thoughts of all kinds, recollections, sometimes of a painful nature, anxieties, hopes—I know not what, in fact; but all that can occupy the vivid imagination of an unoccupied and dreamy woman.

I have finished Tacitus, for I am not always dreaming. While looking for a book, I came upon " Émile," and I am now reading it. But, *mon ami,*

I must be getting old, for I no longer care so much for Rousseau. His paradoxes strike and displease me much more than formerly, and sometimes I find myself saying aloud, "But this is untrue! he speaks falsely here!" And then I am inclined afterwards to regret having become more critical, for in outliving an illusion, one must always give up a pleasure. Fortunately, your affection and the happiness it procures for me are most sweet truths; they will always accompany me on my life's journey, and will be a constant consolation in the sorrowful experiences that await me in life.

## CXLVII.

### TO M. DE RÉMUSAT AT ERFÜRTH.

Paris, October 12, 1808.

Yesterday was a dreadful day to me. I was obliged, at last, to take that poor child back to school. After spending part of the night in soothing him, for he was too agitated to sleep, I exerted myself all the morning to keep up his courage by my own good spirits. At last, at noon, we set out; Albert crying loudly, for he quite well understood that his brother was leaving home. My poor Charles endeavoured to restrain his tears; as for me, I was choking. Our drive, as you may imagine, was not a lively one. We reached the gloomy place. I stayed there some little while, and when I found my courage was leaving me, I made my escape. . . .

While I am passing my days here in making myself alternately miserable and happy by my own thoughts, you are spending yours in a very different way. I ardently wish that your stay at Erfürth would come to an end before you are tired out. You are present at a grand spectacle; all that crowd of kings set in movement by one man, by the impulse of one single will, is a fine subject for profound reflection and observant curiosity. I like the Emperor Alexander for his admiration of our Emperor, and I hope for results from that great friendship ; but I must confess that my alarm will be revived if, on the Emperor's return, he again leaves us for Spain. I cannot bear to contemplate the risks he will run. Those incidental to war are perhaps the smallest. I wish it were possible to close the road against him. I am convinced that, whatever may be the opinion of a small minority, all France ought to place itself between him and Spain.* If he does not stay in Paris this winter, we may prepare ourselves for a very dull one. Talking of winter, when you return we must think seriously of entertaining more company and carrying out our master's wishes. Our sorrows, my want of spirits, my bad health, and my recent absence have prevented our conforming to the orders we had received, but the

---

* If the reader wishes to appreciate the truth of this almost prophetic passage, he will do well to read the Memoirs of Count Miot de Melito.—TRANSLATORS.

time has now come to set about it. What say you? Otherwise, we shall have to reduce our style of living within the narrowest limits, for all our expenses, or, at least, the cost of everything, will be greatly increased this winter. It is extraordinary how all the necessaries of life become dearer day by day. At the present time, an income of a hundred thousand francs a year would not go so far as half that sum in former times. It is true that luxury has greatly increased. We no longer live in times when a good story at dinner would make up for a course the less; at the dinners of the present day, all the wit lies in the *entrées* and the Madeira. Conversation that must take place by the light of thirty wax candles, in a sumptuously furnished drawing-room, is an expensive amusement, and even at that price wit is not to be had for the asking.

I remember to have seen my mother receive her friends in a small room, lighted by one solitary lamp. At nine o'clock boiling water was brought in; she would make the tea, which her guests drank as they chatted, and after this fashion whiled away the time until the night was far advanced. It would be very difficult to attract people to one's house by such means nowadays; but, then, it is also very difficult to be so agreeable as my mother was.

## CXLVIII.

### TO M. DE RÉMUSAT AT FONTAINEBLEAU.*

Paris, Friday evening, November, 1809.

M. Pasquier is going to Fontainebleau to-morrow, *mon ami*, and offers me his services. I had intended to send your nephew; but M.

* A whole year has elapsed between the last letter and this one. At the date of the opening of the present correspondence the Emperor was in Germany. He had left Paris on April 24, 1809, and had fought the battle of Essling on May 21 and 22, and the battle of Wagram on July 6. He had not returned to Fontainebleau until October 16. Despite his victories the situation of the Empire had become much more grave, and this was felt even at Court. In little notes written by my grandfather, and too short for publication, I constantly met with the following totally new phrase : " The outlook grows terribly dark." My grandparents discerned the decline all the more clearly, because their increasing intimacy with M. de Talleyrand opened their eyes to the truth. Their relations with Talleyrand placed them in a political position which at that period was rather disadvantageous to them than otherwise. In his capacity of superintendent of theatres, my grandfather had been obliged to exercise a sort of patronage towards men of letters in Parisian society. Although he derived this appointment from the Emperor himself, he was gradually becoming distrusted by the latter, whose suspiciousness and defects of character had increased. Hence they stood in a special and not easily explained position ; and while M. de Rémusat was considered by many persons, and considered himself, to have fallen into a kind of disgrace, he was at the same time regarded as a probable Minister of the Interior, which post had been for some time vacant, and to which M. de Montalivet was appointed on October 2. The approaching divorce added to these complications.

Laborie's answer, which I add to my packet and which you will show to M. de Talleyrand, renders this unnecessary. I enclose a letter from the Princess of Benevento. I had sent to her house. And another from the Duchess of Courland,* to whom I had also sent. I hope M. de Talleyrand will be pleased with me. Now for our own affairs. I have written to the Empress; I think my letter pretty good, although rather long. When you give it to her, please make my apologies for its length, and then let her have it, whatever the state of her domestic affairs;—unless a violent quarrel is going on, she will contrive to make use of it.

I have seen Corvisart; he will not do anything. "It is rheumatism," he says; "you must be nursed and kept warm; nothing more." I am not feverish, only a little weak; but as I have no occasion for strength, I like my state very well, and thoroughly enjoy my room, my bed, and my quietude. Yesterday, to pass away the time, I sent for Charles. After the classes were over, they allowed him to come. He was as fresh and rosy as possible; we kissed again and again, and had a long talk together. His masters are satisfied with him; his class is very advanced. Auvray† says that the seventh and eighth are very good places. He would have been much higher up, only that he thought the verb after the word *la plupart*

* The Duchess of Courland was a friend of M. de Talleyrand.

† M. Auvray was one of the Professors at the Lycée Napoléon. He was subsequently Inspector of the University.

should always be in the singular, and in speaking of several persons he wrote "La plupart *avait . . .* etc." Muzine continues to bully him a little; he works him hard at Greek; he is translating passages from Isocrates, and is very proud of it. All this he told me while romping with his brother on my bed. Next, he dressed himself in his new coat to show it to me; that coat, you know, that I did not want him to wear lest he should not look well in it. *Mon ami*, how silly I was! As if anything could fail to look well on Charles! He is charming in the coat; I was in despair at having no one to whom I could say so, and I resolved I would write it to you. At eight o'clock my little visitors left me, and Bertrand arrived. He is very sallow and very melancholy. We talked over our illnesses—he of *jaundice*, and I of *rheumatism*. He thought me very good company. I have seen Countess Rumford and my cousin, and that is all. It is said that the King of Saxony * will not arrive before Monday. M. de Talleyrand will be very gay at Meaux. He is designated (not the King of Saxony) as President of the Corps Législatif; others name the Arch-chancellor. People announce the arrival of the Pope at St. Denis; they change the places of all the kings; they know something of the gallantries at Fontainebleau; they narrate these adventures, and ask me questions. To all of them I make my favourite answer, "I don't know."

* M. de Talleyrand had been despatched to Meaux, to meet the King of Saxony, who arrived in Paris on November 13.

I have seen Picard; he has written to you concerning the state of things at the Opera. Everything is going amiss; however, you will have
" Cortez " * and " Orphée." By-the-by, it has
occurred to me, in my wisdom, that you ought
not to have " Athalie " acted at Court; there
are passages which might be applied to the
religious question, such as *" rompez tout pacte
avec l'impiété,"* and that would spoil all, after
your exertions.† People would resent it to you
that their feelings were wounded without their
having the right to complain, and this in presence
of a religious king! I submit this little piece of
advice to you; I carry caution very far, as you
know.

*Mon ami*, the delight that I felt in putting on
my dressing-gown again, and sitting down by my fire
with nothing to do but to rest myself, convinces
me more than ever that I am quite old, and that
if I were sensible enough to adopt the ways of my
real age,‡ I should do well. "But your head," I
hear you say, " and your heart?" Ah! I certainly
still like them to retain their activity; but a good
deal may be done in that way from one's easy-
chair, and though I have not stirred from my
chimney corner, I assure you I have not been
asleep there. I have amused myself with going

* "Fernand Cortez," an opera by Spontini, and a revival of
Gluck's "Orpheus."

† From the previous June, the rupture between the Emperor
and the Pope had been complete.

‡ She was then nine and twenty.

over my past life, and I found you everywhere.
This put me in a good humour, so I ventured a
glance into the future; you were present in all
my projects as in all my recollections, and yet my
reveries were very sweet! Great repose of body,
and some agitation, or rather some emotion for the
heart—this is what I require. But, ah me! I am
involved in a vortex, and I can neither arrest nor
endure the movement that bears me along.

Adieu, my dearest; I wish you a good night, and
am now going to bed, for it is ten o'clock already.
You are very good to have written to me this
morning; I did not expect it, you are so busy!
M. Pasquier will bring me news of you on Monday,
and also news of our friend.* He must allow me
to call him by that name, which by no means
diminishes the respect due to him. Talk to him
about me. If he were here I would tell him all
that I have been thinking of in my solitude; for
he, too, entered into my solitary reveries. He
had the arranging of everything, and it was all
well done. I continue to be amused with his
Gourville, though it is rather confused; I am
going to read Cardinal de Retz over again, so as
to find myself once more in the good old times
I have too much neglected. I am now ready for
" Memoirs " again. Adieu; I am talking a great
deal, and you will have something else to attend
to on Sunday, besides my chatter.

* M. de Talleyrand.

## CXLIX.

Paris, Sunday evening, December, 1809.

*Bonsoir, mon ami*; my day is over, and before going to bed I must say a few words to you. I regretted you to-day; we passed a pleasant time, your boy and I, and I am very much pleased with him. I must tell you that yesterday Madame Pastoret told me the censor, Dumas, had said to her that Charles was one of the most promising boys of this year at the college. This put me in good spirits. The dear little fellow then came in, and behaved very nicely. I saw M. de Talleyrand for an instant this evening; he seemed vexed at not being at Trianon. "Formerly," he said, "when the Emperor was in trouble, he used to send for me." I felt the bitterness of such a reflection, and tried to divert him from it by speaking on other subjects, but he was really grieved.*

I greatly fear that you are having the same bad weather as ourselves; it is raining in torrents,

---

* The divorce was approaching, and the Emperor, after a violent scene with the Empress, had gone to Trianon. That scene had been described in the *Moniteur*. Both of them, in presence of the Imperial family, had declared that they renounced their marriage. This occurrence at Fontainebleau had prepared the way for the event, but the situation was not made public until the *senatus-consultum* of December 16, and the departure of the Emperor for Trianon, where he remained until December 25.

and the country must be very dull. I am going to-morrow to Malmaison. I shed tears this morning over the *Moniteur ;* all the speeches are fine, and make a good impression. Every one I saw yesterday and to-day had been moved by them. People repeat to each other that the Emperor wept! Such tears are pleasing to us women ; the tears of men, and especially of kings, can scarcely fail to produce an effect, and you men are well aware of that.

---

## CL.

### TO M. DE RÉMUSAT AT TRIANON.*

Malmaison, December, 1809.

I had hoped for a moment that you would have accompanied the Emperor yesterday, and that I should have seen you. Independently of the pleasure of seeing you, I wanted to talk to you. I hope there will be some opportunity for Trianon to-day, and I will keep my letter ready.

I was received here with real affection. All is very sad, as you may suppose. The Empress, who has no more need of effort, is greatly cast down ; she weeps incessantly, and it is really painful to see her. Her children are full of courage. The Viceroy is come—he keeps her up as much as possible ; they are both of the greatest use to her.

* This letter has already appeared in the Memoirs, but it is so important in its place in the correspondence that it is thought well to retain it here.

Yesterday I had a conversation with the Queen of Holland. I will repeat it to you as succinctly as possible. "The Empress," said she, "has been deeply touched by the readiness which you have shown to share her fate. I am not surprised at it, but out of friendship to you, I beg of you to reflect. Your husband is placed near the Emperor; all your instincts ought to be on that side. Will not your position be frequently false and embarrassing? Can you bring yourself to renounce the advantages attached to the service of a young and reigning Empress? Think of it well; I give you a friend's advice, and you ought to reflect." I thanked the Queen sincerely, but replied that I could not see any objection to my taking this step, which appeared the only proper one for me; that if the Empress foresaw any difficulty in retaining in her service the wife of a man who was in the Emperor's, then I would retire, but that, unless such was the case, I would greatly prefer to remain with her; that I knew there would be certain advantages for persons attached to the great Court, but that their loss was more than compensated to me by the consciousness of fulfilling a duty, and of being useful to the Empress, if she valued my services; that I did not think the Emperor could be displeased with my conduct, etc., etc. "There is only one consideration, madame," said I, in addition, "which could induce me for one moment to regret the part I have taken. I will tell you very frankly what that is. It is impossible that there should not be, in the interior of this little Court here, some indiscretion, some gossip, something or other which, being repeated to the Emperor, may bring about a momentary annoyance. The Empress, good as she is, is sometimes distrustful. I do not know whether the proof of devotion which I am now giving her will shelter me completely from a passing suspicion which would greatly grieve me. I acknowledge that if it should happen, even once, that my husband or myself were suspected of meditating an indiscretion, on one side or the other, I would immediately quit the Empress." The Queen replied that I was quite right, and that she hoped her mother would be prudent. She then embraced me, and said that she knew that the Empress wished in her heart to have me with her. I needed nothing more, in the mind in which as you know I am, to decide me.

Now let me know what you think. I know that my position will often be embarrassing, but with prudence and true attachment may not everything come right ? Madame de là Rochefoucauld seems to me to want to get away—she has even, I think, said something to the Emperor ; but her position is different. She will render the same services to the Empress, but without annuity or pension. In her circumstances, that may suit her, but I must act otherwise ; and, indeed, the more I question myself, the more I feel that my place is here. Put all this together, reflect, and then decide ; and remember that I have time. We are given until the 1st of January.

One would need to be very happy to find this

place pleasant at this season; but there is an abominable wind, and it is always raining. The weather has not, however, prevented a succession of visitors all day long. Each visitor makes her tears flow. Nevertheless, it is no harm that all her impressions should thus be renewed in succession; afterwards she will rest. I think that I shall remain here until Saturday. I wish you could come then, because we really ought to meet and be a little while together. It is not necessary, in order to appreciate your presence, that I should be deprived of it; and, in good truth, the more I see of agitation and troubles of all kinds around me, the more I feel how dear you are, and that I love the repose and the happiness that come to me from you.

Friday.

I could not find an opportunity of sending my letter this morning. I hope there may be one this evening. The Empress has passed a wretched morning. She receives visitors, who renew her grief, and then every time anything reaches her from the Emperor, she gets into a terrible state. We must find means, either through the Grand Marshal or the Prince de Neuchâtel, to induce the Emperor to moderate the expression of his regret and affliction when he writes to her, because, when he dwells in this way upon his grief, she falls into real despair, and seems to lose her head completely. I do all in my power for her; it gives me terrible pain to see her. She is gentle, sad, and affectionate; in fact, it is heartrending. By affecting her so deeply, the Emperor increases her sufferings. In the midst of all this, she never says a word too much, she never utters a bitter complaint; she is really like an angel. I induced her to take a walk this morning; I wanted to try to fatigue her body in order to rest her mind. She complied mechanically. I talked to her, I questioned her, I did all I could; she seconded my efforts, understanding my intentions, and seemed grateful to me in the midst of her tears. At the end of an hour, I acknowledge that I was almost fainting with the effort that I had made, and for a few minutes was almost as weak as herself. " It seems to me sometimes," said she, "that I am dead, and that there remains to me only a sort of vague consciousness that I am no longer living."

Try, if you can, to make the Emperor understand that he ought to write to her encouragingly, and not in the evening, for it gives her frightful and terrible nights. She does not know how to bear up against his sorrow; no doubt she could still less bear with his coldness; but there is a medium. I saw her yesterday in such a state, after the Emperor's last letter, that I was on the point of writing myself to Trianon.

Adieu, *cher ami*. I do not say much of my own health; you know how feeble it is, and all this tries it. After this week, I shall want a little rest with you. To find anything pleasant, I must be at home with my dear one.

## CLI.

Paris, Monday morning, December, 1809.

A thousand thanks, *mon ami*, for your letter. I was awakened by its arrival this morning. I am rejoiced at what you tell me; I do not suppose that the delay of a few days can inconvenience your business arrangements very much, and I presume that the Grand Marshal, knowing your presence to be necessary here, will help you, later, to obtain the leave of absence that you will require. It is surely impossible that in the solitude of Trianon you can fail to find an opportunity of making explanations to the Emperor, which will restore you to his confidence, and you should neglect nothing towards a justification of yourself, which is necessary on behalf of the other branches of the administration with which you are entrusted. My good husband must needs gain by being heard; I therefore feel great hopes, if you can obtain a hearing.

I should also advise you to have some conversation with the Grand Marshal, provided that you think it well to do so, concerning your attitude towards M. de Montesquiou. Tell him (and it will be the truth) that you cannot entertain the suspicions of his want of good faith towards you, which are generally attributed to him in society, but that you have observed that the narrow mind and uneasy temper of the Grand Chamberlain lead him to take precautions that do harm in every way, because of the misunderstanding they cause between you. It would be well if M. de Montesquiou had a mind like yours; all would go smoothly then, and you would have an easier life. I repeat that, if the Emperor will hear you, your days will once again be peaceful; but if the time of favour is over for us, be quite without anxiety on my account; I shall adopt another kind of life with all the resignation you can wish for. I have attained the age of reason; every day my tastes become more serious, and I assure you, with all the sincerity of a heart that is yours alone, that in any life that would be peaceful for you, I should be perfectly happy. There was a time when I could not have believed in happiness far from Paris; but I have a conviction that my days will be serene in retirement, should we become the victims of the mean intrigues that may be formed against us. May Heaven forbid this, however! Meanwhile, with courage and prudence, you will be able to avoid or endure the trials which are perhaps in store for us. . . .

## CLII.

Paris, April, 1810.

Thanks for your letter of yesterday. I was beginning to grumble at your silence. From the bottom of my heart I pity you for the life you are leading; but I am not surprised that the audience slept, or pretended to sleep, at "Britannicus." It was a brilliant idea of yours certainly, and you had a good answer to give to questions on the subject: "The play was by request!"† Amuse yourself with a safe conscience with the innocent actors of the Feydeau theatre, and be of good courage. If you were pious, you would find plenty of exercise for patience during Holy Week.

* There is an interval of four months between this letter and the last. The year 1810, which was that of the Emperor's marriage (on April 2), was comparatively a year of peace. After his marriage, the Emperor and his new consort went to Compiègne, where they passed the remainder of Lent.

† The Emperor himself selected the play he wished to be performed at Court. He asked for "Britannicus," and no one recollected in time that it contained certain scenes which, after the recent divorce, might be taken as personal allusions. Talma became confused in uttering the following lines:—

> " Non que pour Octavie un reste de tendresse
> M'attache à son hymen et plaigne sa jeunesse . . .
> D'aucun gage, Narcisse, ils n'honorent ma couche.
> L'empire vainement demande un héritier."

The audience were equally embarrassed. The Emperor pretended to be asleep.

I heard of our boy yesterday; he is quite well. He will come on Sunday, to prepare for his first Communion. If the time be fixed for Easter, and you are not back from Compiègne, then I shall ask leave to spend a few days at Navarre, if my health permits.* They say here that the Empress is never coming back; if you can write to me by some safe messenger, whenever there is anything concerning her, you would do me a real kindness.

Did I tell you that Lemercier† was elected? Our old members of the Institute are furious. I amused myself yesterday by teazing Suard and the abbé; for my own part, I am glad of it because of the money. I have read his ode, which he had recited to me. *Ma foi*, all things considered, I think it very bad, with the exception of a few fine ideas, and I return to Esménard, or rather to nothing, for it is all very poor.

M. de Fontanes dined here yesterday; also M. and Madame de Ganay, Bertrand, Lebreton, and Norvins. The Grand Master was quite at his ease and in very good humour; it is true that we all vied in spoiling him. How pompous he is about everything! I made myself agreeable, but in my secret heart his vanity was displeasing to

---

* The Château de Navarre in Normandy had been bestowed on the Empress Joséphine.

† Lemercier had just been elected member of that class of the Institute which represented the French Academy. He had, in spite of his Republicanism, written an ode on the Emperor's marriage, in order to render his election possible. Esménard was an author of some distinction, and wrote some good verses.

me.  He is positively quite in love with Madame
de G——, who, on her side, has not the least
objection ; such things do not displease us women,
do they ?  Are we not, for the most part, curious
creatures ?  We play the coquette, we foresee what
is coming, we do all we can to bring it about, we
amuse ourselves with it, and then, when the crisis
is reached and a declaration is made, we are
angry, we stand on our dignity, and are to be appeased with difficulty.  Nevertheless, *monsieur*,
you may make your declaration to me whenever
you choose.

I enclose you a letter from M. de Lezay-Marnésia.
Two big boxes were brought to me yesterday, with
a request that I would send them immediately to
St. Cloud.  I did not know how to set about this,
so I opened M. de Lezay's letter and perceived
that there was breathing time.  Tell me what you
would like done with the boxes, and whether you
will answer M. de Lezay ; or shall I write to him ? *

*Bonjour, cher ami.*  I am not unwell ; with the
exception of my head and neck, I am much better.
Nor is Joséphin unwell either.  I believe he has
made up his mind to go into Provence with M. de
Villeneuve,† who intends to start on May 5.  He
is in a tolerably amiable frame of mind, and the

---

* The Prefect M. de Lezay-Marnésia had ordered a fancy
costume for the future King of Rome, who was not born until a
year afterwards, and this costume was contained in the two
boxes.  There was certainly no hurry.

† M. de Villeneuve-Bargemon, Referendaire at the Cour
des Comptes, was made a Prefect and Director-General under
the Restoration.

house is very quiet. Lebreton comes to see me every day; he is a kind and excellent friend, whose heart is a hundred times better than his head. I say this so that you may not say I am misled by his cleverness; he is sincerely attached to you and to me. Some of your books were shown yesterday; it was an opportunity for speaking of you; I was greatly pleased at the way in which our friend spoke of you to Fontanes, and you know I am not easily satisfied.

## CLIII.

### TO M. DE RÉMUSAT AT COMPIÈGNE.

Tuesday, April, 1810.

. . . I saw M. de Talleyrand yesterday on his return from Compiègne. He had been travelling for two nights, and looked as fresh as if he had just got out of bed.* He gave me news of you, and hoped to have brought me a letter from you, but I see you have hardly time. I am vexed at the length of your absence. Three weeks more before I shall see you! This is a long and wearisome separation. You cannot picture to yourself how I grieve about it. It was long since we had been parted, and the delightful habit of being with you had regained its old influence over me. Each day I feel your companionship more necessary.

---

* M. de Talleyrand was then in his fifty-seventh year.

I think that our minds are more than ever in unison, that our opinions are more often the same, and that we now know all the charm of union. In youth, a diversity of tastes and opinions, which at that time is more strongly felt, does no harm to love, and indeed contributes to it, by affording opportunities of self-sacrifice ; but when years have crept upon us, quieter and safer joys become preferable, and harmony and unity are then our best happiness.

You will admit, this time, that I am writing for the pleasure of writing, and truly there is nothing in Paris for me to tell you, nor even in my own little circle. I am lazily lying in bed ; the weather is cold ; I have not the least inclination to go out, and find myself very comfortable, with my desk on my knees, writing to you all that comes into my head, or rather my heart.

Madame de Vintimille is better ; this last attack is almost over ; but the future must always be alarming for her. And for whom is it not ? I am often inclined to smile when I hear of some bodily predisposition that is a cause of anxiety for after life ; I laugh at myself, rather sadly, it is true, for my own fears. We fear that such an ailment may cause our death ; we take all kinds of precautions ; we seek all manner of relief, and, poor fools that we are ! the natural course of things leads us more surely than aught else to the death that we would fain escape ! Is not life itself a first cause of death ? The more reasonable plan, perhaps, would be to forecast nothing and to avoid nothing.

# CLIV.

Paris, Holy Wednesday, April 18, 1810.

I have something to tell you that will give you pleasure—Charles is first in his class. I enclose two letters that I received yesterday; you will see that he signs " Charles, First," and that M. de Wailly * is pleased with him. I wrote to Fontanes to ask leave to take him out this week, because I wish him to attend some of the Church services, and to see the *curé*. I shall therefore have the dear boy with me to-morrow; we shall pray together,† he shall go out for walks, he shall

---

* M. de Wailly was Proviseur of the Lycée Napoléon.

† My grandmother alludes frequently in these letters to her tendency towards a piety, somewhat vague indeed, and yet more decided than that of most of her contemporaries. It may be well, perhaps, to mention here what was my father's opinion of the religious beliefs of his parents. " My mother," he writes, " had not been surrounded in childhood by persons of strong religious feeling. She had been brought up in the general creed of Christianity reduced to simple and easy practice, carefully severed from those accessories that, since the seventeenth century, there had been a constantly increasing endeavour to suppress, and she was preserved from difficulties by a general recommendation not to trouble herself about them. Her strongest feeling was, therefore, not so much a fervent faith, as an aversion to unbelief, which indeed had been censured by the Revolution, and a preference for religion, for it appealed both to her heart and her imagination. She was one of those persons to whom ' Le Génie du Christianisme ' made a timely appeal, and she had enjoyed the book. But she was

study. We will try to spend our time well, and we will write a few lines to Compiègne. If you

not disposed to devotion, properly so called, and during her youth it was an unknown element in the world in which she lived. Religion, conceived with moderation and practised with common sense, in no wise resembled the party doctrine abounding in childish superstitions, historical paradoxes, and political calculations, which at the present time is called by that name. As she advanced in age, and also through the influence of my father, who was not a believer, but who had been brought up at the Oratoire on a religious system, my mother, whose mind was more and more attracted to the writers of the seventeenth century, became better acquainted with the dogmas of Christianity, and she also experienced impulses towards piety, of which she gives an accurate description in her letters. For a long time her outward observances had been limited to hearing Mass on Sundays, and even this with irregularity on account of her ill health. In the autumn of 1811, she over-exerted herself in acting Elmire in 'Le Tartuffe,' at Madame de Labriche's house in the Marais (her daughter, Madame Molé, was passionately fond of acting), and she then began to suffer from an affection of the chest that had not been hitherto included among her other ailments. In October she had an attack of pneumonia, which, without being very severe, ran the whole course of the disease. Reflections that are the natural result of illness to Christian minds then occurred to her, and after a lapse of sixteen years she confessed and communicated on Easter Tuesday, 1812. It was thus, as she relates it in a few pages, that she returned to a greater regularity in the practice of her religion. But strict exactitude therein, and severe orthodoxy, were alike unsuited to her. Her clear judgment, her serious sincerity, her dearest affections, forbade her from considering it a universally rigorous duty to believe in and practise certain observances which do not result necessarily from nature, but occur accidentally from the history of humanity. Within this limit, then, she was a Christian, with sincere feelings, and afterwards with the independence which philosophic liberalism gives to religion. By a reverse action, of which there are innumerable examples, the Revolution had helped to place her on the side of religion;

have a spare moment, write him a few words to praise him for being first, and then say something to me, too.

It is weary work to be so long without a word from you; I begin to lose patience, and to reflect that in the salon for the Gentlemen-in-Waiting there must always be some table or other, with a sheet of paper and an inkstand, on which you might write to your wife that you are quite well, and that she is not forgotten. . . .

I send you some papers about the Opera that I found by chance on the table in the anteroom. As for me, I am immersed in the most serious meditations. I read yesterday an admirable sermon on death, by Massillon. It alternately depressed and consoled me ; it would be better to have that read to you at Compiègne than Abbé de Ranzau's * "Passion," which is said to be very commonplace. It is well to speak of death to the fortunate ones of the earth, and the words " dust," " tomb," and " the nothingness of life " ought to be heard in the palace of kings.

The Minister of Police said yesterday, on his return, that Lemercier's ode had been liked at

the Restoration drove her from the Church party. In reality, she differed less than she imagined from the state of mind of the ' Vicaire Savoyard,' if we add to it a liking for the religious writers of the seventeenth century, and consequently for Jansenism, and a marked preference for positive religion over pantheism."

* The Abbé de Ranzau, chaplain to the Emperor, became known under the Restoration by his zeal for the missions that were preached in France.

Compiègne. Have you heard anything about it ?
If so, pray tell me ; it would give such pleasure to
you know whom. Constance is not very well ; this
spring time is disastrous to delicate constitutions.
Take care of your health ; it is my comfort and my
most precious possession. Next in order are
Charles's rosy cheeks ; but I say it from my heart,
they come *next*. I have not arrived at that point
of maternity at which one prefers one's children to
everything. When I was young, people used to say
to me, " It will come." But I have hardly reached
it yet, and I feel that it does *not* come ; whose
fault is that, think you ?

---

## CLV.

### TO M. DE RÉMUSAT AT COMPIÈGNE.

Paris, April, 1810.

I may expect you, then, next week, and I shall
remain in Paris. I am very undecided about
Navarre, not on account of my health, for I am
beginning to accustom myself not to take it much
into account ; but it just happens that I have no
*dormeuse* here, and I do not know in what carriage
to travel. I wrote yesterday to the Empress,
asking how she is. I shall be guided by her
answer, and then if you come here, we can talk it
over.

Did I not send you a nice letter from Charles ?

It arrived last night; and I gave myself the treat of reading it. In the mean time, M. de Talleyrand came in, and I showed it to him ; he was greatly amused, for it is really ingenuous.

There are anecdotes current here, concerning the Court and the life you are all leading at Compiègne. These stories are in general malevolent ; they turn upon the haughty manners of the Empress, and the hardness of her disposition, and then the *other* one is remembered. All this will make her position difficult. It is said that Joséphine is to be Duchesse de Navarre only; that she is to reside in the duchy of Berg ; that Malmaison is to be bought back from her ; that our new sovereign lady has expressed a great objection to her proximity ; and in support of this assertion, expressions are quoted which are clearly inventions, because it is impossible that any one could have had an opportunity of hearing them. I await your return to learn the truth.

## CLVI.

### TO M. DE RÉMUSAT AT COMPIÈGNE.

Paris, April, 1810.

We hear that the Français is going to Compiègne ; the journey to St. Quentin is therefore given up, and also the return to Paris. I am very much disappointed, for I was expecting you home this week, and I see I must give up all hope of that. I am decidedly tired of your absence, however, and of all your side of the house being shut up. . . .

Just at this moment I suppose you are getting up ; it is seven o'clock, and your tiresome day is beginning. You will see our friend * to-day. He is very kind to me in my loneliness, and comes to see me nearly every day. He found me, on Friday, in a state of enchantment over a sermon of Massillon's which is well adapted to the weakness of our poor human nature. From our very defects he augurs our future virtue. The more vain and ambitious we may have been, the more nobly and devotedly shall we serve God ; the more we have loved nature, so much the more shall we love God ; a tender and feeling heart is one step towards the Divinity. I told M. de Talleyrand that I was very glad to find my friendship for him was one of the steps of the ladder by which I might climb to the love of God, and I made him read several passages of the sermon, which it was strange to hear from his lips. After his visit Savary† arrived. He asked many questions about our little Court at Navarre, and also about the future of our son, who seemed to him ready for the army. While I was receiving my visitors, every one was at Longchamps, which was most brilliant, I am told ; but I had not given it a thought. I am unwilling to move whenever the weather is fine, and longing to be out when it

---

* M. de Talleyrand.

† Savary, Duc de Rovigo, was not at that time Minister of Police. He was not appointed to the office until June 2, 1810.

rains. This is being admirably adapted to the seasons!

The *booby* always insists on my mentioning him; he went yesterday to the funeral of poor Chaudet, who, on returning from Compiègne, died of vexation at having been ordered to make a bust of the Empress, in conjunction with another artist.* He was ill, congestion of the lungs ensued, and he died. Talking of artists, they are all wishing for you. I saw Chérubini at the Odéon yesterday, and he wants you to come back, to help him to get his Mass performed at a concert. The Mass is said to be splendid; I asked him to have it performed at my house, and he promised me he would. If it really is so remarkably good, it might perhaps be executed on some occasion of ceremony. However, he did not seem to take to the idea, and appears no longer to care for composing music for the great ones of the earth. He is at work at an *opéra comique*,† and does not seem to be thinking of his grand opera.

* I am ignorant who this *booby* was. Chaudet, a sculptor and painter, had a great reputation. The statue of the Emperor, that until 1814 was on the Vendôme Column, was his work, as was Dugommier's statue at Versailles, and several graceful productions, such as " Œdipe enfant," " L'Amour séduisant l'Âme," " Paul et Virginie," etc. He was born in 1763.

† This *opéra comique*, by Chérubini, is probably the " Crescendo," which met with no success at the Feydeau.

## CLVII.

### TO M. DE RÉMUSAT AT COMPIÈGNE.

Paris, April 25, 1810.

I am writing to you, *mon ami*, without knowing whether my letter can go, or whether the Emperor is at St. Quentin, whether you are to accompany him, whether you are coming home, or remaining where you are. . . .

People are beginning to take their departure. Madame d'Houdetôt is at Sannois. The time is short, and I am sorry when I think that I, too, must go away somewhere. But where? and how? All this uncertainty wearies me, and I try my best not to look beyond the end of each day. I should not dislike this one, if it could bring you back to me in the evening ; I persuade myself this may be the case, and then I am vexed with myself for the delusion. What weak creatures we are ; so easily troubled ; with so little tendency to what is good ! And I—I am the weakest and most imperfect of all ! Ah ! I say it in all humility. Whatever is good in me I owe to you ; it is you who have sheltered, supported, and guided me ; without your sense, your affection, and the happiness I owe you, I should perhaps have been of very little worth, and it is in you alone that I place all my pride.

Amédée * has come back quite enchanted with Italy ; the two together compose elegies on France.

* Amédée Pastoret.

Love of country is not in fashion. What else can I tell you? There is nothing new here, and I know but little about the theatres. Holy Week has kept me away from them. I know that people crowded the Française to suffocation, to see Talma in "Manlius." Madame Corria is not much liked; she is considered inferior to the two others, and rightly so; she is talented nevertheless. Her voice is smothered in fat; she is an enormous mass rolling about on the boards. M. de Forbin's* novel excites controversy in society; he is told of the various opinions on it, and becomes quite indignant. He says that when a man in society takes the trouble to write a book, society, out of *esprit de corps*, ought to defend it. Lemercier went to see the Abbé Morellet. "Monsieur," said he on entering, "this is not a visit of thanks." "Oh! as to that," answered the abbé, "I dispense with your thanks, for if I had been listened to, you would never have belonged to the Academy." "And why so, sir?" "Ah! because, above all, one should speak *French*." "But which of my works has given you this opinion of me?" "Unfortunately, all those that I have met with; among the rest, your ode, which contains forty mistakes in *French*." "And yet, sir, it was on the very day it was published that I was elected one of the Forty. Is not that a striking fact?" "Oh, I

* M. Auguste de Forbin, an amateur artist, who under the Restoration was made Director of the Louvre, had written a novel called "Charles Barimore." He died in 1841, in the sixty-third year of his age.

know you have wit, and plenty of it, but if there are two or three similar elections the language will be ruined."

Lemercier told me all this, with good humour and a certain simplicity which was, however, far removed from humility.

---

## CLVIII.

### TO M. DE RÉMUSAT AT PARIS.

Avallon, Friday, June 21, 1810.

Oh, how delightful a thing it is to travel post,* and how pleasant to wait for postillions, to put on the drag, to toil uphill, to break the traces, and at last to arrive at an inn at Avallon, after spending the whole day in such a cloud of dust that the plan of a landscape garden might be traced on my gown !

I should much like to know what Madame Pastoret, with all her cleverness, could find to say here, and what fine feelings she would have experienced during the journey I have just made ? Such heat, such a stifling wind, dust of which I had never seen the like, such discomfort, in fact, and such weariness, I scarcely had time to think of anything whatsoever. Add to this the pleasant

* The Emperor and the Empress Marie Louise returned to St. Cloud on May 31, after visiting St. Quentin, Antwerp, Brussels, Ghent, Ostend, Lille, Le Havre, and Rouen. Madame de Rémusat left Paris a few days later, to join the Empress Joséphine at Aix, a watering-place in Savoy.

reflection that all these delights are carrying me away from you, and you will have some idea of the day I have gone through! In the morning, however, I had experienced a little patriotic emotion ; *
I had been affected by finding myself once more in Burgundy; but my native dust has rather cooled my ardour this evening, and I beheld Auxerre and the banks of the Yonne with calmness. As for Augustine, she is in a state of perpetual enchantment. Although very far from Val-de-Suzon, the dialect of her own country is spoken here ; she beholds the headgear she was accustomed to, houses like her own, and she is delighted.

I am not over tired. I shall reach Autun early to-morrow, and will write to you on Sunday, and also to my sister, to whom you must tell all my news. Remember me to Madame de Grasse ; next to you and Charles, it is she whom I most regret. I feel this, and she will believe it. Almost every minute I am saying, "If Madame de Grasse were here, we would do such a thing ; she would say so and so." And I am ready to cry! Poor thing! she has been spending the evening in solitude. I have been following you in thought ; you are now at St. Cloud with *Les États de Blois.* It sounds funny at Avallon, *Les États de Blois!* I seem to belong to another world, and do not know whereabouts I am. . . .

* M. de Vergennes' family belonged to Burgundy.

## CLX.

TO M. DE RÉMUSAT AT PARIS.

Aix, Savoy, Friday, June 29, 1810.

I am here at last, and it was time I arrived, for I am very tired. Yesterday was the most fatiguing day of all, and as I know that it is pleasant to hear of what befals one's friends on their travels, and that all I have to do is to narrate my experiences, please to listen. You must know that my stay at Lyons did not rest me much. I explored the town more from human respect than from any wish to see it. I was even then rather unwell; and, besides, my bed was so uncomfortable that I passed the first night in an armchair. The second night, after much turning and tossing about, I suddenly sprang up at three o'clock in the morning, and went off to harangue Augustine, who was sleeping soundly. The effect of my discourse was to stir up the whole house. Horses were ordered, and we set off on our journey; but by the time we had travelled seven or eight leagues the heat became stifling, the air heavy, and we were seized with headache, and with a sort of nervous affection that was most painful. We continued our route, however, but never in my life was I so ill at ease; at last the storm broke. As we were nearing the mountains, a great tempest arose, with showers of hail that devastated all the surrounding crops in a moment. Fortunately, we were able to reach the Pont de Beauvoisin, and I waited at the inn for the storm to be over; it was then four o'clock. I did not want to remain there, and yet was afraid to go on, and we were still, they told me, six hours from Chambéry. At length, when the thunder was passing away, we resumed our journey; but the rain gave us a somewhat melancholy impression of the country. The Échelles road will be a fine one when completed, but at present it is encumbered with stone for the parapets, with carts, and with workmen, and is very inconvenient. We had good horses and a careful driver, yet Augustine was in such a state of terror that I was seriously alarmed. Once, when we were on the mountain side, with a precipice beneath us, she was so overcome with fear that she began to scream. I endeavoured to soothe her, but she had lost all control over herself. I scolded, I coaxed, but nothing was of any avail. I was not in the least nervous myself, but suffered a good deal from the continual jolting. I wonder whether you recollect that last hill, after the Échelles, in which the road has been cut through the rock, and only oxen are used for traffic? The rain was ceasing, so I walked up, for the only means of relief was a change in the form of fatigue. It is really a most extraordinary road, but one ought to be in good health to go in search of a cure in this fashion. I arrived at last at Chambéry, at eleven o'clock at night, quite worn out with fatigue. I slept better than at Lyons, and this morning, at eight, we entered Aix.

I am suffering less than yesterday, and am writing in bed, the most singular bed in the world. There is a paillasse of wheaten straw, and a mattress of I do not know what material. Madame de Grasse, who objects to feather beds for me, would approve of this. The country through which we came seemed very pretty, but this village is ugly. The Empress is living in a small house with Madame d'Audenarde, and I have been put into another with MM. de Turpin and Pourtalis.*  I was not expected to arrive before Sunday. I found a large room destined for me, but without any furniture whatever. Augustine is exerting herself to procure a table, a chair, etc. And I am writing to you, and trying to laugh at all these absurd annoyances.

The Empress has paid me a visit; she is well, seems to be in good spirits, and goes about a good deal. I hope I shall not have to accompany her just yet, for I am really in want of rest. There are no visitors here besides herself and us; she seemed very glad to see me, and, as usual, was all kindness.

This is how things are, *cher ami*. I shall write to you very often; I foresee that will be my only pleasure. I mean to try and profit by the waters here, and repair the fatigues of my journey. I have

---

* Madame d'Audenarde, the mother of General d'Audenarde. She was Lady-in-Waiting. M. de Turpin-Crissé, of the Empress's household, was known as a landscape painter of some talent. M. Fritz Pourtalis, also belonging to the Empress's household, was from Neuchâtel. His elder brother died in Paris, about twenty years ago, leaving a fine collection of pictures and antiquities.

some hopes of receiving letters to-day—the post comes in daily; you must all write punctually and take compassion on my loneliness. I embrace you tenderly.

## CLXI.

### TO M. DE RÉMUSAT AT PARIS.

Aix, Savoy, July 2, 1810.

What are you all about that you do not write to me, and especially that faithless woman on whom I relied, and who has failed me like the rest? What do you imagine us to be doing here, and with what do you expect me to be occupying myself? You really deserve that I also should take to silence, and I see that you are counting on the idleness of my life. Don't deceive yourself, however; I have not quite as much leisure time as you might imagine. I bathe at eight o'clock, and then return to bed until ten. At eleven I breakfast at the palace, and all the rest of the morning we read and work. The Empress, as you know, likes to have people about her, and does not retire to her own room before four o'clock, or even five sometimes. I then go to mine; I read a little or I write; dinner is at six; after dinner we walk about. I am sometimes excused from accompanying her on account of my *infirmities*. . . .

## CLXII.

Aix, Savoy, Friday, July 6, 1810.

*Mon ami*, another day has gone by, and no letter from you. I say to myself that your week of waiting at St. Cloud must have left you but little leisure, and yet I suffer and torment myself just as if this reason for taking comfort did not exist. Yesterday, as we were on our way to Chambéry, the Empress was met by her courier ; he was the bearer of a letter from the Viceroy, containing an account of the accident at the Austrian ambassador's ball.* It seems there were about twenty persons burned. I shuddered as I listened to the Viceroy's letter.  I was expecting to hear your name, and I was in an agony.  When the Empress ceased reading, I burst into tears, and I know not how it was, but nothing could calm me ; a violent headache came on, and in that state I had to endure a drive of ten leagues. Less than this would have sufficed to make me very ill.  I got back at eight o'clock with a frightful headache ; I passed a restless night, and am completely knocked up this morning. . . .

* During the grand ball given by Prince Schwarzenberg on July 2, in honour of the Emperor's marriage, a fire broke out, and a great number of persons perished, the Princess included.

## CLXIII.

At last I have a letter from you! . . . If you care to know what we are doing here, I must tell you things are just as usual. With the exception of a few visits from Chambéry, we live all to ourselves. A little reading in the morning, a drive afterwards, dinner at eight on account of the heat, then cards and a little music. Charles de Flahault is here, and M. and Madame de Chateaubriand. There is also a Madame de Sales, a descendant of the family of St. Francis de Sales. She seems pleasant enough, but you can understand that in presence of the Empress there is always a certain amount of ceremony. Joséphine herself is serene and mild. "Sometimes," she said to me, "repose takes the place of happiness." She behaves with extraordinary circumspection; she need say but one word, and the most assiduous court would be paid her. The authorities of the neighbouring towns wished to pay their respects, but she declined everything, simply and with no appearance of constraint. Great regard and deference is shown for her everywhere. She speaks of the Emperor as she ought and when she ought; in fact, it is impossible to show more tact and moderation. But notwithstanding her resignation, sometimes, when sorrow oppresses her, she makes me

a sign, and comes to give vent to it with me.   I
exert myself to divert her thoughts and encourage
her, and she willingly receives all the consolations
that reason can offer her.   It appears that when
Charles de Flahault left Plombières, the Queen was
more seriously indisposed than we had thought.*
The Empress is not anxious about her, but believes
she is better.   This is a chord I dare not strike.
We are expecting the Viceroy.   There is a report
that the Empress is *enceinte*.†   I can say with
truth that I have been witness to Joséphine's
sincere joy at this news; and, indeed, such an event
would be the reward of her great sacrifice.

## CLXIV.

### TO M. DE RÉMUSAT AT PARIS.

Aix, Savoy, July 14, 1810.

We are alone to-day.   The Empress has gone to
Geneva, to see her daughter-in-law, who stopped
there, being too fatigued to come on; she will not
return until to-morrow.   She took with her MM.
Pourtalis and de Flahault, and Madame d'Audenarde.   The Viceroy, whom we saw yesterday,
gave us the melancholy details of the accident at
that unlucky ball. . . .

* Queen Hortense.

† The Empress Marie Louise.   The report in question seems
to have been rather premature.   However, as the King of Rome
was born on March 20, 1811, we can but admire the rapidity
with which good news is disseminated.

Our circle is very pleasant. Charles de Flahault enlivens us ; he has more in him and more talent for conversation than I should have expected ; he is very gay, he sings well, and we all like him. The country is really beautiful ; it needs better legs than mine to explore it, but I am delighted with what I have seen, and I hear that I shall travel through very fine scenery on my way to Geneva. . . .

Madame Chéron writes that Saint-Ange * will probably be elected to the Institute. Madame de Grasse speaks of a *commission* for the prizes, and seems rather anxious about Spontini. Is this true ? And, by-the-by, what has happened to Madame Festa,† and how have you had the heart to make her begin the " Molinara " again ? Why was I not there to protest against it ? You are really very generous to regret me, for I should have made a strong protest. The *Journal de Paris* speaks very unfavourably of the poor woman.

* Saint-Ange, the translator of Ovid, did, in fact, succeed Domerque at the Academy. He was in bad health, and died soon afterwards, in that same year, 1810. " The shade of the Academician whose place I take is now waiting for my own," he said in the speech he made on his reception.

† An Italian singer. " La Molinara," as everybody knows, is an opera by Paesiello.

## CLXV.

### TO M. DE RÉMUSAT AT PARIS.

Aix, Savoy, July, 1810.

. . . It is impossible to be with the Empress without desiring to repay her by sedulous attention for the pleasantness she infuses into one's daily life, and if I were often to shut myself up in my own room, or if I gave way to my natural depression, it would really be too selfish. She likes to be in company, and is amused by the stories I tell her; I can succeed in making her laugh. She shows her pleasure in my society in a thousand different ways. In short, she is really charming, and of an angelic disposition; so much so that I know my heart will ache when I leave her, although I shall be so happy to be going back to you. I shall probably return home within the month. The Empress intends to leave Aix between the 15th and 20th of August. She is about to take a small house on the Lake of Geneva; this will be her head-quarters while she travels about Switzerland. She wishes me to accompany her to Geneva, and not to leave her until she sets out on her expedition to the mountains. As there is not much time for all she wants to accomplish, I don't think she will remain long on the banks of the lake, nor that I shall be kept long away from you.

## CLXVI.

Aix, Savoy, July 18, 1810.

. . . You might write at great length concerning that awful accident * without making us feel that you say too much about it. I am convinced that we are even more horrified by it here than you are in the whirl of Paris. The Empress was greatly shocked; she was attached by many ties to the Princesse de Leyen, who was, moreover, an excellent woman. The Emperor's danger affected her deeply; she wept, and her tears gave me pain. "How strange is our situation!" she said. "A bond that is still so strong, while our interests have become so different!" Her son's visit was of great service to her, and she is expecting her daughter, who is coming here for the season. The latter is said to be still in a weak and suffering condition. The Empress is glad that I am here; the Queen, as you know, is fond of me, and I shall tend her with my whole heart. I am sure, too, that such an occupation will do me good; my only comfort, when away from you, is in being of some little use, and that amiable and interesting woman is very dear to me. Lebreton †

---

* The catastrophe at the ball, alluded to in the preceding letters.

† M. Lebreton, a member of the Institute and Secretary of the Class of Fine Arts, was a married priest, and a clever and

has written me a very melancholy letter; he seems greatly distressed at the death of the princess. He, too, was very near going to that terrible ball. . . .

Madame Chéron writes that our children are studying with Auvray; * if they could remain with him next year, it would be a good thing. I am not expecting much in the way of prizes; it strikes me that our boy is working less industriously, but I have not the courage to scold him from such a distance. You can sermonize so well, that I depute my powers to you. I presume that at the time of his first Communion you will say a few words of fatherly exhortation. I shall lament very much being absent from that ceremony; I remember how my poor mother wept on the occasion of my first Communion, and that tender recollection would have gone with me as I accompanied my son. By the way—and you will see that the remark is very appropriate—I have found time, in the midst of all the interruptions of the life I am leading here, to look into a serious book, which I find most interesting. M. Pourtales has lent me a

agreeable man. He was on an intimate footing in my grandparents' house, and was considered as a friend. He vanished somewhat suddenly from the scene, and died in Brazil, whither he betook himself at the Restoration. His daughter married Dr. Jules Cloquet.

* M. Auvray was at that time Professor at the head of the Fifth Class at the Lycée Napoléon. He was subsequently Proviseur and Academical Inspector. I became acquainted with him when attending the Concours Général. He superintended us during our compositions, and he has often spoken to me about my father's childhood.

Life of Zwinglius, written by a Swiss.* This seems to me a meritorious book; I have but one objection to it, that it rather inclines me towards Protestantism. Madame de Grasse will shudder at this, but really the Protestants, at any rate just then, seem to have reason on their side. If I continue in this mood, I shall come to your help in your discussions with her, and will bring Councils to bear on her.

## CLXVII.

### TO M. DE RÉMUSAT AT PARIS.

Aix, Savoy, Friday, July 20, 1810.

The longer I am here, the more I wish for you. I am sure you would like this country so much, and would take prodigious walks with your boy! It is really· a charming part of the world. The mountains are less lofty and less gloomy than the Pyrenees, and the valley, which is more open, is wonderfully verdant. I made yesterday a little excursion, adapted to my strength, to see a most beautiful cascade; there are three waterfalls side by side and tumbling into each other, masses of rock breaking the waters into cascades, and at the back a little torrent rushing away through splendid trees. There is not the

* This Life of Zwinglius, the founder of the Reformation in Switzerland, must be Hesse's work, published in that same year, 1810.

same sensation of surprise here as at Cauterets,
but one is more satisfied. The horizon is not so
narrow, and, for my own part, I find that I breathe
more easily here. The town of Aix is very ugly,
and I have a dull lodging in a sort of No
Thoroughfare, with a high wall in front, which
makes my room very dark. If I were to return
here, I should try to get rooms nearer the country,
as I am so bad a walker; but this year it does not
signify much, because I am constantly with the
Empress, whose house stands on the outskirts of
the village. When the weather is fine, I can walk
over to her; when it rains, I am carried in a fine
glass chair, all gilt, that belonged once upon a
time to the King of Sardinia; and in this vehicle,
when I am in full dress, I am the delight of the
little children of the place, and am followed about
by them, as the Arch-chancellor is followed at the
Palais Royal. You can, of course, imagine that
when the Empress goes out, she has much greater
crowds after her. This, in fact, is the one drawback to our outings. We cannot take a step
without attracting the water-drinkers and the
inhabitants; true, our being here is a rather important fact to poor people and gouty invalids.
The elegant carriage, fine horses, liveries, and our
own dresses, all make a great sensation, and in the
midst of it all, the sweet, gentle, kindly countenance of my mistress. People come from Chambéry, from Geneva, from Turin, and from Grenoble
only to see her. She excites the deepest interest.
I am pleased to observe that no one believes she

has become a stranger to the Emperor, for she receives many petitions addressed to him, and people regard her as a mediatrix between the unfortunate and him. She receives every one with extraordinary kindness, and does much unostentatious good in the neighbourhood. She did her best to escape from a really embarrassing welcome at Geneva, and I am always struck with her skill in simplifying a situation that at first seems unmanageably awkward; the reason is that she is absolutely devoid of vanity, and never aims at effect. She speaks of the Emperor as of a brother, of the new Empress as the future mother of the children of France; and if what we hear of the condition of the latter be true, I am sure she will be glad.

## CLXVIII.

### TO M. DE RÉMUSAT AT PARIS.

Aix, Savoy, July 21, 1810.

Pray tell me how my *curé* is getting on? Do you see him? Is he happy? Does he intend to remain? Shall I see him on my return? I am rather offended with him. I hear nothing of him; he is forgetting me. I wrote to him a long time ago, and hardly expect an answer now, and certainly I shall not write again.*

For the last four days the weather has been

---

* The *curé* is no other than M. de Talleyrand.

dreadful—rain, hail, and intense cold. It was snowing on the mountain the day before yesterday, and we had fires. During this wretched weather I finished the Life of Zwinglius. The Anabaptists have rather cooled my zeal for Protestantism. I see there are objections to that religion, too ; but I like the book. I am now reading the Memoirs of Prince Eugène. The Prince de Ligne's pretence was a curious one, and very ill sustained. At the second page one can see it is a mere invention; and the style is that of drawing-room conversation thirty years ago.* . . .

---

## CLXIX.

### TO M. DE RÉMUSAT AT PARIS.

Aix, Savoy, July 25, 1810.

The Empress wishes to make Geneva her head-quarters for ten days, and to travel in Switzerland. When this happens, I shall take my flight. I am strongly advised to return by Lausanne, Neuchâtel, and Besançon. They tell me that route is not much longer, and that I shall avoid bad roads. By doing this I should see the shores of the Lake of Geneva, a great temptation to me, and I should revive some recollections of my childhood. I

---

* The Prince de Ligne had just published his " Vie de Prince Eugène, écrite par lui-même." It will be understood, of course, that it referred to Prince Eugène of Savoy, and not to Prince Eugène Beauharnais.

think it is probable I shall decide upon this course. When I arrive at Geneva, I will tell you what decision I have come to. . . .

Yesterday the Empress asked me which of the two I loved best, you or Charles. "My husband, madame," I replied, in the tone with which you are familiar. Madame d'Audenarde looked up. "Really," said the Empress, "you answer in a resolute tone." "Madame, I answer as I feel." "M. de Rémusat is very amiable, then?" "Amiable! Oh, madame!" and then I did not know how to begin, and a moment after I did not know how to end. "If all this be so, how happy you are!" "Yes." I should have liked to say, "But how much we suffer in being parted as we are!" I did not say this; I restrained myself; but the tears came into my eyes, and I talked I don't know what nonsense to escape from my thoughts. I promise you that you shall not have to complain of me in this respect. Nobody knows that I suffer from my separation from you and from my children. As the holiday time approaches, my heart sinks more and more, but no one shall be let into my secret. It is ridiculous to trouble other people with one's affairs, and the poor Empress is sorrowful enough on her own account. The affairs of Holland distress her greatly, and she is much troubled about the future of her daughter and the position of her grandchildren.* I do my best to

---

* Louis Bonaparte had just broken with his wife and with the Emperor, and Holland had been united to the Empire on the 9th of July, 1810.

quiet her, urging her strongly to trust the Emperor, and also not to go faster than the time. At an epoch so full of strange events, an excess of foresight is a mistake ; one must submit and hope, and I say to the Empress what I believe : "The Emperor will not visit the faults of their father upon his nephews. You are placed in a painful position, apart from the action of the Court, while you are obliged, all the same, to feel and suffer from its troubles. It requires great firmness of character and extreme reasonableness to act wisely in the midst of all this." The Empress is deeply sensible of the services which I render her ; she is very happy to have me with her ; she calls me and looks for me incessantly. I listen to her, console her, and try to amuse her by talking of other things ; for it weakens the judgment to dwell too long upon certain subjects, and our reasonable course is to wait, not to make long and anxious forecasts, and to trust to a superior authority, which we may be sure is a beneficent one.

## CLXX.

### TO M. DE RÉMUSAT AT PARIS.

Aix, Savoy, July 21, 1810.

I do not understand what M. de Talleyrand has said to you. He declares that he has written to me, but as I receive all my other letters, I cannot suppose that his only do not reach me, and I conclude that he has yielded to his usual indolence. I beg you will tell him this, but at the same time say that I forgive him.

Yesterday we made a long excursion, but it was not too fatiguing, because it was partly by water. We drove about two leagues on the opposite side of a lake, called Le Bourget, which is of considerable extent, to see the ruins of an old abbey, which formerly belonged to the monks of the Cistercian order. The situation of the abbey is very picturesque. It is built on a tongue of land in the middle of the lake, which is surrounded on all sides by peaked and barren mountains. No vegetation is to be seen; profound silence reigns all around. The aspect of the place is so entirely solitary, that I can easily conceive this retreat having been chosen by persons whose object was to break entirely with the world. The abbey is called Haute Combe. Two popes came out of it. It dates back to very remote times, and the remains of the church are very fine. Within a quarter of a league of this building, there is an intermittent spring, which yields water in abundance during several hours in the day, at various and uncertain periods. The cause of this phenomenon has never been ascertained. We remained for an hour and a half beside the rock, but the water did not appear, and the naiad was deaf to our entreaties.* On returning here, we found one of

---

* In this account of the expedition of the Empress to the abbey of Haute Combe, the tempest which she encountered on the lake, and which made a great sensation at the time, is

the Queen's Chamberlains come to announce her Majesty's arrival for to-morrow. This intelligence gave the Empress great pleasure.

---

## CLXXII.

### TO M. DE RÉMUSAT AT PARIS.

Aix, Savoy, July 30, 1810.

. . . The Queen has arrived. She is thin, pale, down-hearted, and always ready to cry without exactly knowing why. " Madame," said I to her, " take courage, and take care of your health. Your misfortune is not a misfortune, for your heart is not wounded by it. The Emperor has received your children perfectly well ; he takes care of them ; he watches over them ; they are in France ; you will see them again this winter. You are with your mother. You must think of all this ; sleep, eat, and leave the rest to God and the Emperor." She smiled at my little harangue, but I believe she thinks I am in the right. Oh, if we could but limit ourselves to the evils that we must bear ! " May God deliver us from our friends ! " says the Portuguese proverb ; I would add, " May God deliver us from ourselves ! " I have my reasons for saying

purposely omitted. My grandmother's first intention was to conceal the danger which she had incurred from her husband, but knowing that others had mentioned it in writing, she changed her mind, and sent him a detailed account in a letter which has been lost.

this; there are moments when I would fly away from myself, on condition, however, that it should be you who would find me. . . .

## CLXXIII.

TO M. DE RÉMUSAT AT PARIS.

Aix, Savoy, Friday, August 10, 1810.

It is all settled. I shall leave Aix this day week; there is no more question of Geneva and Switzerland. I shall come by the shortest way, to Jura, Dijon, Troyes, and Paris. I shall be five or six days on the road, so make your own calculation when to expect me. Do not write to Dijon, as I shall arrive there late, and the post will be closed.

I am charmed with the Trianon arrangement,* because you can give me a few minutes sometimes. I feared lest you should not go there. All is for the best. Heaven is on our side this time; my joy is too natural not to be approved on high, and I feel that I merit the happiness which awaits me. Do what you can for my cousin. I approve all that you do. You are really excellent; your kindness delights, but can never surprise me. . . .

M. and Madame de Tascher arrived here yesterday. The poor little woman is very sorrowful, and talks a great deal of her mother. As you may suppose, I listen to her gladly. The young husband was taken ill with gout on the way, and so

* The Emperor had taken up his abode at Trianon.

seriously that he cannot put his foot to the ground, and is in terrible suffering. . . .

The Empress is growing fat, and looks better than I have seen her. She grieves at parting with me, and I feel that my heart will sink at bidding her farewell, for she is very, very good to me. Her daughter is still extremely delicate, but she no longer spits blood. Peace of mind and the variety of a journey in Switzerland, which she proposes to make, will do her a great deal of good. They are to set out from hence on the 25th, and they do not return until October. Thus, you see, I shall be able to pass the month of September in perfect quiet. I shall devote it to delightful idleness. Our life here is one of continual movement; we come, we go, we are always together, we dress, we play cards—in short, we are never quiet, and that dear idleness that I love so much escapes me. I am astonished that I could have found time to write so much and so often to you as I have done, for the interruptions are perpetual. Everybody here has been very amiable to me. M. d'Audenarde is a pleasant companion; Mademoiselle de Macau is charming and agreeable; the two young people, attentive and polite; Charles de Flahault, very amusing. In short, it is a little society which pleases me and is pleased with me; it would not be my place to say that it regrets to lose me. You know how gay I am, and they say there will be no more laughter when I shall be gone. It will now be your turn to pet me and spoil me, which I shall allow you to do, quietly submitting to be waited on and made much of. My heart beats when I think that within a fortnight from to-day I shall be with you ; that is my unchanged song, and you must let me sing it in every key, for I have no other. . . . To-morrow is my fête ; the Queen is kind enough to give a breakfast. You will think of me, I am sure, and Charles will drink my health. I do not hope for prizes, and I must not reckon upon them, but I feel so much pleasure at the thought of seeing the dear little fellow again, that I care little about them. You are content with him ; he is happy ; all is well.

## CLXXIV.

### TO M. DE RÉMUSAT AT PARIS.

Aix, Savoy, August 12, 1810.

. . . Yesterday was my fête. Did you and the child remember it? It was quite a grand day here. The Queen gave a charming breakfast. We went to her house, which is outside the town and delightfully situated ; a splendidly served table was set in the garden, verses were read, and a pretty little proverb played. My health and hers were drank with great heartiness. The Empress gave me a very pretty necklace. Both mother and daughter were as charming as they could be, and I was quite embarrassed and moved by their kindness. I could have thanked them much more eloquently, if my heart had not been full of a thousand recollections, but all this revived the sentiments of the occasion to an almost painful degree.

---

## CLXXV.

### TO M. DE RÉMUSAT AT RAMBOUILLET.

Aix, Savoy, August 13, 1810.

I cannot make up a packet for Paris without writing to you. I do not want to commence my budget by my letter to you, because I know what would then happen to me; I should not know how to leave off, and time would fail me. I have therefore written the three little letters which you will find enclosed, and am now allowing myself my reward. My friends will not complain; a few more days and I shall have fulfilled all my promises. I have not so much time here as might be supposed. It is true that we do not breakfast until twelve o'clock, but the business of drinking the waters, taking the baths, and dressing, occupies a great part of the morning. Then we remain at the château until five or six o'clock. There we talk, we work, we read stupid tales, to which nobody listens, and which are thrown aside half finished. The newspapers and our letters arrive, the gentlemen sleep for a while, and at six o'clock we go to dress for a carriage drive until eight. You may easily imagine the effect which is produced in a miserable town like this by the *calèche,* the horses, and the elegant equipage of the Empress; and, besides, her *toilettes* are always very impressive. The water-drinkers and the inhabitants all turn out to see us pass, and the other day the Empress said to me, "Why, we are like Cambacérès!" In fact, we were followed by quite forty little urchins. At eight we dine; after dinner come cards and music; so we go on until eleven, and the history of one of our days is the history of all. You will therefore see that I have only one hour to myself before I begin to drink the waters; when I wake at six, the time when I am in the water, during which I read, and the two driving hours when I am not well enough to go out.

The Empress went to Geneva the day before yesterday, and she has just come back. She travelled all night, and it is now six, and I am told she is about to take a bath and go to bed. She took leave of me in the kindest way before this short absence, regretting that she could not take me with her. In every respect it is impossible to be more amiable than she is, and I am very happy, notwithstanding the grief of being separated from you, that I had courage and strength to give her this proof of my devotion. If she had been in happier circumstances, I should have hesitated, on account of my health; but her solitude forbade any hesitation on my part, and up to the present time I certainly do not repent, for the quiet life here agrees with me. You will believe I do my best to enliven it. I keep my regrets, and certain secret causes of disquiet, to myself, and I succeed so well in being one person in the salon and another in my own room, that yesterday M. de Toupin expressed the greatest surprise, on hearing me sigh, that so gay an individual as myself should ever need the solace of sighing. I answered him that I was not so gay as he thought. He maintained the contrary. I continued the discussion smilingly, and nevertheless I might say that even then I had tears in my heart, for talking of gaiety, and of true gaiety, recalled to me that painful recollection, the impress of which I have never lost.*

## CLXXVI.

### TO M. DE RÉMUSAT AT FONTAINEBLEAU.

Paris, October 13, 1810.†

*Mon ami,* I beg you not to allow it to be doubted for a moment that you wish to have me with you, and to arrange for my being summoned to join you as speedily as possible. Since I have been thought of at all, I consider that it would be unbecoming on my part not to show readiness and eagerness; besides, when our child has left me, I shall be

* This allusion is to her mother, whose cheerfulness she frequently mentions.

† Madame de Rémusat had returned to Paris, having left the Empress Joséphine at Aix in Savoy. The Emperor and his Court were at Fontainebleau, and it was now a question of presenting the Empress Joséphine's ladies, after their sojourn at Aix, to the Empress Marie Louise.

dull and melancholy in this big place all by myself, whereas at Fontainebleau I shall be good for something, and I want you to want me. Ask the Duchesse de Montebello to fix my personal presentation for next Sunday, on condition that I may remain at the château after it, for I am not strong enough to go and come back and return again. If the thing can be simplified so that I shall only be named to the Empress, then I will not come at all until Sunday or Monday; otherwise I will set out on Saturday, if I am not countermanded, provided that I have a room, and that the Grand Marshal has given his sanction to all this. I will write more at length to you this evening. Answer promptly, because if I am not wanted, I ought to know it at once. Alix has no news from her husband; she worries herself about this, and does not know what to do. I think she would much rather take the road to Semur than that to Fontainebleau. Adieu. I boasted too much of myself when I said I wanted to stay here quietly without you; I am already weary of this separation. I have suffered so much this year, that I assure you that I desire very sincerely not to pass the month of October away from you.

---

## CLXXVII.

Paris, Friday, October, 1810.

. . . My little preparations are made; I can set out on Saturday, if I am to be presented on Sunday. If it will be enough to name me to the Empress, which I should like better, I shall not leave Paris until next Monday, but I think it would not do to wait fifteen days longer. Besides, as the season advances, my health becomes worse; I am much more sure of myself in October than I shall be in November, and I would rather be at the Court when I am in a state to bear the bustle of it. I think I shall make out some quiet life for myself even there, in the midst of the duties to be done and the pleasures to be enjoyed. I can always find some hours for rest, which I will employ in talking with you, or in my own occupations. I shall take my books, my writing, and my work, and if I am pretty well, the time will pass more pleasantly than in Paris, where I should be so long without you. I am bored to death here, and go to bed at half-past eight. I brood over these last days with Charles, and you alone can console me for being parted from my son.

He is in very good health, and working diligently. I do not take him to the play, lest the contrast should be too strong beween his life during this week and that which awaits him, and so, not to give him pain, I do not go myself. In fact, I conduct myself very well; I talk classes and school to him, and reconcile him to the best of my ability. . . . Deschamps has just left me. The Empress told him to come and see me, and to thank me. She understood that all my advice was dictated by sincere affection. She was about to come here when my letter reached her; * it was that which prevented her return. She charged Deschamps to ascertain from me whether she ought positively to remain here, and I believe that the Queen of Holland also received a commission in the same sense. Her mother's plan is to remain at Geneva, to go to Milan, to return to Aix, and not to re-appear at Navarre until the next September. Every one there seems to be perplexed; I am asked for advice on all sides, but I cannot give it. Speak to the Grand Marshal. I do not suppose, however, that there is anything for me to do, since the Queen is here.

## CLXXVIII.

### TO M. DE RÉMUSAT AT FONTAINEBLEAU.

Paris, October, 1810.

I must really tell you how well I have been managing since yesterday, *mon ami.* I have

* The Empress passed the winter at Geneva, following in this the advice of my grandmother, which was given by order of the Emperor.

arranged for our children to perfection. Yesterday I was reflecting with regret that to-day Charles must return to school, and to that Muzine,* who has come back in pretty good health, but more strange and irritable than ever. The children, too, were anxious on the subject. "But who," I asked Charles, " could be put in his place over you? " Charles began to consider. " None of the professors," he said, " live at the school, and they are too well paid to be willing to undertake what we want. But there is a master in the place, named Leclerc, who would be very suitable." On hearing this, I sent for Amédée Pastoret, who came to me and strongly recommended the said Leclerc, who has been appointed second professor in I know not which class ; he obtained two prizes of honour and twenty-five prizes in one year. He is a perfect Greek scholar, never teaches out of the school, is devoted to poetry, and knows both English and Italian. Accompanied by Amédée, I proceeded to the school, and sent my carriage for Leclerc. He is little, very shy, and absurdly afraid of me. He informs me that M. de Wailly had asked him in vain that very morning to take charge of young Thibaudeau, but that he knows our children, and will agree to everything I wish. I then asked for M. de Wailly, but he was out. We consulted with

* My father retained an unfavourable recollection of this man's harshness (Muzine was in bad health and not quite sane); but he was grateful for his excellent teaching of Latin syntax, and attributed to him a great deal of his success at the University.

Madame Chéron; she was much afraid of Muzine, thought he would refuse to change his quarters, and overwhelmed me with words. You know her style. I begged her not to interfere in any way, and we retired. I was at the school this morning by half-past seven, and spoke frankly to M. de Wailly about Muzine. He agreed with me on many points, and perfectly understands that I am determined to have done with him. I asked for some one to take his place, and the first name mentioned was little Leclerc's ! * He answers for his moral character, his attention, his capability; I begged him to arrange everything, and to bring Helen to dine with me on Thursday. When we had come away, Amédée, who was with me, wrote to Leclerc, telling him to appear as if the first intimation on the subject had reached him from M. de Wailly; and so our business is done, the children are delighted, and I must own I am extremely pleased at having rid them of Muzine. If you can come on Thursday, you will see your boys, and we can go away on Friday. I am now expecting M. Pourtales, and am ready for an argument with him. I am in the vein, and hope all will go off well. I have heard endless stories of Muzine's absurdities this morning, which prove that I have acted wisely. I hope

---

* This *little* Leclerc is M. Joseph Victor Leclerc, who died in 1865. He was a member of the Academy of Inscriptions, Dean of the Faculty of Letters in Paris, and author of some celebrated works on the literary history of France. He was for a long time my father's tutor, and was always one of his most valued friends. From his school days almost my father had assisted him in his translation of Cicero.

you will be of the same opinion. Leclerc's moral character being so good, I think his youth is no objection; Charles and he will get on the better. He likes talking, and they will converse; my boy tells me, moreover, that he has seen him occasionally in the school, and that he can be severe with the pupils when necessary. I am charmed at getting rid of this business, for it was a great trouble to me. My poor boy's spirits fail in proportion as the day approaches for going back to school; when he leaves me I must be with you, for I miss him very much. We have had some talks together since we have been alone, and we agree admirably. He made himself most agreeable to M. Lebreton yesterday, and I asked him whom he liked best of all my friends. He replied that it was Lebreton, because he was kindest to him. Lebreton embraced him thereupon with tears in his eyes. He is a good boy, and I almost worship him.

---

An interval of nearly three months occurs between this and the following letters. When the correspondence is resumed, Madame de Rémusat is again in waiting on the Empress Joséphine at Navarre.

## CLXXIX.

### TO M. DE RÉMUSAT IN PARIS.

Navarre, January, 1811.*

I am hoping to receive a line from you to-day, *mon ami.* Alix wrote me a few words which have done me good, but only you or your secretary, Madame de Grasse, can entirely relieve my mind. While I am full of Thursday's difficulties, you perhaps are engrossed with a thousand other cares; these are the delights of absence!

My health continues tolerably good, with the exception of slight rheumatic pains, which are an excuse for remaining by the fireside. Our present abode is really only adapted for royalty: it is only by lavish precaution that we can escape the rigours of the season. But it must be a charming place in summer, and I, who have very little curiosity, nevertheless feel a great wish to see it

---

* The year 1811 was one of the most peaceful of the Empire, and the birth of the King of Rome in March diminished many anxious apprehensions. Far-seeing politicians, however, and especially M. de Talleyrand, still entertained serious fears, founded on the Emperor's character, and without actually losing all hope, felt neither secure nor confident. It was at this epoch that the Duc Decazes said to Maréchal Marmont, "We are lost, depend upon it, and the Emperor is mad." During this year, M. and Madame de Rémusat were separated for a short time only, and there exist but a few letters written by the latter from the Château de Navarre (Eure), where she had joined the Empress Joséphine. I am unable to fix the precise date of these.

again in fine weather. Moreover, the Empress has pleasant surroundings; her associates here are kind and nice, like herself, and the town of Evreux is not without its charms. The greatest is its bishop.* He is eighty years of age, agreeable, lively, well-informed, and ready to talk on any subject. He and I get on uncommonly well, and of an evening, when the card tables are filled up, we enjoy a little talk, which ends the day pleasantly. I do not prolong it much; you know my taste for going to bed early, and the Empress, who likes to sit up late over her cards, has no need of my services, and leaves me at full liberty. Our party here consists of the Duchesse d'Arenberg, Mesdames d'Arberg, de Vielcastel, d'Audenarde, Ducrest, three or four young girls, MM. de Turpin, de Monaco, de Vielcastel, and Pourtales, and of Deschamps, who is admitted to the drawing-room, and does very well. We draw or work in the mornings while some book is read aloud; then we pay visits to each other until dinner, or else retire to our own rooms to write, as I am now writing to you. At six o'clock we separate to prepare for the evening, as some change of dress is necessary, and then there are cards and music. You perceive that our time passes pleasantly enough, and I should like it as much as others do, were it not for the anxieties I packed up and brought with me in my travelling-bag. From

---

* M. Bourlier, Bishop of Evreux, was very intimate with M. de Talleyrand, and stayed at his house whenever he came to Paris.

those I hope your letters will relieve me by degrees. I contrive to devote a short time to my favourite pursuit of reading, and in the gardens here there are fountains by Lenôtre, and in the house old portraits that go marvellously well with the books I brought with me. I think I have already told you, *mon ami*, that I am quite reconciled to the idea of passing a winter in the country. Your company would be no objection, for I feel certain beforehand that you would like the quiet and tranquillity, and I think that in bad weather the country is less dreary to look at than the streets of Paris. There is always some sort of verdure to be seen, and the least ray of sunshine gives a look of spring to the meadows.

I have had some sensible conversations with the Empress. She seems to be in the best possible frame of mind, wishing only for quiet and the means of gratifying her tastes, which she cultivates that they may take the place of her memories. She has no wish to reside in Paris, but she is strongly bent on Malmaison for the cold season, and there would certainly be some risk in repeating every winter the experiment she has made with tolerable impunity this year. Her idea is to leave this place in the spring, to return again for the summer, to go away in autumn, and perhaps to pass next winter in Italy. She says that had she known anything of this house beforehand, she would not have accepted it. She is alarmed at the almost inevitable expenditure in which it will involve her. In fact, the château is in a dilapidated state, and is a very inconvenient abode; and, however undesirable it may be to undertake building operations in her position, one cannot reasonably endeavour to dissuade her, when one sees how greatly she is inconvenienced at present. It is really good of her to feel so much pleasure at having me here, and when I see how affectionate and caressing she is, I rejoice at the slight sacrifice of my vanity that I thought it right to make out of gratitude for all I owe her. We often speak of the Emperor; she likes to talk of him, and to persuade herself that he still cares for her, and she does this with the most admirable tact and moderation always. *Mon ami*, a woman's heart contains a thousand good things, and on several points we shall always be superior to you.

## CLXXX.

### TO M. DE RÉMUSAT AT PARIS.

Navarre, Friday, February, 1811.

I had vowed that unless I received a letter from you to-day, I would never write to you again, but the oath was worth no more than that of a drunkard or a lover. The post came in, no letter for me, and yet I am at my writing-table, and the worst of it is you owe me no thanks, for it is to please myself that I am there.

I am in the best of spirits this morning. The weather is splendid; I shall find winter again in

Paris. This is a spring day ; the sun is shining, the meadows are green. I am writing, not in the chimney corner, but close to my open window, and my room is scented with hyacinths and lilacs. I am well, and if you were with me, this would be one of the happy days on which, although there is not one single additional reason for tranquillity of spirit, we yet find ourselves inclined to trust in life, and to enjoy it calmly, without either grieving over the past or dreading the future. This pleasant frame of mind is not usual with me, and can hardly occur in town, where some little circumstance is constantly happening to upset one, be it only an unseasonable visitor. As I was telling you this morning, I have aged. I need the sun ; he warms and does me good, and if he always shines in Provence as he is shining to-day, I believe I shall make friends with this part of the world.

I read great praise of " Pirro " * in the papers ; our friends write to us from Paris that Madame Festa and Crivelli are restoring the right style of singing. When you see Spontini, congratulate him for me ; I think he must be pleased, and that he is now on the right track.

---

* The date of the first performance of " Pirro " or " Pyrrhus," an Italian opera by Paesiello that Spontini had modernized by the addition of recitatives, will assist us to determine the date of this letter. M. Regnier, who has been good enough to supply me with much useful information for the notes of this work, tells me that it took place on January 30, 1811. Spontini conducted the orchestra, and it was one of the first successes under his management.

I drove out this morning in an open carriage.
The country here is very pretty and gay.  I should
like to come again in summer, and bring you with
me ; for to enjoy it properly we must be together,
and your presence will but enhance the beautiful
sunshine.  In my character of an old woman,
I amuse myself with recollections of the past.  It
seems to me that when I was young, there were
oftener such days as this, and I recognize the
same atmosphere that I used to breathe at St.
Gratien.  *Mon ami*, how happy we were ! and
how we let those blessed hours slip by !  Youth
is a season that we squander away ; we hurry over
the present moment because we feel so certain of
the future.  But the lapse of years and a *very
little Court life* soon cure us of such pleasant
improvidence, and oh, how sorrowfully proficient
I have grown in the art of fearing and guarding
not only the passing hours, but the very minutes !

Our time passes here in a strange way ; we are
always together, we do very little, there is hardly
any conversation, and yet we are not dull.  You
know how I like sameness ; it accounts for the
rapid flight of time, for the same occupations
return at the accustomed hour, and we scarcely
know whether it is yesterday or to-morrow.  Ah !
if we only chose, life need be neither so burden-
some nor so difficult as we make it for ourselves ;
it is partly our own fault.  Happiness and repose
are close to us ; we move round them, we see them,
and for the most part fly from both.  All this is
not very new, but you must listen to it, because

I feel it so strongly that I must needs put it into words. Besides, I know to whom I am speaking.

Would you like to learn how I pass my day? I am in the humour to give you an account of it. I wake at eight o'clock; I write numberless little notes, and then several pages; I rise at ten; at eleven we breakfast; then people begin to come and go. I sing, I play chess, I work a little; if it is fine we go out; at two o'clock there is reading aloud. If the book is some stupid story, I don't listen, but think of whom I please. Do you understand what that means? At four o'clock we are free again, and I lie lazily back in an easy-chair, and read my "Cardinal," who is very amusing. At six o'clock we dress; then come dinner, cards, music, and Madame Lazy is in her bed by half-past ten. We might spend the day worse, might we not? Here are seven women living together on the best of terms; only one of us is really pretty—we allow her the pleasure of knowing it; some of us are agreeable, and accordingly have the privilege of pleasing. As for me, I have leave to be idle, absent-minded sometimes, and even sad when so inclined; in fact, we enjoy entire liberty. The men of our party are polite and attentive; if they were not, we should not complain; but they are attentive because we are not exacting, and the mistress of the house sets us an example of sweet temper and willingness to be pleased. When I look around me, I feel disposed to believe that the human species is composed of good people; but if I look farther afield, if I think of you and of some others, I think—— In truth, I think so many things that I will not say another word.

I am called; I had made my escape from the drawing-room to come and talk with you, I must now go back. Adieu, *mon ami;* by summoning me away, my friends deprive you of the pleasure of listening to a good deal more frivolity. I was in the humour for writing. Adieu; but it is a settled thing that I write no more; it is a sheer folly to do nothing but think of the absent.

## CLXXXI.

### TO M. DE RÉMUSAT IN PARIS.

Navarre, February, 1811.

You must receive a quantity of little letters from me, *mon ami,* for I lose no opportunity of writing to you. Madame Gazzani * leaves Navarre to-morrow, and has promised that this shall be delivered to you the same evening. The post would be much slower. I wrote to you this morning, saying you had better send again to Madame de la Rochefoucauld for the parcel you had sent to her house, for she is ill, and may not

---

* Madame Gazzani, the wife of a Receiver-General in Italy, and a singularly beautiful woman, had been Reader at Court. She became attached to the Empress Joséphine, and remained with her after the divorce.

arrive here until after my departure; thus the letters would be lost. I received one this morning from Madame Chéron. She is enchanted with "Pirro." The papers are full of it, and so are all the letters we get; it is, in fact, a splendid success, and I should like you to have some share in it. But, to deserve well and to be unappreciated is the usual thing with you. I will not say that success lies in the exactly opposite direction, but I begin to *think* so.*

## CLXXXII.

### TO M. DE RÉMUSAT IN PARIS.

Aix-la-Chapelle, June 21, 1812.†

This place is really too melancholy, *mon ami;* we are getting quite dismal. It is raining in torrents; it is horribly cold; we have a wretched coal fire that covers us with smoke, and of the sun

* At this time the Court was becoming more and more intolerable, owing to the Emperor's gloomy moroseness and ill temper.

† Madame de Rémusat had gone to Aix-la-Chapelle with her sister, Madame de Nansouty, and her second son, Albert, in the beginning of June, 1812. Her ideas of medicine, like those of most persons of her time, were altogether erroneous, and on a careful perusal of her letters it seems probable that the waters she took every year, at a cost of great fatigue, regret, and suffering, both mental and bodily, did her harm. Her correspondence on the subject is full of details and complaints not suitable for publication. This will explain why her letters at this period are fewer in number and shorter than at the beginning.

not a glimpse! This bad weather has brought back my rheumatic pains, and I am suffering a little from my chest. I see that I must henceforth take the waters much more cautiously. They have retained their strength, while. I have become weaker. Albert, unlike his mother and his aunt, does not find the place dull. He will not hear of returning to Paris. I cannot think what the poor child finds to like, for he is very lonely. I do my best to amuse him; but when I am tired or in pain, I have to send him away, and then there is nothing for him to do. If the fine weather ever comes, and he can go out, he will think Aix-la-Chapelle a paradise. Alix is well; the baths are curing her cold. She does well to rely on her own strength, and to laugh at my precautions.

We are at war in a small way with the Prefect. When Madame Ney and Madame de Lavalette arrived here, he called upon them, while he has not even inscribed his name on the visitors' book for us. We were waiting to receive his card before calling on his wife, but we will not make all the advances; he has just invited us to spend the evening at his house to-morrow. Alix thinks we ought not to go. I will do as she likes; I leave her to regulate the ceremonies. I care little, as you know, for new acquaintances, for these new ones, like all the rest, could not alter the fact of your absence.*

---

* M. de Lameth was no longer Prefect of the Department of Roër; he had been succeeded by the Baron de Ladoucette, who was born in 1770, and died in 1848. He was a deputy in 1834.

To-day is Sunday, and Charles is with you. I hope this deluge of rain is not universal, and that he will have been able to take his ride; I prayed that he might not break his neck. Tell him, when next you see him, that my second pleasure consists of thinking of him; you and he together may guess what is my first, if you can.

In sober truth, *mon ami*, now that I have told you about the rain, I hardly know what else to say. Our days are somewhat desultory. Alix comes and goes; Albert wants me for his play-fellow, and the poor child puts on such a melancholy look when I send him away, that I devote myself willingly to his pleasure, feeling quite certain I shall succeed in securing that, whereas I am gravely in doubt as to my own. The slight pain in the chest, from which I have been suffering the last two days, prevents me from writing or working for any length of time. Reading is my only resource, and I devour *Mademoiselle's* * gossip. It amuses me because she mentions all my friends, but she terribly travesties them. In reality she understood little of what she relates. I am far better acquainted than she with all she professes to have seen, and I often feel inclined to exclaim, " Mademoiselle, with all due respect to your Royal Highness, you are entirely mistaken. The persons you mention never thought of the

* Mademoiselle de Montpensier, or *La Grande Mademoiselle,* who died in 1693, and whose Memoirs were first published in 1729. My grandmother was enthusiastic about Louis XIV. and his times.

things you attribute to them, and I can answer for it they cared not at all for your opinion." To keep myself in practice, I amused myself in thus arguing with her; but the good princess is very obstinate, and I do not think I shall succeed in convincing her.

I saw the mayor of this town yesterday. From what he tells me, my friend Lameth seems to be greatly regretted; and, for my own part, it is a disappointment not to find him here. The Constituent Assembly was a never-failing subject that we had by no means exhausted. People always like to talk of the times when they were somebody , were it even for evil, and both vanity and conscience urge them to alternately boasting of their deeds or endeavouring to justify them. But in default of this subject we harp on Mr. Frizell's travels in Italy.* Sometimes, when he describes the beautiful Italian skies or splendid buildings, I find myself wishing to go there some day; then my thoughts revert to you and Charles, and I make plans that I shall never carry out. Alix is more consistent, and declares that the buildings of the Rue de Lille are quite enough for her. But after all, the happiness of being with you is sufficient for me, and should fill my whole life; and were my health good—I say it with due respect

* Mr. Frizell was one of the few Englishmen who remained in France during the war.[1] He was a friend of M. de Chateaubriand's, and had written a pamphlet on the English Constitution.

[1] Mr. Frizell was an Irishman.—TRANSLATORS.

to all the circumstances and disappointments of life—I should have been too happy for this sublunary world. All then is well, since you pardon my want of health, and still love me in spite of my complainings.

---

## CLXXXIII.

### TO M. DE RÉMUSAT AT PARIS.

Aix-la-Chapelle, June 23, 1812.

. . . The Queen * is suffering from the effects of the waters, and much depressed by the bad weather. She regrets Savoy, and thinks that in this rain St. Leu would be pleasanter than the streets here. As you may imagine, we all sing pretty much in the same key, and we end our evenings with her, with elegies on absence. We pass our day in our lodgings. This morning, on the sun's condescending to show himself, we went out, but were driven back by a storm.

Well then, *mon ami*, do not go to Lafitte,† since your engagements will not allow of it. I am vexed with Spontini for giving you so much trouble. This is an opportunity for showing firmness, and treating him with some severity, so that

* Queen Hortense was at Aix-la-Chapelle.
† The estate of Lafitte (Haute-Garonne) had been repurchased by my grandfather from the heirs of M. Bastard, in 1809, and our family thought of settling there.

the others may see you always act with justice.
He needs a good lesson; don't be afraid of letting
him have it. Financial reasons will prevent your
even coming here; and yet health is before everything. Think of the winter; think of me. I have
just strength enough to endure my own ills; yours
would be more than I could bear. . . .

---

## CLXXXIV.

### TO M. DE RÉMUSAT AT PARIS.

Aix-la-Chapelle, Monday, June 29, 1812.

It is still raining, the weather is cold, and I
have a coal fire which stifles while it warms me.
One of the delights of Paris will be to see a log
of firewood; I shall also salute the sun, for he
remains apparently on my terrace. . . .

I went to the theatre yesterday evening. Both
Albert and I enjoyed ourselves very much; "La
Petite Ville" was the play, and was very fairly
acted. There was also a vaudeville, in which I
recognized several of Charles's airs. This was a
great pleasure. By-the-by, I hope he will write
some verses on M. Deghen's balloons,* and on the
difficulty of directing one's course in this lower
earth. I fancy something might be made of it.

---

* Deghen had excited a momentary interest in Paris, by
announcing a novel acrostatic experiment. He proposed to
support himself in the air by wings.

By going to the theatre, we missed Madame de Salm's * (Pipelet) presentation at the Queen's. She brought with her an album in two volumes, full of verses by Lemercier, Chénier, Lalande, and Co. She recited some of her own. She installed herself in the Queen's armchair, and displayed all her possessions. It seems to have been a most diverting scene, and I regret very much that I was not present. Mr. Frizell gave us a capital account of the evening. By-the-by, I think I am beginning to like him extremely. We were speaking of the men of our circle this evening, and passing them in review. " But you do not mention," said he, "the cleverest man of all, who is no other than the master of the house. To begin with, he is more highly informed than any of the others ; in the next place, he is pleasant, unaffected, perfectly free from self-conceit, and has something worth hearing to say on every subject." He has won my heart, of course ; as if there were any merit in appreciating you ! But in this world we naturally esteem people who say what is true. His words roused me ; I spoke of you. I said that even they did not know you thoroughly, that life with you

---

* Constance de Théis, born in 1767, was the daughter of a distinguished man of letters, and had shown from early youth a poetical turn. At eighteen she wrote the well-known novel " Bouton de Rose." She married M. Pipelet de Leury in 1789, and a few years later an opera by her, entitled "Sappho," was produced on the stage with great success ; then a drama in verse, called " Camille," which failed completely. In 1802 she married Prince de Salm-Dyck. Her works were collected in 1842, and published in four volumes in 8vo. She died in 1845.

was like the cloudless sky of Nice. I like this comparison; it is so true; and Mr. Frizell, who loves the south, approved of what I said.

I am still keeping company with *La Grande Mademoiselle.* She says things to me about Louis XIV. that I note carefully. My little book will be charming; I shall make it my album; quite equal to that of the Comtesse de Salm. *Mademoiselle* is much less commonplace when she comes to M. de Lauzun. Women can always write well on the subject of love, and I have a weakness for that sentiment, which makes me like her so soon as she falls in love. It is a great pity you have never been able to *inspire* me in any way; perhaps I should have been a superior person had my lot been different! But, jesting apart, I really believe that a serious passion, that lacks the merit, or the *misfortune*, of being legitimate, greatly develops a woman's qualities? If Madame de Grasse were reading this, she would say, "Here is another of her queer ideas suddenly making its appearance; we must let her talk." And yet, when one has never met with contradiction, how can one know one's deserts? United to you, *mon ami*, one is simply happy, without deserving it, without effort, and consequently without meriting a reward in the next world. It is for this reason that I was declaring a little while ago to my sister that I am not what is called *a worthy woman*; she nearly beat me! You know it has been my conviction for a long time that I owe everything to you. And as a crowning *mis-*

*fortune* I had to become the mother of Charles! Are people to conclude from this that I am a good mother? And then comes Madame de Grasse! Is there much merit in loving you all? In good sooth, *mon ami*, notwithstanding my ill-health and all the rest of it, I am a terribly spoilt person.

---

## CLXXXV.

### TO M. DE RÉMUSAT AT PARIS.

Aix-la-Chapelle, July 3, 1812.

I awake, I look out of window, I see the pouring rain, I heave a deep sigh and sink back in my bed, but sleep will not come again to me. Then I draw up my table to write to you, and having re-read the dear letter I received yesterday, I begin. How good you are to write to me as you do! Your words sink sweetly into my heart, and fill the long hours of absence with thousands of happy thoughts! Ah! I say it again with gratitude, I have no right to complain of anything whatsoever.

I think it has never rained so much as during the last three days. Before this there used to be a few moments of sunshine; but now there is a leaden sky from seven in the morning until eleven at night, and it is as cold as in November. I think the waters must be bad with all this rain. The reservoirs are not in good order, nor properly roofed; the rain gets through and lowers the temperature very much. Albert is well, and behaves well about the shower bath. He does not like it yet, but resigns himself; I continue to be pleased with him. He plays every morning with the little princes. As the eldest is very fond of being coachman, he gets on capitally with Albert, who manages the *Monseigneur* very well now, and who is happy and seems to improve a little with all these games. The day before yesterday he thought proper to strike Prince Louis,* who was disputing with him; but the Queen would not allow me to reprove Albert, as her son was in the wrong. Albert looked at me to see what I thought; and on our return home I gave him a little lesson which he understood.

There are some new arrivals here : Madame de Bartillac, who has left her card for me; Alix knows her a little, but I have not seen her yet.

* The following note by my father relating to this incident, may be of some historical interest:—" I remember that at the time Louis Bonaparte was a candidate for the Presidency in 1848, I was dining one Sunday with Odillon Barrot at Bougival, and he arrived there, as if unexpectedly, at the beginning of dinner, with his cousin, Jérôme's son, and Abbatucci. Naturally, he took my place next to.Madame Barrot, and sat between her and me. I was not pleased at his arrival, and being, besides, no partisan of his, I restricted myself to a cold politeness. He wished for something more, and told me I was one of his oldest acquaintances in France, and that he had seen me at Aix-la-Chapelle. I replied that it was not I, but my brother. He persisted, so did I; and I think he was inclined to believe this was a stratagem of mine to avoid any excuse for greater intimacy. The incident caused a certain stiffness between us during dinner."

Madame Rapp * and her sister, who, unfortunately for them, are living opposite us, and who wanted to be *incognito;* they are always hiding behind their curtains, and will lead a dull life of it here; and M. de L——, who has already visited the *tripot,* where he is received with great ceremony. The banker gives him up his armchair, every one rises to do him honour; in fact, he has become an institution. But the great attraction of all is Madame de Salm. Unfortunately, she is only a bird of passage, for I confess she would entertain me immensely. I met her at the Queen's the day before yesterday. She is certainly very clever, and so full of self-confidence, so eager to recite her own verses, her egotism is so unremitting, and yet so odd, that she is most amusing. She is connected with all the second-rate people of the Institute, and is for ever quoting Lemercier, Arnaud, Laya, etc. She never stirs without her album; in the very middle of the drawing-room she will stand and sing verses of her own composition, and yet she seems to be a good woman, and very unaffected. All this rather tires the Queen, who is so sweet and simple in her ways; but I, who am not obliged to join in the conversation, am greatly diverted by it, and I own that I shall regret this Sappho.

I cannot tell you how charming I think the Queen. Hers is really an angelic disposition, and she is quite a different creature from what she is

---

* General Rapp, aide-de-camp to the Emperor, married first Mademoiselle Vaulerberghe.

generally supposed. Mr. Frizell, who had come here with an unfavourable impression of her, is quite fascinated. She is so true, so pure-minded, so completely ignorant of evil; there is so sweet a melancholy about her, and so great a resignation as to what the future may bring forth, that it is impossible not to feel very strongly for her. Her health is not bad; she dislikes this continual rain because she is fond of walking; she reads a good deal, and appears anxious to repair the deficiencies of her education in certain respects. She studies closely with her children's tutor. Since the trouble she takes amuses her, it is well she should take it; but I should like to see her studies directed by some wiser head. There comes a time when one should learn in order rather to think than to know, and history should not be taught at twenty-five as it is at ten years of age.

Adieu, *cher ami;* I am grateful to you and to my son for being quite well. I hope we shall all be well this next August. If Madame de Vintimille will lend you a little collection of Charles's verses, and you send it me through M. de Lavalette, I would show it to the Queen, who wishes to see it; or Charles might send me his book of manuscripts, and I would bring it back to him. But it must be very carefully forwarded.

## CLXXXVI.

TO M. DE RÉMUSAT AT PARIS.

Aix-la-Chapelle, July 8, 1812.

We have been rather anxious since yesterday about Prince Napoleon. He got up in the morning feeling very feverish and sick. The fever is on him still. M. de la Serre does not think it is of a serious nature; he suspects some eruptive malady, but is not certain as yet. The poor Queen is in a distressing state of anxiety. Everybody tries to comfort her, but mothers are not easily comforted. In any case, I shall keep Albert away from the house, and I shall not go into the sick room. Say nothing about this in Paris, on account of the Empress Joséphine. Her daughter might not wish her to hear of it so soon; besides, it may be nothing, and in that case it will be better not to have mentioned it. The Queen's habitual ill luck makes one more alarmed at this illness of her son's, for, after all, it is but what many other children go through safely; but some human beings seem born to misfortune only, and she appears to be one of these. May my fears prove erroneous!

I wrote yesterday to Madame de Grasse, who complains of us in her last letter. You would be frightened if I were to send you a list of my letters since we have been here. I receive a great number, which I am obliged to answer. I find this fatiguing, and, between ourselves, a great labour. I liked writing when I was younger, but now I only care to correspond with you and two or three others, and, next to that, to write for myself alone. In early youth one likes to expand, if I may make use of the expression, on every side; but afterwards one becomes more reserved, and indifferent to pleasing those who are not the very first in our affections. This is what I experience. Every day I care less for the world. On one side are my friends; on the other is a great gulf of emptiness, with which I concern myself less and less.

The night before last I went to the theatre and shed half a dozen tears over "Omasis." It was not bad for provincial actors, as Madame de Sévigné would say. In that dark and smoky theatre, full of fat Germans smelling of tobacco, Madame S—— appeared in the loveliest toilette, and displayed all the elegance customary at a first night at the Opera. I was greatly amused by it. However, there is nothing like bankruptcy for having everything nice about one.

* "Omasis," or "Joseph en Egypt," a tragedy by Baour-Lormian, was performed for the first time in 1806.

## CLXXXVII.

Aix-la-Chapelle, July 16, 1812.

I always said you were a bad husband, and every day I discover fresh reasons for supporting my theory with all the eloquence I possess. I was at Madame de Lavalette's * yesterday. She had just got her letters, and I was congratulating her on receiving one from M. de Lavalette. She told me that whenever they are separated, he invariably writes to her every day, and that in the course of several years he has never failed even once. You perceive, monsieur, that on this point he is much more of a paragon than you, and on other points —well, I have my own opinion! I must resign myself, however; for " where the goat is tied, there it must browse." . . .

Now as to our leaving this place. I think we shall start on the 25th, that is, on Saturday week. We have done well to delay a little, for I am wonderfully better ; the waters are warmer because of the fine weather, and by taking them cautiously they no longer disagree with me. So we have not come here for nothing, after all.

My grumbling over your negligence as a corre-

* This Madame de Lavalette (Mademoiselle Tascher) is the same individual who distinguished herself by her wifely devotion when her husband was condemned to death under the Restoration.

spondent is all the more gracious that a thick packet of yours has just been delivered to me. I shall now leave off and read it. Wait a moment. Ah! ah! in your present humour Heaven knows how you will take the false news of our return, and yet I do not think that we were wrong in delaying it. Your wish to see us again sets you against the waters unless they do me very great good. Ah! *mon ami*, what do you expect will ever do me great good, unless it be the pleasure of seeing you, which really and truly does influence my health?

Aix-la-Chapelle is beginning to be quite brilliant. We shall be leaving it at its best, and, nevertheless, without regret. Numerous visitors are arriving, but society entails a certain amount of ceremony. We are living very quietly. I have not seen the Queen for a week, and from excess of prudence I do not even go to the Maréchale's.* In the morning we go out, we write, and so on until six o'clock. We retire early, and our evenings are filled up with needlework and one or two visits. Between ourselves, I believe that only for me, Alix would lead a different kind of life. I do not interfere with her, however, but as I stay at home, she stays. I am not dull in her society, but I think she is rather dull in mine. She loves me very much, but I am not altogether suited to her. Keep all this to yourself, and if you write again after receiving this letter, say nothing about it.

* Madame Ney (Mademoiselle Auguié) had been a schoolfellow of Queen Hortense at Madame Campan's.

Adieu, *mon ami;* I must go to dinner. I have written every day since Thursday, and if Albert will let me, I shall keep up this good habit until our departure. I have received the money and the verses ; * a thousand thanks for them.

* My father's verses have been alluded to in these letters several times. A taste for singing and composing songs, which he had shown from earliest childhood, had been greatly culti-vated at his school, where it was shared by several school-fellows older than himself, viz. Amédée Pastoret, Scribe, Naudet, and others. He kept only a few of his compositions at that age, although he often thought of publishing a collection of those written at a later date, after he had left school. In order to prove, however, that what is said in these letters is not entirely the self-deception of a tender mother, I think it well to quote one of the poems in question; not one of those that he sent to Aix-la-Chapelle, but one of the earliest that he did not destroy, and which is dated November, 1813. He was then sixteen, and was studying philosophy at the Lycée Napoléon, which subsequently became the Collége Henri IV.

### LE REVE, OU MON HOROSCOPE.

*Air—*" Vaudeville du *Jaloux malade.*"

" On dit qu'il est un Dieu des songes
   Qui s'éveille toutes les nuits,
   Et qui, par de vagues mensonges,
   Du sommeil charme les ennuis.
   Dès que je ferme la paupière,
   Il vient de pavots couronné :
   Grâce à lui, j'ai, la nuit dernière,
   Rêvé que je n'étais pas né. (*Bis.*)

" Je n'ai pas besoin de vous dire
   Comment on est, quand on n'est pas :
   Dans sa nullité, l'on respire
   Plus à son aise qu'ici-bas.
   Le néant est un lieu tranquille
   Qu'aucun bruit jamais ne troubla :
   Mais le détail est inutile :
   Vous avez tous passé par là.

" Or, voilà que mon bon génie,
   Un matin, se met dans l'esprit
   De m'envoyer en cette vie ;
   Il ouvre son livre, et me dit :

' Mince effet d'une grande cause,
Demain, sans faute, tu naîtras,
Mais, avant d'être quelque chose,
Viens savoir ce que tu seras.

" ' Être futur, c'est une femme
Qui te portera dans son sein ;
En attendant, voici ton âme
Que j'ai prise au grand magasin.
Ne crains rien, je l'ai bien choisie,
C'est une âme de ma façon :
J'ai mis deux doses de folie,
Pour une dose de raison.

" ' Écoute-moi bien, je t'en prie !
Ce registre-ci te promet
La France et Paris pour patrie.
Veux-tu savoir ce qu'on y fait?
Guide par la mode et les femmes,
En guerre, en procès, en amours,
Heureux, on fait des épigrammes,
Et malheureux, des calembours.

" ' Là, tu viendras à la lumière,
Et tu criras incessamment.
N'importe, ton père et ta mère
Diront : *C'est un enfant charmant !*
Mérite leur amour extrême
Quant à moi, je te réponds d'eux :
Tu les aurais choisis toi-même,
Que tu n'aurais pas trouvé mieux.

" ' Après une sereine enfance,
Au collége tu passeras.
Persécuté par la science,
De la science tu riras.
En faisant ta philosophie,
Tu chanteras sur ton pipeau
L'amour, sans avoir une amie,
Et le vin, en buvant de l'eau.

" ' Pendant quinze ans, ta gaîté folle
Par des chansons aura fêté
Les jours d'un âge qui s'envole :
Mais adieu chansons et gaîté !
Bercé d'une vague espérance,
Ton cœur qui semblera s'ouvrir
Avec ta première romance,
Laisse éclore un premier soupir.

" ' Vois-tu, le banquet de la vie
Cesse parfois d'être joyeux.
Si l'on n'y goûtait qu'ambroisie,
On deviendrait l'égal des dieux.
Pour toi, sous l'aile de ta mère,
Auprès de ceux que tu chéris,
Tâche d'attraper sur la terre
Quelques moments du Paradis.'

An interval of eleven months occurs here.

## CLXXXVIII.

TO M. DE RÉMUSAT IN PARIS.*

Vichy, Friday, June 18, 1813.

. . . I am quite settled, and am leading the life of a hermit. We have so much time on our hands that I waste a little on principle. In the morning we gather flowers in a small garden belonging to the house; at eleven o'clock we breakfast, and then go out. I have discovered some rather nice little walks. The country about here is neither pretty nor ugly. It is a plain of large extent, surrounded by grass-grown hills. At this season of the year all is bright; the corn, the fruit trees, and vines are in their prime. There is a hill that reminds me of the Valley of Montmorency. There are nice walks in the neighbourhood, and we do not need horses. We return to the house about noon. Albert is really a good little fellow; he

> " Ainsi disait mon bon génie,
>   Lorsqu'à grand bruit, notre tambour
>   Vint annoncer l'heure ennemie
>   Où, pour le collége, il fait jour.
>   Le réveil à l'erreur m'enlève ;
>   Revenu d'un premier émoi,
>   Je n'ai rien perdu de mon rêve,
>   Car j'ai trouvé que j'étais *moi*.   (*Bis.*) "

* In 1813 Corvisart ordered Madame de Rémusat to Vichy, the waters at Aix-la-Chapelle having done her serious harm. She had been very unwell all the winter, and was falling into the habits of an invalid. She had, however, taken her turn of service as Lady-in-Waiting to the Empress Joséphine at Malmaison, and had started for Vichy on June 12, 1813.

brings the tears to my eyes twenty times a day.
He is my only occupation, and all that I do is
with reference to him. At two o'clock I send him
out for a walk with his attendant. They walked
nearly two leagues yesterday without the least
fatigue. Meanwhile, during their absence, I work,
or read, or pray ; I review my past life, and endeavour to disentangle my thoughts, and to reason
with myself. At four o'clock Albert comes to me
again, and we read " Cinderella " while waiting for
dinner, after which I take a walk ; and yesterday
I made a few visits. I intend to devote this part of
the day to social duties. I come in at eight o'clock,
and play dominoes with the boy until his bedtime ;
I sit up until ten, and then I, too, go to bed.

After this fashion, *mon ami*, I have passed my
days since Monday, and shall continue to pass
them in the same way unless my health should
unfortunately interfere. I shall not be inconvenienced by society here ; there are several invalids, and people live as they like. I paid my
visits yesterday. Madame Ducayla,* the mother,
was at home ; she is very nice and gentle, with an
appearance of suffering that grieved me. She
would like M. de Jaucourt to accompany the
Queen, who is expected to arrive here to-day.
Her daughter was out. I left my name at Madame

* Madame Ducayla was sister to M. de Jaucourt. Her
daughter, or rather her daughter-in-law, became celebrated, as
every one knows, under the Restoration. Madame Jars, of
Lyons, obtained a divorce shortly afterwards, in order to marry
Ellevion the actor.

de Choiseul's and at Madame d'Aumont's, who goes by the name of " the duchess " in this place. I have for a neighbour Madame Jars, the wife of a Receiver-General. She confided to me her complaints of the bad food given to the horses here, and the uselessness of the horses on account of the bad roads. Madame d'Orvilliers is here also, but I did not find her at home. And these are all. I have not yet spoken to a single man; I see them passing my windows both on foot and on horseback, but they do not seem desirous of my acquaintance, nor am I of theirs. Madame Regnault is expected; I shall be just as well pleased if she delays her coming a little while. I have now given you a faithful account, which would hardly be amusing but for the interest one takes in all the sayings and doings of those one loves. I have been tolerably well all the week. The doctor * is so busy, that I have only caught a glimpse of him; he is well spoken of, and liked by every one, and is very clever. I am going presently to his house to pay him a little visit.

I have received a charming letter from my sister; I wrote to her yesterday. She tells me that nobody had yet heard from me, and she writes on Tuesday! I posted a short letter at Montargis on Saturday; it must have been lost. A severe storm had forced me to remain six hours in a cottage; only for that I could easily have reached Briare,†

* M. Lucas.

† Briare is a small town in the department of Loiret. In one of the letters I have suppressed, a pretty château was described with admiring envy. She alludes here jestingly to this.

notwithstanding the wretched posting arrangements in the neighbourhood of Paris. During the storm I amused myself watching the love-making between a servant girl at the inn and an ostler, who were very little incommoded by my presence, and were taking advantage of the storm and of the absence of the girl's kinsfolk. Gestures were more abundant than dialogue between them, and I thought as I looked on of the difference made by education in people's notions of a subject which each one develops after his own fashion. A big brush was used to lay on the colours in this instance, as *ma chère amie* * would say; yet there was something about it more frank and natural, and there was also the feminine instinct, everywhere the same, to impart artifice and coquetry to the girl's proceedings. I am inclined to think that education makes more difference to men than to women. To whatever class a woman belongs, she is well aware that she must affect to part reluctantly with that which in the end she is willing to grant.

When the storm was over I left the loving couple, and reached Montargis at eight o'clock. The next day I travelled through the beautiful country of which I told you, and began bargaining for my château, where I want to make arrangements to sleep on my way back; or I can do so at my friend the postmaster's, in case you should have delayed sending your authorization. It is four leagues beyond Briare, coming from Paris.

* Madame de Sévigné.

Nevers is an ugly and uncomfortable town; Moulins is better, and Vichy very ugly indeed.

You may imagine that I often think of Madame de Sévigné; I inquire for her and for her house. If I found it I should almost be tempted to leave my name there; but when I speak of her, no one can answer. I know more about her than the people here.

I read Grimm's * rubbish as I came along; it is just the thing to take up during a day's journey. It occurred to me that we are very silly to attribute so much importance to the Present, which is of so little account when once it has become the Past. All the extracts he gives, all the little anecdotes of the day, the society verses, the eagerness of every one over a thousand trifles, are tiresome to read of, and yet these things pretty well sum up the life of the rich in a great city, and occupy the greater part of our time. There is something pitiable in all this. Happy am I to be able to devote my life to loving and being with you! Ah! *mon ami*, life is worth living, and it is worth coming to Vichy in the endeavour to retain it. . . .

* Grimm's Letters had just been published, in 1812 and 1813.

## CLXXXIX.

Vichy, Sunday, June 20, 1813.

. . . To-day is Sunday. I went to Mass. The Queen * was there, so was everybody else ; she saw me among the crowd, and came very kindly to speak to me. On my way back I met the water-drinkers, to whom I paid my civilities. I have called upon a stout Princesse de Rohan here, who seems a good sort of woman, and made great advances, saying she knew all my family ; can you tell me, any of you, who she is ? I have seen M. de Boisgelin, and M. d'Harcourt, and M. and Madame d'Orvilliers.† You will not be much interested in all this ; neither was I ; and I returned to the house and to my desk. Madame de Sévigné says that in order to take the waters properly, one should be *spensierata ;* and you say the same when you tell me to forget everything, but you will admit, *mon pauvre ami*, that this is not easy. However, I am doing my best, and making the most of my little stock of common sense and patience.

You overwhelm me with your account of

---

* The Queen of Spain, wife of Joseph Bonaparte. She was at Vichy with her sister the Maréchale Bernadotte, Princess, and subsequently Queen, of Sweden.

† M. de Boisgelin and M. (afterwards the Duc) d'Harcourt were slightly related to each other. M. d'Orvilliers was the son of a *valet de chambre* of Louis XVI. He died a peer of France.

your exertions about the Comédie. All these pleasures seem to augur well for peace. Charles writes to me that he fears you also may be sent for; I don't know whether to wish it or not— what say you? I foresee that your journey is at an end; * and this disappoints me a little, but yet I can understand your remaining. I must resign myself and wait, and take life, at present, much as I take it at Vichy, that is, not looking beyond each day. Madame de Vintimille writes to me that she has gained her lawsuit. *Mon cousin* † has also sent me a kind of certificate of friendship. He protests in every way that he loves me, that he regrets me more than anybody, and that his life is going to be dreadfully dull. I concede his affection for me, and that he would have preferred my not leaving Paris; but in order to carry on the argument I shall not yield the last point, and I shall tell him that I believe there are persons who love me even better than he.

Monday.

It is not raining to-day, and I am in a better humour; you must resign yourself to hearing of all the changes in the weather from me. First, because the sun is very important here, and secondly, because the doctor forbids us the waters when the weather is damp, on pain of fever, and that a day without the waters counts in the matter of absence, though not in the matter of treat-

---

* A journey to Lafitte which did not take place.
† M. Pasquier. He was at that time Prefect of Police.

ment. However, it does not rain, but it is cold, and I am still living in smoke. I went yesterday to visit the hospital which is situated in old Vichy. It is a large, clean house, kept by Sisters of Charity. They were at vespers when I arrived. I returned thither this morning. They were anxious to see me, and were already great friends with Albert. I was charmed with the appearance of these good Sisters, and with their expression of repose ; their speech is full of Divine Providence, and their welcome was most cordial. They received me first in their surgery, where, as you may imagine, I felt quite at home. They took me through the wards—four very large rooms, for men, children, and women. They have baths; they feed the poor, while they are themselves extremely poor ; for their sole resources are a small farm worth about four thousand francs a year, and the collection made for them every season ; but with those small means they relieve much suffering. God helps them, they say, and they never find themselves obliged to deny an alms to any supplicant.

Two or three of them are young—one is a really beautiful girl; the others are old. The Superior told me she was anything but happy when set at liberty during the Revolution, and that she had resumed her nun's habit and the duties belonging to it with delight. When I told her that I venerated her state of life, she answered with the greatest simplicity, "Ah, madame, you who are in the world have many more duties and difficulties than we, and much more merit in the sight

of God! You are continually tried; while as for
us, we have some little labour indeed, but such
inward joy that we must almost fear it will be
reckoned against us some day." I confess that
I was so much touched by these words that my
eyes were wet. They showed me their chapel,
where I prayed heartily, and promised to come
there to mass. I foresee they will often have my
company. As I was going out, I met the pretty
nun I told you about; she is in delicate health,
and has come from Nevers, for the waters. I
smiled when she said Nevers and thought of
" Vert-Vert," and I came home with a mixture of
serious reflection and lively thoughts that made
my walk interesting and amusing.

The Comtesse Laure * arrived yesterday, with
two carriages, a courier, and a good deal of fuss.
The house was quite upset; every kind of honour
was paid her, for she is the real "countess" of the
house, while I glide in silence through all the com-
motion she makes. She brought a lady with her,
and some man, I know not whom; perhaps she
took literally some note like the one I received
from M. Lucas. Do you remember? I mean the
wax candle, the chocolate, and the humble servant.
I saw the Queen and the Princess of Sweden for a
moment on the Promenade; not being "coun-
tesses," they make no fuss. Madame de Magnitôt

---

* Madame Regnault de Saint-Jean d'Angely was by birth
Mademoiselle Laura de Bonneuil. She was considered very
handsome.

is in attendance, and also M. de Jaucourt,* with whom I passed part of yesterday evening, and whom I like, as you know. His sister is very pleasant, and makes me welcome. The gentlemen here pay me very little attention as yet. Is this a good or a bad sign ? I shall ask my little Sisters of Charity the next time I see them, for I am tempted to consult them about everything.

## CXC.

### TO MADAME DE RÉMUSAT'S SON CHARLES IN PARIS.†

Vichy, Tuesday, June 22, 1813.

You are a little rogue, M. Charles, let me tell you. You are not in the least in earnest when

---

* The Comte François de Jaucourt, nephew of him who laboured so ardently and so successfully at the " Encyclopédie " of Diderot and D'Alembert, was born in 1757. He was a gentleman-like and most agreeable man. He held some post at the Court of Spain. He had been a member of the Legislative Assembly, and was a great friend of M. de Talleyrand. He was a member of the Provisional Government of 1813, Naval Minister under Louis XVIII., and finally peer of France under the Restoration and the Government of July. He died in 1852. He was the real head of the Protestants in France.

† My father had preserved a great number of little notes that his mother had written to him in his childhood, in which her maternal tenderness was expressed with grace or with gaiety. I consider her affection for him has been made sufficiently apparent in her letters to her husband. But in 1813 my father was sixteen years of age, and some of her letters to him are worth preservation. He was destined to become, in subsequent

you try to persuade me that you are afraid of writing to me lest I should find your letters tedious. You deserve I should let you believe the very worst on that point by way of punishment. Unfortunately I do not know how to lie with an air of truth in this matter, and, in the second place, you would not believe me. So, my dear child, I will merely say your letter amused me very much, and that if you want me to endure my exile patiently, you will write to me very often. I will allow you to put loops to your *p*'s, and to use as many hyphens as you please, etc., etc., and I shall receive everything with delight and gratitude.

I have much less to tell you on my side. I could certainly write a certain endless chapter, but in the first place you do not like to have your feelings touched, and in the second I do not want to touch my own; and if I once began I know not how it might end. I find absence and the complete isolation in which I live very hard to bear. Affection apart, if indeed the love of a foolish mother can be put on one side, it is difficult to find an equivalent for the pleasure of being with you and your father. I do not even seek one; memories of the past and a faint gleam of hope, on which I dare not reckon as yet, since it is very distant, keep me up pretty well. I walk out; I think; I build castles for you, not in the air, believe me, but close to Paris and to me; I ask God to

years, her most active correspondent. I select for publication here only one of his letters, in which I believe there is proof of a development of mind very unusual at his age.

preserve you; I read; I teach Albert; and the time slips by, for, happily or unhappily, Time never halts.

But can you guess what I am reading? Pretty well, I fancy. My beloved Madame de Sévigné. *I had never read her so thoroughly before*, and I am charmed. But what, think you, is the consequence? Why, that I feel ashamed and disinclined to write afterwards! I should like to copy out her letters and send them to all of you. I might certainly sign my name to all the affectionate things she says to her daughter, and address them to you without any hesitation. That dear and charming woman has felt everything, and said everything, and if I do not copy her, I must restrict myself to telling you simply that I love you with all my heart, which will be neither very new nor very amusing.

I do not know why you do not like M. de Villemain's * quotations. I like some of them; but, at any rate, I agree with you as to the young professor's prose. It is not at all juvenile, and has a flavour of the olden days that I love so much. You will perhaps say, "But if you admire his style so much, how can you also admire that of the author of 'Le Désert,' which is very dis-

---

* M. Villemain, born in 1790, was already a professor at the Lycée Charlemagne, and Maitre de Conférences at the École Normale. He had just obtained a prize at the Academy for his "Éloge de Montaigne." He afterwards became, as every one knows, a great author, and died in 1867. As to the writer of the "Désert," it is probably M. de Chateaubriand, who had just brought out his "Itinéraire de Paris à Jérusalem."

similar?" My dear boy, one must try to like everything as much as ever one can.

Every day I receive fresh versions of the death of poor Madame de Broc,* and of the reflections occasioned by it. All those who write to tell me of it think it necessary to descant on the readiness with which Death lays hold of us, and God knows how ill suited to me, as I am here, are all such melancholy thoughts! It is true, nevertheless, that we must needs think sometimes of that our inevitable end, and meanwhile live well in both senses of the term, which are by no means the same, and yet may be completely harmonized. . . .

Do not forget to tell me how you are now placed, and what are your expectations for the next examination, and also whether M. Leclerc has spoken to M. de Wailly, and then beg your father to ask M. Villemain to dinner some Sunday. I want him to keep all my little circle together, that I may not feel quite lost on my return.

Madame Chéron tells me that her son made her very happy by writing her a nice letter on his seventeenth birthday. Tell Henri this. To hear of the pleasure felt by his mother will give him pleasure too, for he also is an excellent son. I wonder why I say *also?* Can you explain this association of ideas? If you cannot, you must ask your father, who has been greatly pleased by all your little attentions to him since I left you

* Madame de Broc, a friend of Queen Hortense, was accidentally drowned in her presence, while visiting a waterfall at Aix in Savoy.

both. Ah! you are trying, perhaps, to console him for my absence? That is too much! I must make haste to come back, for you might get on so well together as not to leave me the least little place between you.

Adieu, my dear and good child. Above all, keep quite well, and, next to that, love me. As for me, I shall continue to take the waters, and to bathe in them, so as to be stronger this winter. All I ask from God is strength enough to watch your life and to see you happy. Once again, adieu. I feel that tears are very near, so I must fly from them.

---

## CXCI.

### TO M. DE RÉMUSAT IN PARIS.

Vichy, Sunday, June 27, 1813.

I like being near the Ducayla household; we suit each other admirably, and yet without interfering one with the other. I see little, however, of M. de Jaucourt, who is obliged to be frequently in attendance on the Queen, and as she lives in *Le Grand* Vichy, our lives are quite apart. I meet this kind and unaffected little Queen at the spring every morning. She comes on foot to drink her glass of water, quite quietly and alone, in a simple grey silk gown, with a parasol in her hand. The Princess of Sweden is here, trying to get cured of something in her blood, which quite spoils her complexion, and makes her melancholy and inclined to solitude. I go to see them now and then in my morning dress, and that is all. When I come to think of it, if you were to ask me what I do *most*, I should say I *walk* more than anything else, and I am consequently quite sleepy by nine o'clock. Pray tell Madame Chéron and Madame de Grasse to make their minds easy, and that I am not a bit clever in this place. I never take up a pen except to write letters, and, with the exception of those to you, I make them as short as possible, the waters being a good excuse. It wearies me to write letters. I have always to speak of myself, and repeat the same things, and when I have just finished a letter to you, or to Madame de Grasse, who is almost you, I have nothing more to say. Good night.

Monday, 28th.

After writing to you yesterday, I spent an hour with young Madame Ducayla, who is a pleasant and a good woman. We had some agreeable conversation. Like me, she wants to be religious. She often sees the Abbé Duval,* and likes him; so, you see, we had a good subject for our talk. I told her of the uneasiness I sometimes feel at the large share of happiness that you bestow on me, and which must find its makeweight somewhere. This gave me an opportunity of speaking of you, and when I had begun on that topic, I did not

---

* The Abbé Legris-Duval was a clever man, of gentle piety, and a great favourite in the Faubourg St. Germain.

soon come to an end; and then I said a word or
two about Charles, and, in short, about all my
happiness. But I fancy, now I am on the subject,
that you are afraid I may go to an extent that
would be inconvenient to you in the matter of
piety. Do not alarm yourself. I am far indeed
from any deep devotion at present. My will is
good, but the least thing discourages and cools
me, and I cannot explain why; but my imagination, which plays a part in other feelings or actions
of my life, is not excited on the subject of religion.
On the contrary, the occasional meditations I
make on that subject lead me to calm and serious
reflections; therefore you may be quite at ease, for
I am still far from becoming a good Carmelite.

## CXCII.

### TO MADAME DE RÉMUSAT'S SON CHARLES IN PARIS.

Vichy, July 7, 1813.

I should have written to you again before now,
my dear boy, only for the monotony of my life
here, which furnishes me with nothing to tell you.
There is one subject which could not easily be
exhausted, but I know you dislike having your
feelings ever so slightly touched; and, besides, it
would interfere with the vow of patience which I
made on arriving here. So I cut short all my
regrets and all my tenderness, and I sit opposite
my desk without venturing to refer to them. Yet

I must not be an ungrateful mother either, nor omit to tell you that your dear letters are the greatest pleasure of my solitude.

Your father is right in saying that I do not wish for your philosophical treatise. You must know that since I have been here I no longer care to write. With the exception of a few occasional letters, I do not touch a pen ; for writing tires me, and is, besides, against my doctor's advice, and you know my reverence for the Faculty. What do you think of my new passion, which perhaps you have heard of, for the doctor here ? Thanks be to Heaven, we have now three doctors in this house. If we are not well in health, we are at least sure of dying according to rule. But my doctor is a very pleasant man ; he agrees with me about my favourite century, reads Massillon to me when I ask him, and has a portrait of Madame de Sévigné in his room. How could any one resist such attractions ? His society is certainly the pleasantest I have met with here, and the only companionship I care to seek. Towards other people I own that I am rather unsociable, and I prefer my rambles with Albert, and thinking of you, or reading over your letters and Madame de Grasse's (with or without comparison between them), to talking of the waters and their effects with everybody I meet at the springs.

I can see that you, too, are leading a quiet, regular life. Your father has taken a liking to his occupation that you will not find contagious, and that we shall laugh at when I come home ; for

2 E

laugh we shall, since you say that my *so-called melancholy* suits well with your bright temper. I assure you that this gaiety of mine that you have discovered is a kind of reflection of your own, for here I can hardly perceive it. By seeing you, and listening to you, and observing your happy nature, I am invested, it seems, with a character that disappears with you. I ought to be ashamed, perhaps, that the humour of a mother should depend in such fashion on that of her son, but the fact remains, and I decline to investigate the depth of such an offence against maternal dignity.

But, though I do not write or do my woolwork, neither do I read anything to speak of. " But, mamma, how do you employ your time ? " My dear son, I take the waters, I bathe, I eat, and I sleep. What more would you have ? I have, however, begun your "Discours sur l'Histoire Universelle." I don't know why, I find it rather dull. Keep this a secret. It is because I am quite stupefied by it. I do not understand how one can help getting into confusion amid such admirable order. I have already thought it over, and get lost among those brackets. You will set me right. My favourite work * is the only one that I can stick to. I am quite distressed at the death of the Duc de la Rochefoucauld, which I learned yesterday. By-the-by, he used to say, " *We have not sufficient strength to follow out our reason,*" and Madame de Grignan used to say, "*We are not sufficiently reasonable to follow out our strength.*" What do you

* Madame de Sévigné's Letters.

think? Which of them was right? If you are for Madame de Grignan, I will tell her mother, who will be delighted, and M. de la Rochefoucauld will not mind, as he is dead.

I brought with me here a volume of selections from Massillon that I should like you to look at. They are models of thought and style. I should wish you, my dear boy, to like Massillon, and to be helped by him to be a good Christian. Your friends of the time of Louis XIV. were such, and were none the less great men.

But to return to our own times. Tell me what is going on at the Institute since the death of Cailhava.* Are you a candidate? I would certainly vote for you. Tell me about the prizes, and try to get some, for my sake, if not for your own. I do not like you to be so philosophical; it does not suit with your youth. Nothing is good before its time. The age of indifference will come quite soon enough. As for me, I feel very great ambition for you. For your sake I have become a schemer; and it would take little to fill me with envy on your account. Only remark the vices I shall owe to you.

Do write those verses and send them to me; above all, let there be one for the Feast of St. Clare, whether I am there with you or still here. Adieu, my dear boy; the sun is setting, and I cannot see to write. I too will go to bed. Adieu, my dear and good son. I must tell you sincerely

* Cailhava, a member of the French Academy and a dramatic author, had just died, on June 20, in his eighty-third year,

that you are the joy of my heart, and indeed of my mind too, and I think I am very silly, and shall end by making you ungrateful for so much love.

## CXCIII.

### TO MADAME DE RÉMUSAT'S SON CHARLES IN PARIS.

Vichy, July 10, 1813.

You are the dearest and best son in the world. This is a truth that I will defend at the point of my eloquence, or rather, that I shall have no occasion to defend, for I shall meet with no one to controvert it. Meanwhile, I feel it to the core of my heart, and I own that I thank God for the child He has given me. I must inform you, however, that notwithstanding all your good qualities that I love so much, I think you are a little *roguish* towards your mother. You praise that poor woman very much; you feel you must gain her good graces and correct her natural antipathy, and, in default of anything better, you compliment her on her letters. Alas! my child, I do not know what you can find of any value in what I write to you. I seem to have scarcely an idea in my head in my solitude, and as to my feelings, you know I have made a vow of silence about them. But it is all the better for me if my emptiness pleases you.

There is some truth in what you say of the

facility with which women can write. I can
hardly give a reason for it, unless it arise from
our habit of attaching greater importance than
men do to the thousands of little daily occurrences
which arouse emotion in us, and we are thus led to
talk of them with more liveliness and interest, but
without making too much of them; for it is a
feminine gift to touch lightly on everything, without pausing on any. Observe the piquant turn
which a Parisian lady of society can give to the
conversation in her salon; how skilfully she eludes
an embarrassing dissertation, and how she con-
trives to include in one general conversation a
number of men, who all want to talk, but who
would often have said nothing, if they had not
been drawn on, or if their interest or their vanity
had not been awakened by some adroit word or
other. This is the grand art of women, and the
reason that there is no real society except in
countries where they hold a certain place. True,
this is said to have its drawbacks; but it is the
business of you gentlemen to defend yourselves,
and it is ours to take advantage of your need of our
modest means of pleasing you. To return to the
letters. I assure you that yours, too, give me extreme pleasure. You write very well, because you
write naturally and pleasantly. All that you write
is exactly like yourself; in a letter of yours there
are a thousand different things, just as there are
in your own head, and the bright tints of your
sixteen summers animate the whole. I thank you
for calling me *your best friend*. Remember, my

dear boy, that you have given me this name, and
that I shall not relinquish it.    To tell you the
truth, I had reckoned on it in a measure, but I
like you to assure me of it.    In a few years you
will be entering the world ; you will make friend-
ships of your own ; you will meet with both joys
and sorrows.    In the latter case especially, I
would wish you to think of me, and to feel the
need of confiding in me.    We may not always be
able to cure these sorrows, for grief, in this world,
has a tenacious grip ; but it would be strange
indeed if we could not assuage them in some
measure.    There is, moreover, a sweetness that
you will know some day, in confiding in a person
who understands you, and can even divine your
feelings.    Confidence is one of the best gifts given
to us ; your confidence will be the reward of my
tender affection.

The thought that you are now going to love me
as a friend, after having during your childhood
loved me as a mother, brightens my life, and
makes it delightful and serene.    But this, too, is
a subject which I must cut short.    How difficult
it is to keep one's heart out of the conversation
in writing to one's child !    But now to business.
You think that M. Fercoc * requires too much of
you, and that your youth also makes requirements
that you cannot refuse to hear ?    You would be

---

* M. Fercoc was a disciple of Laromiquière and Professor of
Philosophy at the Lycée.    My father was at that time in the
second class, and in those days philosophy was studied by way
of supplement in the second and in the rhetoric class.

wrong not to listen to it; one must be civil to every one, and not snub poor Youth—who, besides, presents itself with such grace—too rudely. It bids you to seek pleasure? And who, my dear child, could say that this is wrong? M. Fercoc, or rather, wholesome philosophy, would certainly allow that this short life may be brightened; only they warn you beforehand to avoid those pleasures that would sully your soul and would oppose themselves to the inward content that can resist all things, and in which the true independence of the mind consists. "But," you will perhaps say, "I do not care particularly for independence of mind." Let me explain: there is independence and independence. Yield sometimes to an amusement that pleases, to a feeling that interests, to a pretty face that notices you; but retain to yourself the power of doing without all these things, should they fail you, without feeling inclined to hang yourself; and that you may be able to do this, do not exhaust yourself by exhausting pleasure. On the contrary, accustom yourself to refuse it sometimes, substituting for it the satisfaction of having enhanced your strength. This is a compensation invented by reason, and perhaps, also, by vanity, to console us under privation. Men who have lived and who are wise, will teach you the way, not, indeed, to be always content on every occasion, but to render life happy as a whole. Believe in their theory, and take what you can of it into practice, adopting nothing exclusively, not even reason. You see that mine is an easy philosophy.

Perhaps you like my jargon better than Fercoc's, but I know to whom I am speaking, and you have a clear head, and are quite capable of understanding everything, and abusing nothing.

I am delighted that you are going up to the examination. I have my hopes that I cherish in secret, and consolations quite ready in the event of reverses. A mother is a curious mixture, my child, but there is really something good about it.

---

## CXCV.

### TO M. DE RÉMUSAT IN PARIS.

Vichy, July 17, 1813.

. . . The *cousin* writes, warning me against intimacies that might last beyond the Vichy season. My sister has whispered her fears to him; but tell them to make their minds easy. I do not usually throw myself at people's heads, and I shall come back as free as I departed. The count is now quite well, but I hardly see him. He comes in, talks of the Institute or of literature very pleasantly for a few minutes, and then goes away and there is no more of him. Yesterday morning, three acts of " Iphigénie " were performed at the house of a lady of their acquaintance. Madame Regnault acted Iphigenia. She wore a severely classical costume which suited her beautiful features. Her voice is good, and that is enough when backed by Racine and a Grecian nose; the other actors were not equal to her. In the third act, when she was declaiming the grand tirade, her husband wept, and when it was over he could not resist going up and kissing her before twenty persons, who all stared at him. The costumes of the other actors were rather in Carnival style. That Madame de Latour * of whom I spoke to you recites well. The *Achille* was a ridiculous person who caricatured *Lafond* with a snuff-coloured coat, and a yellow shawl worn as drapery over his trousers. The *Eriphile* was indifferent. M. de Bernis, son-in-law to the Princess de Rohan, was *Agamemnon;* he is accustomed to recitation, but he is stout, wore a frock coat and boots, with the inevitable shawl over his shoulders, and held the play book in his hand, for he did not know his part. All this took place in bright sunshine at three o'clock ; but towards half-past four the dinner bells began to ring, and the family of the Atrides and ourselves retired to dinner. We are bidden to expect proverbs this evening. As talking is not required on these occasions, they suit me perfectly. I can hear the preparations and rehearsals going on, and the discussion of the costumes ; meanwhile I gargle my throat, I give Albert his writing lesson, I write to you, and this evening at eight I shall go to witness the performances.

* Madame de Latour was by birth Mademoiselle Buffaut and aunt to Madame Regnault.

## CXCVI.

CHARLES DE RÉMUSAT TO MADAME DE RÉMUSAT AT
VICHY.

Paris, Tuesday, July 24, 1813.

I received your letter, my dear mother, with as
much pleasure as surprise to find you so zealous in
the fulfilment of your epistolary duties. Your
letter is a *volume*, and that is what I like. I do
not think Madame de Grasse quite understood
me.* First of all, if I said you were too clever for
me, I did not mean that your conversation was
too lofty or too serious; but only that when one
converses with you, and that you really take a
share in the conversation, you are so brilliant and
so original in your views, that it is difficult, for me
especially, to follow and to answer you.

Secondly, I want your advice for my compositions during these holidays. I have analyzed in
vain; I know not whether to employ the syn-
thetical or other method. The subject is nature,
mankind in general, persons in particular, the con-
ventions and relations of society and literary
works. As I do not want to produce a folio
volume, the task is rather puzzling. My idea is
this. I purpose to make, at once, notes, more or
less confused and entangled, of my present opinions
and feelings, which date only from yesterday, and

* This refers to a letter from Madame de Rémusat to her son,
which will be found in the preface to the Memoirs.

which may change by to-morrow. I purpose to relate all the variations they have undergone, whether from circumstance or from the passage of time, until the present moment, and thus to prepare materials for a serious work, which I shall write several years hence. It will be a history, or a novel, as you please, which might be entitled, " Metamorphoses, or Memoirs of a Young Man, belonging to what is called High Society, from his Birth until the Age of Twenty." You understand that it would contain neither adventures nor events; for even had I experienced any, they would have to be suppressed. It is a man's ordinary life, especially his moral life, that I should try to depict, and the various ways in which he is influenced by his family, his friends, his position, and every outward circumstance. What do you say to the verb *to influence?* It is in fashion, but certainly does not belong to the time of Louis XIV. To return. I should therefore begin to make my notes at once, for in three or four years' time, not only will my ideas be changed, not only shall I not think then as I think now, but I shall not even be able to imagine that I have ever thought differently to what I shall then think. I already find it difficult to persuade myself that I have not always been what I am now in this month of July, 1813, and to recollect my thoughts during the years that are past. The question is therefore pressing, for the older I grow, the more do these recollections fade and the footsteps of childhood disappear. What think you of my project? I fancy you will like it. M. Fercoc is continually exhorting us to write a treatise on imagination. I obey him literally, for is not a history of youth a treatise on imagination ?

I am certain that at this moment you are saying to yourself, "How lucky he is ! What a lot of paper he will have to cover ! " You would like to be sixteen and to do as much. But listen : write the memoirs of a mother ; give an account of the manner in which, as years pass by, her feelings towards her son and her feelings concerning him, become altered. The subject is perhaps less fertile than mine. Never mind ; we shall be working at the same time, but shall tell each other nothing. While I shall be describing a son of fifteen, you will be describing a mother of thirty ; and afterwards we will compare notes. As we shall necessarily have to treat of the same subject, it will be amusing to discover the different points of view from which the same thing will have presented itself to each of us. Think this over, and give me a categorical answer.

To come now to the *historical* part of my letter. Last Friday I wrote a Greek composition. I showed it both to M. de Wailly and to M. Leclerc. Neither of them has mentioned it to me since. Yesterday, from eight in the morning until half-past seven in the evening, I was on a straw chair, trying to mount Pegasus, that is, trying to compose Latin verses. I wrote forty-eight, and, unfortunately, I cannot call them *short and good.* We are doing nothing here, absolutely nothing.

M. Pottier,* not knowing how to fill up the time, spends it in reading " Vert-Vert " to us, which is not a very laborious occupation. We begin our competition of themes to-morrow, and philosophy on Friday. After that the *concours* is over.

Pray return as soon as possible to relieve papa from his celibacy; for frankly, whatever you may say, the society of Madame de Grasse is not enough for him. My aunt's husband has been here for the last few days; he arrived last Thursday, and ought to have started on Monday—that is yesterday. He is really very well, and I hope that the waters will be equally beneficial to you. We dined with my aunt on Sunday, with M. Pasquier, Madame Chéron, and Madame de Grasse, and there was plenty of talk. We began dinner with a discussion, which has lately come into fashion. It is concerning Mademoiselle Gosselin, who, so far, has no one against her but my aunt and Geoffroy. In vain did the dear baron, in vain did my uncle, make the finest speeches. My aunt was adamant, and Madame Gardel can find no more obstinate champion.†  Nor was this all; Madame Chéron, who apparently is no great judge of dancing, and who was inwardly groaning at not having said a word since the beginning of dinner, *i.e.* for three quarters of an hour, suddenly emerged from silence by a

---

* M. Pottier taught the second class.

† Mademoiselle Gosselin, a young dancer whom Geoffroy called *désossée*, was at that time greatly admired. But the *classicists* preferred Madame Gardel.

pompous panegyric on Mademoiselle Leverd's admirable and original acting in "Tartuffe" the evening before, and on her superiority over her enemy.* Oh, what an apple of discord! My aunt exclaims; my uncle echoes her, vowing he has never seen either one or the other. M. Pasquier begs and entreats that such a chord as this may not be struck, and pours out a glass of water for my aunt, who is choking. In vain does my father wait for a moment of silence, in which to make them hear reason, while I hold my tongue and say to myself, "Analyze, analyze!" But there was no analyzing it. Madame Chéron misuses all her words, and piles up sophisms in order to prove the greatest of sophisms, viz. that she was right. However, that did not surprise me. Only imagine! After "Tartuffe" she went to see two farces at the Variétés, and after that she is ready to criticise the actors of Molière. Elmire submitted to the censor of "M. Dumollet"!† So be it. Moreover, without this I should not have known how to finish my letter, and you must accept it, such as it is. Adieu.

* The enemy was Mademoiselle Mars, whose acting was at that time always compared with, and not always preferred to, that of Mademoiselle Leverd.

† A vaudeville by Désangiers and Gentil.

## CXCVII.

### TO M. DE RÉMUSAT IN PARIS.

Vichy, July 27, 1813.

I am breathing again, for I think my letters of yesterday must have relieved you all, and that, after reading them, the husband and the wife will settle down to their occupations again, saying to themselves, " The poor darling has suffered a good deal, but it is over now! She is well again, and has gathered up her courage. Time is getting on ; let us be patient, and to our work again." And every one sits down, while Madame de Grasse says, " Those waters are too strong for her; I knew they would be." " But you hear what her doctor says ; he believes they will do her good." " Ah ! that is because he wants her to stay at Vichy." " Ah ! that is like you, always thinking there is some motive besides the ostensible one." " Mon Dieu ! am I wrong in that ? Men are so deceitful ! Why should not that man tell lies as well as another ? " " You mean, why should he not be mistaken as well as another ? " " Bah ! it is the same thing." " No, to deceive or to be deceived are different things." " Well, but did I not say those waters would do her harm ? " Will not the conversation run after this fashion on Tuesday, amid long intervals of silence ?

As for me, I passed a quiet day yesterday. I remained in my own room all the morning ; it was

positively raining in torrents. I worked; I wrote
to Madame de Vintimille; I read a little of La
Bruyère. At four o'clock I paid a short visit to
the count and countess, who had sent me an
invitation to dinner, which I had declined on the
score of health. We talked on several subjects,
the musician * among others, the count telling
me he thought the business was settled. I told
him I was " glad to hear it ; that he and his family
were deserving of interest; that as for him, he
would have to pay dearly for his great blunders ;
that you had given him the means of an honourable livelihood ; that the desire of gaining more,
and of providing for extravagant expenditure, had
brought him into difficulties and occasioned behaviour that any one else in your place would have
found it hard to overlook, but that we should
forget such things in presence of misfortune, and
that this is what you had done." The count
replied " that he knew nothing about the rights
of the business; that Erard had asked him to
befriend his son-in-law, and that, therefore, he had
done so ; that his opponents seemed to be rather
questionable people ; that the poor fellow must
have a chance given him of making use of his
talents," etc. After this we talked of operas,
poems, verses, the Institute, etc. For the most
part we did not agree, but I let everything slide
and took nothing up seriously. Every now and
then I paid some little compliment. It was a
delightful conversation, without effusion or sim-

* Spontini.

plicity; each of us saw what the other was going to say, and fell in with it—at least, that was the case with me. Afterwards I returned to my little hermitage, and at eight o'clock I went to Madame Ducayla's, where everybody assembled—the countess and the other members of society, Guelphs and Ghibellines. There was music and work; I played a game of whist. The evening went off well, and at eight o'clock the convent was shut up.

But, oh, what beautiful bits I read of Massillon! How delighted I am with La Bruyère! How full of thought and knowledge are all the writers of those times! How much we may learn from them by reading them slowly and with attention! We may positively converse with them; we question them, and they give admirable answers; in their turn they ask a question, but we cannot reply as well as they, especially when Bourdalone or Massillon is the questioner. We stand before them with downcast eyes, begging for time, which they do not seem much inclined to grant.

Madame Devaines has written to M. de Jaucourt,* informing him of her son's marriage; he is delighted, I assure you. I wrote to both mother and son, and also to Countess Rumford yesterday. I am an admirably punctual correspondent, and keep my turn with a great many persons. Between ourselves, I do not always find it very amusing; but, after all, one must answer letters and escape a scolding. I have received a somewhat melancholy

---

* M. Devaines had just married Madame Dillon (Henriette de Meulan), sister-to the first Madame Guizot.

letter from Corvisart. Try and show him some mark of interest. He might be flattered by your calling on him. Charles amuses me very much; his letters are bright and gay, and sometimes tender; but so soon as he perceives that, he makes a joke so as to cut sentiment short. He ended a letter the other day by saying that "he loved me and kissed me as—— " then he hesitated and resumed, "as a mother kisses her child," saying he could not improve upon that. He assures me I shall always be his best friend; in fact, he wants to turn my head altogether, and I am afraid he will succeed.

THE END.

Printed in Great Britain
by Amazon

84228262R00264